The Skeptical Moderate

A Guide for the Ambivalent About Religion, Economics, Politics, and Knowledge

By Chad Gregory

Table of Contents

Acknowledgements

It is with great reluctance that I ask friends and colleagues to read a manuscript and increase their work load, for I doubt that perusing this manuscript was a proper endeavor of leisure. So, I would like to take this opportunity to thank Tim Holder, Art Scheck, and John Mauer for their input and helpful suggestions. I have incorporated many of their insights and counterpoints. They often vigorously disagreed with how I framed an issue, objected that I had overly-simplified a complex topic, or said that I had not adequately presented the opposing side's refutations or qualifications. All errors of fact and interpretation – and shortcomings in, or lack of, style, organization, and humor – are my own and do not represent the views of my employer or the above individuals that agreed to read the manuscript.

A World Of Books

My knowledge is derivative. I accumulate new tidbits of information, and then try to organize, interpret, and digest all of it, often connecting this new knowledge with what I already know or think I know. Students scan my bookshelves in my office and ask the standard question: "Have you read all of those books?" "Well, maybe three-fourths of them," I reply. "Any knowledge that I possess is almost entirely derived from those books and reading original sources." People often assume that college instructors are nearly omniscient about their disciplines – they are not. My students frequently ask questions that I cannot answer. My stock response is that I am not an encyclopedia. Usually, a joke that demonstrates my limited knowledge will get me off the hot seat when my students perceive that I am out of my element. In the midst of their increasing number of questions to demonstrate their cleverness, I will imitate a student asking an arcane question almost impossible to answer: "Uh, exactly how many bears were in

Alaska in 1881?" The students will laugh and eventually get it, that those college professors, or at least this one, do not have all of the answers. I can feign profundity and humility once again by comparing myself to Socrates and embracing his assertion that it is wiser to admit that you know nothing than to be unaware that you know nothing, and yet claim that you know something. Yes, I have built up a store of knowledge about history, philosophy, religion, economics, and other disciplines. But the more that I read, the less I seem to know; I become increasingly aware of how multifaceted a topic can be – full of arcane details and little-known minutia. The context of a fact, story, topic, or interpretation gets bigger and bigger, it seems.

Perhaps it is better not to be omniscient about your discipline or specialty. I seemingly would be a better teacher if I was all-knowing, able to deftly answer every query in class. That lack of knowledge, however, justifies my appetite for reading books. A sense of wonder and discovery would be lost if my mental capacity and memory were god-like. The feeling of intellectual competence that comes with having grappled with and successfully followed an author's line of argumentation would be gone if one already knew everything. Not knowing the answers in class is actually beneficial for discussion. A firm answer for every question immediately ends discussion. Open-ended questions with partial answers encourage open-ended conversations that engage students' interest.

I was not a serious reader until I reached my junior year in college. Up until that time, though, my affinity for written text was largely limited to a consistent, daily reading of the Bible, a product of my early, moderate fundamentalist upbringing. A youth pastor encouraged this habit, and prodded me and other Sunday School scholars to underline, circle, or mark key passages in the Bible. Even though it was God's Word and each word was holy, he assured us that we would not deface or profane it by underlining words and sentences. A well-marked, worn Bible, I thought, would establish my studious spirituality before others. I reveled in pride as I thumbed through my Bible and glanced at page after page of underlined text, markings, and marginal sophomoric comments.

My habit of underlining key passages in the Bible carried over into my undergraduate academic life. Once my love of books began to flower in my junior year at Murray State University, I felt oddly ill-equipped if I did not have a pen in my hand while reading a book with a Mountain Dew at my side. Throughout the years, my professors would often share books and copies of articles, and I would see how they would mark topic sentences, put question marks out beside certain passages, draw a wavy line vertically in the margin to flag a particularly long passage, and add erudite comments or pesky questions in the margins. I tried to imitate them sometimes or experimented with different types of pens, highlighters, or arcane symbols denoting agreement, disagreement, confusion, or laughter. Those sentences underlined or flagged often contained the thesis of the book, evidence that backed it up, amusing examples, or were simply well-wrought expressions or turns of phrase that I savored. I needed etchings within the book to prove that I had struggled with the text. Once finished with a book, the shelf would await with a prized spot and I was off on my search for the next book to digest. After graduation, and throughout graduate school, the books would accumulate on my shelves. A sense of satisfaction would envelop me. Sure, I would be convinced of one thing until I read another book on the same subject and pondered the probability of this new thesis or perspective. I can nod in agreement with David Denby, a prominent film critic, and his struggle with the great texts of Western civilization, only that my primary engagement was with non-fiction works of scholarship and other serious books aimed at literate, intelligent non-specialists:

> You read a persuasive argument and it filled your mind; you became an adherent of that text, swelling with it, enlarged by that implacably correct way of looking at the world – for a week. You were a rationalist, an empiricist and skeptic, a Hegelian, a Marxist. Taking on one identity after another, you were, for a while, blissfully irresponsible. . . . Out of this early promiscuity, if you were smart and disciplined, would come something like intellectual experience and readiness for more.[1]

A proper liberal arts education should produce students who love to read, or at least can tolerate the chore. I am thankful that my education did just that, and there are voices out there confidently asserting that goal. Denby, who went back to college after 30 years to reengage with the "Great

[1] David Denby, *Great Books: My Adventures with Homer, Rousseau, Woolf, and Other Indestructible Writers of the Western World* (New York: Simon and Schuster, 1996), 279.

Books," downplays literary theory and the need for background and "context" for ill-prepared undergraduates. What's wrong with reading for pleasure, asks Denby? "Readers! That's what undergraduate education should be producing."[2] Cultivating readers is needed now more than ever in a nation of increasing aliterates, and I hope that is not a circular argument. Unfortunately, to a certain extent and at certain periods, American education has always been seen in utilitarian terms. Americans valued education as a vehicle toward ensuring social order, producing a qualified yet disciplined workforce, and promoting upward mobility and personal advancement – not for developing a critical intellect or gaining knowledge of the best that has been done and thought.[3] An undue focus on intellectuality and aesthetics would produce too much leisure and decadence, like Europe.[4] And proper Americans don't want to be like Europe. If Morris Berman is correct, a nation of serious, critical readers, critical thinkers, and patrons of art and culture may just serve as a cell of enlightened individuals that will preserve these intellectual, aesthetic pursuits in a country and world that is engulfed in corporate culture, consumerism, and entertainment.[5]

I am not disparaging entertainment, though. Let me use an example from the popular sitcom *Seinfeld* to establish my endeavor. The character of George Costanza broke up with a girlfriend, I think, and told Jerry Seinfeld that he needed to get back into her apartment to retrieve a book or two

---

[2] Ibid., 204

[3] Insisting that a college education should result in a well-paying job is certainly understandable given the high cost of tuition.

[4] Richard Hofstadter, *Anti-Intellectualism in American Life* (New York: Vintage Books, 1963), 299-309; Peter R. Mitchell and John Schoeffel, *Understanding Power: The Indispensable Chomsky* (New York: The New Press, 2002), 236: When it comes to education, Noam Chomsky claims that a close friend concluded, and Chomsky is in agreement, that "The important thing is to be able to obey orders, and to do what you're told, and to be where you're supposed to be. The values are, you're going to be a factory worker somewhere – maybe they'll call it a university – but you're going to be following somebody else's orders, and just doing your work in some prescribed way. And what matters is discipline, not figuring things out for yourself, or understanding things that interest you – those are kind of marginal: just make sure you meet the requirements of a factory. Well, that's pretty much what the schools are like, I think: they reward discipline and obedience, and they punish independence of mind.

[5] Morris Berman, *The Twilight of American Culture* (New York: W. W. Norton and Company, 2000).

without having to confront or interact with her. Seinfeld, in one of his perennial digressions about nothing, asked why people were so intent on storing their books on a shelf like trophies. Once you have read it, why the need to hang on to it? Well, I could have just as easily interrogated the TV screen with a related question: Why do people download songs on their I-pods or hang onto their DVDs? After all, they have already heard or seen them. Why hang onto them? But I digress. Anyway, I am certain that all of the books on my shelves have forged me into the person that I am. Should they just sit there gathering dust, though, as past lofty trophies? Perhaps I need to revisit them like old friends and ponder the stuff I underlined.

Please suffer another example from popular culture. In the acclaimed movie, *Good Will Hunting*, Matt Damon's character, Will Hunting, a book-absorbing genius without a college degree, confronts a Harvard graduate student in a college bar who is demonstrating his knowledge of American colonial history to upstage an attempt by Will's friend to pick up a Harvard coed by pretending to be a college student. The grad student has succeeded in stalling the flirtation, but Will intervenes and cites the book the grad student has been filching from without attribution down to the very page number. He confidently asserts that this snooty book-bully will be convinced of one viewpoint during grad school until he reads a book or two from another perspective months later. I admit that I was once like this brash young grad student, albeit without the confrontational showcasing of my reading regimen. As stated above, immersion in books from one political or religious orientation would solidify that outlook until one began seriously reading books from a different perspective. Granted, some people can read opposing viewpoints without seriously questioning their own ideological or religious orientation. I do not wish to say that I am simply more open-minded, but I have always found it fascinating, and frustrating, that two equally intelligent and credentialed writers or scholars could reach such different conclusions about the same topic, as noted here by one bewildered historian:

> This has always troubled me. We both had taken advanced degrees at eminent universities. . . . We used the same documents and read the same biographies and memoirs in preparing our respective books – and came up with quite different interpretations. . . . Is there something wrong with our methods?[6]

In somewhat the same way, one encounters lots of competing claims from different religious, political, and economic groups in American society today about big questions. If bleary-eyed grad students and well-trained scholars often scratch their heads about contested truth claims in a variety of disciplines, can you imagine how everyday folks try to decide who's right about any number of religious, economic, and political questions?

Perhaps I am still adrift on an epistemological sea of information and viewpoints, always in the end taking a principled, yet safe, stand of healthy skepticism. Such a stance conveniently complements my noncommittal attitude concerning religion and politics, or at least the organized versions of them. Perhaps it is time to revisit all of those books about the above topics and consider them collectively in a systematized way – systemized, yes, but certainly not as a specialist. I will embrace and imitate Montaigne as "the patron saint of amateurs," in Denby's wording, and luxuriate in all of these books and ideas for the pure enjoyment, if not for a skillful dissection or exegesis.[7] Montaigne encouraged readers, when struggling with difficult books, to blame the author for being unclear, rather than judging themselves too dense to understand[8]. I will assume that density will be present on my part, but I will draw upon the thinking of writers less dense. Harold Bloom suggested that we turn to genius authors with the hope that some of that genius will rub off on us, even though he was referring to literary giants like Shakespeare and Chaucer while I will focus on secondary works of scholarship.[9] I can relate to a statement by one of my revered colleagues who teaches English: he said that the only way that he could grasp a subject was by sitting down and writing about it. Transforming yourself into a critical thinker will not be the result of simply reading books.[10] In like

[6] Andrew Delbanco, *College: What It Was, Is, And Should Be* (Princeton: Princeton University Press, 2012), 97.

[7] Denby, 272.

[8] Alain De Botton, *The Consolation of Philosophy* (New York: Pantheon Books, 2000), 158; Montaigne is an appropriate figure to mention when discussing skepticism and moderation. See Harry Clor, *On Moderation: Defending an Ancient Virtue in a Modern World* (Waco, TX: Baylor University Press, 2008), 4.

[9] Harold Bloom, *Genius: A Mosaic of One Hundred Exemplary Creative Minds* (New York: Warner Books, 2002), 5.

manner, public philosopher Bryan Magee affirmed the need to write in order to understand:

> Lord Acton said that one should learn as much from writing as from reading. It is a profound saying. Writing about a subject forces one to study it in an organized way and with a focused aim; to read all the important literature about it; to cover the whole ground, not leaving material gaps; and it gives one a powerful motive to get even the most trivial details right. . . . Most important of all, it forces one to *think* about the subject – and to organize one's thoughts, as well as one's material, into coherent structures.[11]

Before the widespread use of word processors, I wrote out college papers and book reviews by hand. Then I ventured into the brave new world of composing while typing. I was pleasantly surprised. The slight clicking noises of the keyboard as I wrote somehow imparted clarity to my thinking (or so I thought). I cannot explain it. The rest of this book will hopefully fall under the same magic as I grapple with the big questions, viewpoints, and worldviews encountered in a world of books, and I wish to see if revisiting these old friends will help me hammer out a coherent outlook on important topics, hopefully replete with reasonableness and moderation.

Early in my intellectual awakening, I was drawn to books about Christianity, religious history, biblical theology, and the crossroads where religion and philosophy met. It was not until I was seemingly treading water in graduate school, and especially after the challenge of teaching American history surveys years later, that I began taking an active, willing interest in economic and political topics. Religion, politics, economics, and the nature of knowledge are fundamental topics that try to address basic questions that affect all of our lives:

- Does God exist, and how can we know?
- Which religion is true, and how can we know?

---

[10] John Chaffee, *The Thinker's Way: Eight Steps to a Richer Life* (Boston: Little, Brown and Company, 1998), 21.

[11] Bryan Magee, *Confessions of a Philosopher: A Journey Through Western Philosophy* (New York: Random House, 1997), 33.

- Can we accumulate evidence to prove religion, when religion, subject to a certain definition, deals with a supernatural order that is beyond sense experience, the very realm from which we derive evidence?
- What ideology or political plan is the best way to govern people and ensure their happiness and liberty, yet simultaneously bring about social order and stability?
- What is the proper role of government? Especially on the federal level.
- What is the best way to ensure that a nation's store of material goods is fairly distributed on the basis of ability, hard work, justice, and emergency?
- Does competition or cooperation ensure excellence? Should it be a combination of both? In what proportion? Under what circumstances?
- When it comes to our knowledge of religion, politics, or economics, how do we know?

American conservatives and liberals, capitalists and socialists, Republicans and Democrats, Christians (and followers of other religions as well) and nonbelievers, empiricists and skeptics, moralists and libertines will answer those questions in very different ways. Each group and organization has very intelligent members, not to mention those who are ignorant or stupid, and perhaps proud of it. Each group has their own intellectuals and experts ready to deploy a host of arguments, data, and evidence to prove their point of view. Frequently, each accuses the other of lacking reason or being uninformed. Who's right? I will not even pretend that I know, but correctly sketching out the contours of thought from multiple perspectives will help us sharpen our focus. Perhaps I will irritate Morris Zap, a fictional literature professor in one of David Lodge's many hilarious send-ups of academic life: "[Postmodernist lit profs] liked to begin a paper with some formula like, 'I want to raise some questions about so-and-so' and seemed to think they had done their intellectual duty by merely raising them. This maneuver drove Morris Zap insane. Any damn fool, he maintained, could think of questions; it was *answers* that separated the men from the boys."[12] Fair enough. But honestly presenting the best of what each side has to offer will help develop what I will call "contextual awareness." It is a humble recognition that there are unrevealed facts and angles that we are simply unknowledgeable about that may, when brought to the surface and considered, alter our outlook.

I remember taking a road trip to a trailhead two or so hours away from Lexington, Kentucky. My hiking companions and I would enjoy discussing a wide range of things to pass the time. When I expressed something about a current political topic that seemed wishy-washy and ambivalent, one of my conservative friends firmly, yet playfully, proclaimed, "Pick a side!" Which side of the issue do you support? You are either a Republican or a Democrat. And more broadly, either you believe in God or you do not, and more specifically, you are either a Christian or not. Are you a capitalist or a socialist? A liberal or a conservative? I had learned well how an academic is supposed to respond to such either/or dichotomies: "Well, you see, it is more complex than that . . . ." But I certainly sympathized with the upfront, manly declaration of allegiances for clarity's sake.

Is it possible to take an intellectually defensible position that is intermediate among these religious and political poles of opposition? It certainly is possible, but is that position much more subject to vacillation and watered-down blandness? Who likes to take a bath in lukewarm water or be accused of being a milquetoast? There are books that abound to the tune of "the courage of a conservative" or the "courage of a liberal," for it takes fortitude to stick to one's guns and cling to cherished principles even when the chips are down. When your political team is on the bench, or your religious persuasion is not popular, you man the fort, fly your flag, and keep fighting until better days arrive. "The courage of a moderate" just doesn't have the same vim and vigor. Conservative talk-radio host Rush Limbaugh once groused, "By definition, moderates can't be brave – they don't have opinions! . . . I mean, brave moderates? 'Great Moderates in American History?' Show me that book."[13] So, one central question about the whole idea of moderation is whether one that maintains a "centrist" position can

---

[12] David Lodge, *Small World* in *A David Lodge Trilogy* (New York: Penguin Books, 1993), 38.

[13] Quoted in David S. Brown, *Moderates: The Vital Center of American Politics, From the Founding to Today* (Chapel Hill, N.C.: University of North Carolina Press, 2016), 268.

authentically adhere to any cause, belief or principle. Unapologetic partisans may point out that political or religious moderation "can only mean a disposition to tepid, middling compromise between opposing ideals," that it is "a weakness, a timid unwillingness to take a clear and decisive stand, a mere utilitarian 'splitting of the difference.'"[14] What do moderates believe, anyway?   True believers and partisans charge that wavering moderates pick and choose from the Bible, world religions, and political/economic systems like a buffet, and present an addlepated worldview. Or my favorite analogy/warning: if you are in the middle of the road, you are going to get hit (since this is a metaphorical road, I've never been sure by what).

My approach to these questions, I hope, will be moderate, cautious, and honest. Instead of searching out evidence, arguments, and examples that support one's economic, religious, and political viewpoints, let's adopt the rule of <u>disconfirming evidence</u>: be alert to evidence, data, arguments, or questions that disconfirm – or at least complicate – what you believe and honestly try to incorporate these into your worldview, and modify it, if need be. Charles Darwin, for instance, meticulously jotted down any objections to natural selection upon immediately encountering them so that he would not forget them later, for he "had noticed that we are all more apt to forget what we have an interest in not remembering."   So, let's cultivate "an unspecialized critical alertness," in the words of Anthony Flew, and examine the scaffolding and window-dressing of these ideologies, credenda, and worldviews.[15]

This book is designed to provide a litany of points and counterpoints concerning politics, religion, economics, and knowledge so that the jaded, educated moderate can be aware of, understand, and even appreciate, the arguments from opposing ideological camps.   I've culled together observational gems from authors and scholars from a variety of religious and ideological perspectives and have placed them side by side. The aim is not to find some position in the middle of the ideological spectrum in order

---

[14] Harry Clor, 3, 10.

[15] Anthony Flew, *How to Think Straight: An Introduction to Critical Reasoning* (Amherst, NY: Prometheus Books, 1998), 73, 109, 115; Quoted in David Henige, *Historical Evidence and Argumentation* (Madison, Wisc.: The University of Wisconsin Press, 2005), 200.

to stay safe and free from contention. Political and religious moderation should not be a stance of studied ambivalence masquerading as cleverness, or stem from the desire to inject complexity that springs from a playful cynicism (as appealing as that is for me), or result in an inability to commit oneself to a position and defend it. Instead, the moderate honestly considers several viewpoints, requires evidence for positions taken, and strives to acquire accurate information. He is aware of how each camp tries to spin information to their advantage, and has a passing familiarity with the various logical fallacies that are employed to persuade. This is not to say that only moderates can be honest and seek accurate information. I am sure that many conservatives and liberals strive to acquire accurate information and honestly employ it. But are they willing to consider accurate information and good argumentation from the other side?

Moderates also have to deal with the reality that those true believers and ideologues usually have more charisma because of their conviction that their sacred cows have been certified from on high, whether from a deity or an academic/think tank press. We need to construct a moderate code of belief and practice that appeals to reasonable, open-minded people. Entertaining multiple perspectives does not mean some epistemological free-for-all, but an honest evaluation of positions and arguments that may lead us to accept a Republican policy or embrace a Democratic one; castigate a liberal stance on some issue and award kudos to a conservative one on a case-by-case basis; dismiss a religious belief as irrational, or side with the Catholic Church on a moral issue; deride a statist measure as requiring too much government bureaucracy or voice skepticism about scrapping needed regulations to prevent corporations from taking advantage; or reject a view of knowledge that is overly relativistic and/or acknowledge that an embrace of uncertainty produces hesitancy and can stifle decisive activity.

Having the major arguments and contentions laid out in a systematic manner may serve as a way for both sides to engage each other with meaningful discussion. Just as discussion in a classroom helps nurture democracy and the ability to see, and maybe even appreciate, different perspectives,[16] it is helpful if both ideological and religious camps can first

---

[16] See Stephen D. Brookfield and Stephen Preskill, *Discussion as a Way of Teaching: Tools and Techniques for Democratic Classrooms*, 2nd ed. (San Francisco: Jossey-Bass,

properly understand the position of the other and not perpetuate straw man arguments. We need to clear away misperceptions about opponents and pursue dialogue that may foster a more democratic society. My litany of bolded truisms, principles, and observations will hopefully reflect the "big ticket" items of these major topics, but they also are simply nuggets of wisdom – as partisans and advocates see them – that I have cherry-picked in an idiosyncratic manner simply because they peaked my interest. I have strived to present their point of view with accuracy and fairness.

For all of you non-joiners out there, the skittish of the world reluctant to declare allegiance to any party or ideology, the "squishies" on the street that endure good-natured ribbing or verbal abuse for your careful navigation between the shoals, take heart and embrace your complicated, wary view of the world and gather some intellectual ammunition to justify your seemingly slapdash worldview. If you are skeptical about those who denounce any form of governmental regulation or intervention into society or the economy, and are equally unsure of those that want the government to regulate and protect almost everything, from the "womb to the tomb," or sneer at those who promote a rigid, authoritarian theological view based purely on dogmatic revelation, and are equally put off by atheists and nonbelievers who seem to *know* that God does not exist or that Christianity is obviously a scam or delusion, then maybe this book can assist you. I am not trying to manufacture more moderates with no substantial political or religious allegiance; neither am I persuading people to abandon the Republican or Democratic parties, or conservative and liberal principles; nor am I trying to seduce people into forsaking Christianity (or any other religious belief) or embracing atheism/agnosticism. My goal is to enlighten people about the improbability that any one set of people has a monopoly on the truth, that the context of the issue gets bigger with more information, that people should be willing to admit that they were wrong if overriding evidence is at hand, and that everyone should sharpen their practice of, in the words of Thomas Cathcart and Daniel Klein, bullscatology: the art of detecting bullshit.[17]

2005).

[17] Thomas Cathcart & Daniel Klein. *Aristotle and an Aardvark Go To Washington: Understanding Political Doublespeak Through Philosophy and Jokes* (New York: Abrams Image, 2007), 12.

I can foresee the possible reactions to this effort. Theistic readers may think that my treatment of religion has only a thin veneer of balance laced with contemptuous remarks about religion, while atheistic readers may think that I skirt the edges of academic respectability by too seriously considering a religious argument about some topic. Conservative readers may complain that this book leans slightly, or too far, to the left – liberals, to the right. I can only address this by relating it to my teaching experience. When it comes to American History textbooks and courses, many conservative commentators often complain that high school and college history classes are "biased" because of an excessive focus on the negative things in the American past (a roast). Responding to that demand, conservative scholars write histories of the United States that uplift the "traditional" or patriotic version of American history (a pep rally). Neither roast nor pep rally, I always say. I walk to the board and draw a slanted line. How do we know that this line is slanted, I ask? Because we know what a straight, vertical line looks like. In the same way that you can only describe a line as slanted by comparing it to a straight one, the only way that you can tell that a version of history is slanted or biased is by comparing it to the straight, objective version. Well, I ask, can you show me where to find two volumes of American history on a college level that represent the absolute, accurate, objective truth about United States history? If you can, and demonstrate its objectivity, I promise I will adopt it as the course textbook next semester. I still have not received an answer – although some brave liberals and conservatives conceivably might suggest a few titles that are in line with their own ideological inclinations about history. In other words, if they largely agree with it, then it is largely objective. If they largely disagree with it, it must be largely biased.

I doubt that anyone can ever produce a work that represents a reasonable, well-balanced, accurate version about religion, economics, politics, and knowledge (or U.S. history) that captures the assent of the vast majority of people. I can only offer my attempt in the next few chapters to forge a fair and moderate account of these topics.

I will employ categories for the sake of comparison and convenience. However, one must keep in mind that religious, economic, political, and epistemological opinions are often ranged on a continuum. Any agreement about what "moderate" is depends on where one is located on the spectrum.

A reasonable question is, moderate "compared to what?" Or extremist compared to what? A liberal may see someone who supports the free market with needed regulations here and there as conservative, while a laissez-faire libertarian may see the same person as substantially liberal. With religion, an atheist may see a member of mainstream Protestantism as a traditional Christian believer while a fundamentalist may see that same person, and even some evangelicals, as a heretic. Regarding American political history, for example, one's opinion about Franklin Delano Roosevelt and his New Deal programs depends on where one sits on the ideological spectrum. Those to the far right of FDR, like the Chamber of Commerce, the National Association of Manufacturers, and the American Liberty League, thought his programs bordered on socialism and undermined individual liberty as well as economic incentive and stability – i.e., his programs were doing too much – while those to his far left, like Father Coughlin[18] and Huey Long, thought that his programs *were not doing enough* to alleviate the Great Depression. Was FDR trying to introduce socialism or save capitalism? It depended on who you asked and where they were located on the ideological scale.[19]

The challenge here is to craft a zone of reasonable moderation that can appeal to the widest possible range of positions on this continuum, a *methodology of caution* in evaluating information to which most good-willed, reasonable people with all types of religious, economic, and political perspectives can subscribe. I have mentioned some of these above, but let me offer more explicitly the "marks of moderation." A moderate conservative or liberal, or a reasonable atheist or Christian, or an open-minded laissez-faire advocate or regulator:

1. Requires evidence and accurate information.
2. Pays attention to disconfirming evidence.
3. Understands the actual argument of an opponent before responding and does not perpetuate a caricature of the opponent's argument to create a straw man. Or, as Richard Paul and Linda Elder ask, "Have I

---

[18] Textbooks often describe Coughlin as residing on the right. His advocacy of nationalizing banks places him on the left, I think, given conservatives' loathing of government ownership.
[19] Clor, 8-9.

entered the opposing views in good faith, or only enough to find flaws in them?"[20]

4. Is willing to change his mind when met with a convergence of evidence from different sources.

5. Sees moderation not as a cozy notch half-way between two positions or policies, but as a habit of mind and outlook, "an attitude, a disposition, an orientation."[21] If you are a politician, it means that you are not simply a moderate because your vote is "up-for-grabs." Your position is born of "genuine conviction," not because you are currying favor with your donors, desiring to draw attention to yourself, trying to win a popularity contest with lobbyists, or tilting your stance to reflect the political pulse of your district.[22]

6. Adopts a "case-by-case" mentality unencumbered by strict adherence to principle in every case and every situation. As Harry Clor has noted when discussing Aristotle as a "philosopher of moderation," "A course of action, policy or pronouncement that is valid in some or most cases would be wrong, even disastrous, in certain situations, and there will be exceptions to any proposition you could affirm."[23] Determining those unique situations, of course, requires more deliberation.

7. Sees moderation as a "recognition of limits." The imposition of a social, economic, political, or religious blueprint for society, despite the best of intentions, will not easily dissolve, cure, or fit over the imperfections, flaws, and rough edges of human beings. We must grudgingly tolerate these blemishes and realize that a campaign to eradicate vices, evils, annoyances, and anomalies, and all other parts that won't fit, may make them worse.[24]

8. Exalts reason tempered by humility. Reason is a wonderful tool of the human mind, and it must be defended in the face of those that

---

[20] Linda Elder and Richard Paul, *The Art of Socratic Questioning* (Dillion Beach, CA: Foundation for Critical Thinking, 2007), 9.
[21] Clor, 45
[22] Jacob Hacker and Paul Pierson, *Winner-Take-All Politics: How Washington Made the Rich Richer – And Turned Its Back on the Middle Class* (New York: Simon and Schuster, 2010), 237, 239.
[23] Clor, 23
[24] Ibid., 12.

see it as an oppressive epistemology that masks self-interested power and those who naively believe that all opinions or judgments are equally valid. It must be practiced, though, with a meek acknowledgment that humans are not omniscient and are prone to mistakes in thinking and fact-gathering.

9. Is able to distance himself from a partisan stance; and
10. Recognizes the limitations of moderation itself. For instance, too much moderation can debilitate decisiveness.

Laying out the arguments, statistics, principles, and emphases of these different ideological and religious groups will hopefully give readers many perspectives from which to consider the major questions I raised earlier, and they can keep these marks of moderation in mind to consider judiciously the viewpoints of these contending groups. I can only be a guide, moderator, and occasional commentator by imagining how a liberal, conservative, Christian, atheist, laissez-faire enthusiast, or government official would respond.

A plea for an informed moderation is certainly not a path-breaking endeavor. Abler scholars and writers have outlined this orientation for several years now: David Brooks, David S. Brown, and Aurelian Craiutu, for instance. Brown has surveyed the political history of the United States and has identified numerous individuals that he describes as embodying the "moderate persuasion," men like John Quincy Adams, Abraham Lincoln, and Theodore Roosevelt. Although these individuals may not have seen themselves as moderate, they carefully navigated a path between "Jacksonianism and Cotton Whiggery," "radical abolitionism and radical state's rights," and powerful trusts and labor extremism respectively. The conservative-liberal contest in many political narratives overlooks these individuals and pragmatic coalitions. Brooks, for his part, has issued "a moderate manifesto" replete with signposts of moderation that resemble the points above. For instance, moderates are humble about the limits of their current knowledge, strive to make situation-driven policy decisions, and do not predictably sit squarely in the middle of the spectrum – it depends on the case and the situation.

Aurelian Craiuto, in his book *Faces of Moderation*, has also identified key elements of moderation. Although he focuses mostly on European figures and politics, he does include American exemplars of moderation. The elements or orientations that he identifies mirror my own list above (or my list mirrors his): moderates value discussion as a reasonable route to an imperfect consensus, see decisions and policy adoption as driven by circumstances and the situation, uphold civility as an ideal for society, shun absolute dichotomies between good and evil, and are open to syncretism and "hybridity." Practicing moderation is akin to maintaining balance, like a high-wire performer (as depicted on the cover of his book). He also notes that other scholars have recently published books about moderation or topics that intersect with it, so the concern about developing a philosophy of moderation is far from being an innovative scholarly enterprise. Craiuto's "main goal is to continue a conversation about an important but still surprisingly neglected virtue that is worth having today in our heated political environment."[25]

I wholeheartedly agree and would like to join this conversation. My goal is to lay out a series of bolded principles or arguments from each side of these debates – interspersed with actual or imagined criticisms and occasional references to possible logical fallacies and relevant cautions derived from our list of exhortations about moderation. Again, my list is not comprehensive at all; it merely registers what I think are standard arguments and emphases within these ideological camps, or are focal points that I happen to find interesting. After having summed up these themes, I then try to find a way forward based on a reasonable consensus.

---

[25] David Brooks, "What Moderates Believe", *New York Times*, August 22, 2017, https://www.nytimes.com/2017/08/22/ . . . /trump-moderates-bipartisanship-truth.html; "What Moderation Means", *New York Times*, October 26, 2012, www.nytimes.com/2012/10/26/opinion/brooks-what-moderation-means.html. Accessed February 24, 2018; David S. Brown, *Moderates: The Vital Center of American Politics, From the Founding to Today* (Chapel Hill, N.C.: University of North Carolina Press, 2016); Aurelian Craiutu, *Faces of Moderation: The Art of Balance in an Age of Extremes* (Philadelphia: University of Pennsylvania Press, 2017), 1-33.

Chapter Two

Religion and Unbelief

I have never seen a design that had no designer, a law that had no lawgiver, an order that had not been ordered, information that had no informer.[26]

James P. Keener

[In response to the question, "Why is there something rather than nothing"?] *How do you know the universe didn't always exist? . . . . Couldn't something be the default position, with nothing being the truly extraordinary thing?*[27]

Peter Boghossian

Let's start with probably the major topic, since it deals with ultimate issues like the existence of God and the meaning of man's life on earth: religion. Although I will try to address religious belief in general, my primary focus will be on Christianity because it is a system of belief and a lifestyle with which I am most familiar, and also has been the most influential in the United States and Western civilization.

---

[26] James P. Keener, "Confessions of a 'Weird Mathematician'," in *Professors Who Believe: The Spiritual Journeys of Christian Faculty,* ed. Paul M. Anderson (Downers Grove, Ill.: InterVarsity Press, 1998), 91.
[27] Peter Boghossian, *A Manual for Creating Atheists* (Durham, NC: Pitchstone Publishing, 2013), 149.

No matter how educated or uneducated, I'm reasonably certain that every human being has, at some point, wondered if there is something beyond this world and typical human experiences. Are we exclusively embedded in a material or natural world of cause and effect, or is there an extra-material or supernatural order of things/entities/existence beyond our five senses that we can only know by revelation and faith, extrasensory perception, or some other unusual means of knowing? Answers to this question produce spirited, sometimes bitter, disputes. Atheists and agnostics often see religious believers as ignorant and intolerant, while Christians and other types of believers in the supernatural view the former as arrogant, dismissive, and even immoral.

My steady regimen of reading books has impressed on me the necessity of disclosing biases and points of view before setting out on a topic. So, here it goes. As for me, I converted to evangelical Christianity in my teens. One of the monumental memories of my life is when I "got saved," or accepted Christ as my savior. Admittedly, this salvation event happened several times, and I have no idea which one sealed the verdict, if any of them did. The church I attended was moderately fundamentalist but good-natured about the challenge of living in a secular world, and I still have fond memories: the Bible was inerrant; Jesus was God and had saved me and the rest of humanity from sin by dying on the cross; and my behavior was supposed to reflect the moral teachings of the Bible. It was not morally strict, however, for we could wear shorts and bathing suits on the beach during a Christian retreat.

When I went to college, my beliefs started to buckle under exposure to my college majors: history and psychology. When I began graduate school, though, I discovered that evangelical Christianity did have an impressive array of degreed defenders. I read their books and gained an appreciation for their able defense of the Christian faith, even though church attendance and bible study groups went into a temporary eclipse in my life. I was intellectually engaged with Christianity, but not emotionally. The "praise and worship" craze in contemporary evangelical churches – along with backslapping and sucrose piety – left me cold, and still does. Even during my early stage of Christian belief in high school, studying the Bible and reading Christian books were more appealing than the emotional hoopla of revivals and retreats even though I participated with some enthusiasm. After a few years of wide-eyed Christian spirituality, I gradually came to greet the alter calls at the end of the service with indifference – even discomfort, inward groaning, and interior eyerolls.

Today, I try to steer a middle course between a culture of belief that is encapsulated by the bumper sticker, "God said it, I believe it, and that settles it," and a more complex approach that risks diluting the essential elements of Christianity that make it historically distinctive. On many days, a simple belief in God and ethical behavior is sufficient. I guess I can say that my religious beliefs range on a continuum from appreciation of well-wrought Christian theology to a general ethical theism, with recurring agnostic moments. I like reading about theology and the history of Christianity, especially in the United States. I appreciate a good, exegetically-savvy sermon, even if I do not believe all of it, or my normal routines, behavior, speech, and attitudes remain undisturbed the rest of the week. I like the age-old Baptist tradition of going out to eat after church. I treasure my Christian friends and family. That's about it, though. Praying is an infrequent chore. I shun touchy-feely, piety-infused Bible studies (especially the call to hold hands while wrapping up the session with prayer). I doubt all the time. I don't have faith that there is an afterlife; but I hope there is, if only to reconnect with family and friends that were taken from this life and those that will be. [28]

This doubt is often tied to my states of mind and heart. Moments of extreme doubt often arise from a gloomy mood, as noted by the acclaimed Christian theologian C.S. Lewis: "Now that I am a Christian I do have moods in which the whole thing [Christianity] looks very improbable: but when I was an atheist I had moods in which Christianity looked very probable."[29] I continue to think about these ultimate issues no matter what mood.

---

[28] There is a difference between hope and faith, I think, as Peter Boghossian has noted in *A Manual for Creating Atheists* (p. 26-27). I don't have faith that I will win the lottery. I don't purchase a ticket and then go sell my house and quit my job right before the drawing, dreaming of where I will relocate and how I will spend my millions. I hope that I will win, though. Hoping implies that I am aware that what I hope for may not come about. I hope that the probability of a pleasant afterlife is much greater than that of winning the lottery, though.

[29] C. S. Lewis, *Mere Christianity* (New York: McMillan Publishing Company, 1960), 109.

THE EXISTENCE OF GOD

In any discussion of religion, the foundational issue is the existence of God/gods. Simply put, belief in God often depends on faith. For others, though, faith is not enough; they want to know that God exists through the additional means of reason and sense experience. The following is by no means comprehensive, but is simply a comparison of the traditional and most interesting arguments for the existence of God and subsequent critiques.

Assertion: The idea of God proves his existence

This formal proof for God's existence was put forth by an Italian cleric, Saint Anselm, in the 12th century. When I first read about it, I must admit that it took me a long time to get my head wrapped around it. He argued that we can form an idea of the most perfect Being. But a Being like this that actually existed in reality outside of our head would be even more perfect. But if this Being did not exist in reality, then there would have to be a conception of a being more perfect than the one originally conceived, and subsequently one that existed in reality that was superior in perfection. If that Being did not exist, then there would have to be a conception of a Being even more perfect, and on and on. Rene Descartes later added that our notion of "imperfection" would be impossible if we did not already have an idea of perfection. God is perfect, and nonexistence would take away from that perfection. [30]

Criticism: The idea of something does not prove its existence because that line of reasoning can be applied to almost anything

Challenges to Anselm came quickly for the medieval era. A pesky monk replied that we do not necessarily have the mental capacity to imagine a perfect entity and, even if we did, that conception does not prove anything. He said that we could imagine the most beautiful island, but that does not prove that it exists anywhere [31] – or the most perfect goblin or pixie, for that

---

[30] Karen Armstrong, *A History of God: The 4000-Year Quest of Judaism, Christianity and Islam* (New York: Alfred A. Knopf, 1994), 300; Simon Blackburn, *Think: A Compelling Introduction to Philosophy* (Oxford: Oxford University Press, 1999), 155.

[31] Richard E. Rubenstein, *Aristotle's Children: How Christians, Muslims, and Jews*

matter. Centuries later, the famed German philosopher Immanuel Kant also pointed out that Anselm's questionable, unstated assumption was that existence was more perfect than non-existence.[32] I guess that means that if entropy is true, then existence will tend to get sloppier over time. Non-existence will maintain its undifferentiated, simple state of nothingness. As for a method of thinking in general, Anselm's argument demonstrates that deductive reasoning, although a powerful tool, is inadequate and needs to be supplemented and disciplined by the empirical rigor of the scientific method.

Assertion: There cannot be an endless chain of cause and effect, for something or Someone had to exist in order to start the sequence

This assertion is known as the cosmological argument, or the first cause principle. Why is there something rather than nothing? All things in existence had to come from some previous cause, which was preceded by a cause, which was itself preceded by a cause, until you trace this line of causation back to some beginning. The ultimate cause's eternal existence is a given; it has existed before the beginning of the universe, time, and the chain of causation.

Objection: It is contradictory and arbitrary to use cause-and-effect reasoning and then suspend it at some beginning point

Mathematician and philosopher Bertrand Russell argued that the conclusion contradicts the premise. The premise is that everything has a cause. But when you argue that the ultimate cause does not have a cause, then you have made a huge, arbitrary exception to your premise. This supernatural uncaused Cause is no more probable than a natural, uncaused material cosmos that has always existed. And, as skeptic Michael Shermer has simply asked, along with others, what caused God? If God does not need a cause, then not everything in the known universe needs a cause, which complicates the premise of the cosmological argument. If God does have a cause, then an endless hierarchy of higher-level deities can be postulated. [33]   Atheist

---

Rediscovered Ancient Wisdom and Illuminated the Dark Ages (New York: Harcourt, 2003), 103-104; Blackburn, 156.

[32] Richard Dawkins, *The God Delusion* (Boston: Houghton Mifflin Company, 2006), 83.

[33] Blackburn, 160, 162; Michael Shermer, *How We Believe: The Search for God in an Age*

Richard Dawkins takes the objections even further: if we grant that one can give a good reason for arbitrarily stopping the chain of causation that is crucial to one's case, why does this uncaused entity get all these different attributes ascribed to it, like omniscience, omnipotence, wisdom, love, etc.? Dawkins goes on to ask, which god? If you do not believe in Zeus, does that make you an atheist? [34] Not only does the entry of an uncaused deity into the chain of cause and effect make no sense, but those who claim that there cannot be an uncaused cosmic sequence of cause and effect are also arguing from ignorance. Their assertion is simply that – mere assertion. How do they <u>know</u> that there cannot be an unbroken chain of cause and effect without beginning nor end? It is a clear case of the appeal to ignorance fallacy: since I cannot explain X, Y, or Z, it must be God, aliens, green goblins, or a government conspiracy, a conclusion that does not have warrant.

Pascal's Wager: If you believe in God and He does not exist, then you have lost nothing. If you do not believe in God and He does turn out to exist, then you are in trouble

Blaise Pascal famously posed a choice that people could make based on common sense and reason. He concluded that it was wise to believe in God no matter his existence or nonexistence. If God does not exist, your belief does not net you any type of suffering after death. If God does exist, and you believed, then your own existence after death would probably be pleasant. However, if God does exist and you did not believe, presumably your experience of the afterlife would be horrific, or at least unpleasant.

Objections: The assumption that God will punish unbelief is debatable, and one cannot turn off their unbelief like a light switch if taking the wager

Philosopher Simon Blackburn has noted that Pascal simply postulates God's schedule of rewards and punishments, an actuarial table that he just assumes. That God would punish unwarranted belief is just as plausible as

---

of Science (New York: W. H. Freeman and Company, 2000), 15, 92; Jennifer Michael Hecht, *Doubt: A History, The Great Doubters and Their Legacy of Innovation from Socrates and Jesus to Thomas Jefferson and Emily Dickenson* (New York: HarperSanFrancisco, 2003), 452.
[34] Dawkins, 53, 77.

the rewarding of the same. Someone that took the wager starting from a position of serious doubt cannot automatically start genuinely believing in God with a snap of the fingers and – presto! – I'm a true believer, now. Besides, if God is all-knowing, then he can perceive that the newly-adopted belief is insincere or pragmatic and merely adopted to avoid some expected punishment.[35] In addition, Pascal's wager does not tell us anything about the nature of this deity. Is this God all-knowing or simply smart enough to manipulate or threaten humans? Fundamentally good or evil, or something in between? Finally, Jamie Whyte has noted that Pascal had Christianity in mind when postulating the bet. What about other religions and belief systems? His bet works just as well – or badly, as we have seen – for any other religion that punishes disbelief with an unpleasant afterlife and rewards belief with eternal bliss.[36]

Assertion: The universe is so fine-tuned for the existence of mankind that it points to God

This assertion is known widely as the anthropic principle. It seems that every physical or material variable and constant is tweaked to such a specific extent as to allow the comfortable existence of life on this particular planet in this particular universe. If just one of these factors was increased or decreased by a minuscule amount, like the binding power of atomic nuclei or the ratio between gravity and electromagnetic forces, then life would be unsustainable. God is the only explanation. He creates and maintains the conditions for our existence by monitoring and keeping his hands on the knobs and tuners (yes, I am using anthropomorphic language to describe God's operations for the purpose of illustration. More about that later). This argument is one of the most powerful and persuasive, theists argue, and is related to the concept of an Intelligent Designer.[37] Not only is the survivability of life in this finely-tuned world amazing, but our position in the universe is incredibly suitable for observing this universe and detecting these beneficial constants and variables. Our stadium seats provide a great view of the action, almost as if some Divine Alumnus purchased the tickets

---

[35] Blackburn, 188-89; Dawkins, 104.

[36] Jamie Whyte, *Crimes Against Logic: Exposing the Bogus Arguments of Politicians, Priests, Journalists, and Other Serial Offenders* (New York: McGraw Hill, 2005), 38.

[37] Michael Shermer, *Why Darwin Matters: The Case Against Intelligent Design* (New York: Times Books, 2006), 54-55

for us to use. The ability to survive – if not to flourish – *and observe* is further proof of benevolent design.[38]

Objections: If there is a multitude of possible worlds, then the seemingly perfect conditions for life would have arisen on one or more of them by chance

The field of physics has made some amazing theoretical advances. According to string theory, it is plausible to imagine realistically a number of worlds approaching 10 to the 500th power. If that is true, then it would be incredible that at least one or two of these possible worlds did not have intelligent life with the optimal conditions for existence.[39]   Besides that, if the world and the universe were designed by a Designer, then one could justifiably ask, echoing the question in the cosmological critique, who designed the Designer? And if you are relying upon the argument that the Designer is undesigned, then that is clearly arbitrary if your premise is that *everything* in the universe has the appearance of design. Further, if you simply cannot believe that the universe and life on it came about by the happy concurrence of the right atoms at the right time in the right combination under the right conditions, that such an occurrence is statistically improbable, then isn't God also statistically improbable? God's awfully smart and powerful – being omniscient and omnipotent – so that speaks of an entity with incredible complexity. So, if he did not come about by some previous designer or cause, then his spontaneous appearance (or eternal existence) would be *even more statistically unbelievable* than the appearance of a universe with the optimal conditions for life.[40] Further, those who advocate design in the universe often dodge questions about the

---

[38] James Daniel Sinclair, "At Home in the Multiverse? Critiquing the Atheist Many-Worlds Scenario", in Paul Copan and William Lane Craig, eds., *Contending With Christianity's Critics: Answering New Atheists and other Objectors* (Nashville: B & H Publishing Group, 2009), 22.

[39] Ibid., 57

[40] Shermer, *How We Believe*, 94; Dawkins, 120-21, 153; William Lane Craig, "Dawkins's Delusion", in *Contending With Christianity's Critics*, 4-5; William Lane Craig has critiqued this notion of a statistically complex deity being just as improbable by asserting that God is an incredibly simple being, and that Dawkins has conflated the idea of God (simple) with His thoughts (complex). But Craig asserted in a footnote that God is "an unembodied mind." If that is true, how can you separate the idea of God from God's thoughts?

nature of that Designer. If one postulates a theory, it must have "explanatory power" along with evidence. Ruling out other explanations for the origin of the universe and life is not enough. Design advocates "simply estimate probabilities and use them to eliminate chance or necessity" but do not go on and provide positive evidence of a designer. In addition to evidence, one must also sketch out the characteristics and properties of the purported explanation left.[41]   Finally, wouldn't it be even more amazing – and convincing – if God maintained human life on earth in conditions that were clearly *unsuitable*, critics could ask? Living in a world that is exactly suitable is not evidence of God's design, but simply one grand circular argument: if life was not precisely good here, it would be systemically bad.

Christian retort: The idea of multiple worlds is just a grand hunch dressed up in academic garb, and evidence of design is still obvious in the face of ignorance about the ultimate cause

William Lane Craig, a professor at the Talbot School of Theology, points out that the premise is not that <u>everything</u> requires a cause, but that which comes into existence requires a cause. All that is needed is a simple word change in the premise. God is timeless and never came into existence: He does not need a cause. One has to admit that it is a nifty, tidy verbal fix. As for the multiple worlds theory, these possible universes are not empirically available to us to investigate. They are merely metaphysical speculations. That skeptics have to resort to such elaborate explanations is proof enough that they will come up with almost any scenario to avoid conceding divine design and fine-tuned conditions.[42]   As previously noted, in Christian intellectual circles, God is often obliquely referred to as an intelligent designer. Stephen Meyer answers the "who designed the designer" question with two responses: 1) The inability to explain the previous cause responsible for the cause in question does not invalidate the former's explanatory power about an effect: "A proximate explanation of one event is not negated by learning that it does not supply a comprehensive or ultimate explanation of all the events in the causal chain leading up to it" and 2) the

---

[41] Matt Young and Taner Edis, eds., *Why Intelligent Design Fails: A Scientific Critique of the New Creationism* (New Brunswick, NJ: Rutgers University Press, 2005), 193-95, 196.
[42] Lee Strobel, *The Case for Faith* (Grand Rapids, MI.: Zondervan Publishing House, 2000), 76-79.

same objection about an infinite regress of an endless series of designers could also be applied to material causation, for if material causes are sufficient to explain life, then what *previous* material factors caused the material causes of life's origin, and the previous material causes before that?[43] Craig has offered a useful analogy to support Meyer's first point: if archeologists dig up some artifacts, they reasonably infer that ancient people constructed them even though they may not know who these people were and their origin. Or if astronauts discovered mechanized objects on the moon or some other planet, we can attribute the gadgets to intelligent life without knowing anything about these entities' ultimate beginning or whereabouts.[44]

Secular assertion: The presence and prevalence of evil disproves the existence of God

The classic formula goes something like this: If God is all-powerful and good, he would prevent evil. If evil happens, then either God is not omnipotent because he could not stop it, or that God allowed the evil, which would make Him much less than good – sadistic at worst and mischievous at best.[45] Either way, whether it's a significant reduction in His omnipotence or His goodness, this incomplete, imperfect being does not merit godhood or adoration. Besides that, the existence of evil itself says nothing about God's existence or nonexistence. It just occurs and proves or means nothing. If I can paraphrase Hugh Laurie's award-winning character, Dr. House, who, when questioning why bad events in peoples' lives must have meaning, merely asserted, "people just get what they get."

Theological response: Evil tests peoples' faith and character, and one cannot know what evil is unless they have a firm sense of what good is

Here are the basic responses:

---

[43] Steven Meyer, *Signature in the Cell: DNA and the Evidence For Intelligent Design* (New York: HarperOne, 2009), 388-392.

[44] William Lane Craig, "Dawkins's Delusion", 4.

[45] Armstrong, *A History of God*, 376.

- Suffering breaks us down for repentance and then clears away the suffocating underbrush to prepare us for spiritual growth and greater understanding
- Suffering and evil remind us that morality is its own reward. We should not be moral in expectation of rewards, otherworldly or worldly. The continuance of moral behavior after evil events reinforces the principle
- Our limited minds cannot foresee the possible long-term benefits brought about by short-term evils and suffering [this argument sounds a lot like the utilitarian argumentation put forth in the discipline of economics by authors like Henry Hazlitt – more about that later]
- We cannot call evil that happens to otherwise good people "unjust" without first having some notion of what "just" is. Now, where does that notion come from?
- God may indeed have a purpose for allowing a certain evil to transpire, but why should He be obligated to reveal to us why? Secondly, even if God revealed why, the revelation may thwart the full effect of the providential purpose of the evil. Thirdly, if God did reveal why, one may not be able to understand it given our limited capacities
- God could have chosen to create a world without suffering, but such a world would be largely devoid of human comfort and responsibility for others. It is in suffering that human connections become the most vital. We would not have opportunities to show compassion and sympathy if there was no evil and suffering in the world
- And the old standby: God allows evil because he does not want to violate our free will to choose. Some people will choose to inflict harm on others by direct or indirect action, or by no action at all[46]

---

[46] Richard Swinburne, "The Vocation of a Natural Theologian" in Philosophers Who Believe: The Spiritual Journeys of Eleven Leading Thinkers, ed. Kelly James Clark (Downer's Grove, Ill.: InterVarsity Press, 1993), 200; Peter Kreeft and Ronald K. Tacelli, Handbook of Christian Apologetics (Downers Grove, Ill.: InterVarsity Press), 123; Lewis, Mere Christianity, 31; Michael J. Murray, "Seek and You Will Find" in God and the Philosophers: The Reconciliation of Faith and Reason, ed. Thomas V. Morris (New York: Oxford University Press, 1994), 66-67; Strobel, The Case for Faith, 32, 44; David J. Wolpe,

- Well, to make this issue even more complicated, what if you are a Gnostic? The ancient believers known as Gnostics thought that God existed in isolated splendor, but somehow God's energy or essence branched off or was seeded throughout the universe, creating more types of deities, which spawned even more. The farther out the "emanations" were from the original Spring, the more incompetent, ill-intentioned, and grumpy they became (depending on which Gnostic cosmology one consults – and actually understands). One of these incompetent deities created man and the material world, both being very imperfect and corrupt. The goal for humankind was to escape from this mortal prison by connecting with the faint spiritual spark within, and Jesus was sent to help people get in touch with this unworldly essence and climb their way back up the waterfall to the Eternal Spring. Anyway, Gnostics could dismiss evil by blaming it on one of these incompetent deities – a demiurge. Therefore, the original, inscrutable God was off the hook.[47]

From a logical standpoint, even the atheist philosopher Antony Flew admits that Christians may have a case if they can demonstrate that you cannot have Good and good things without the Bad and bad things, for it would be "logically impossible." For instance, it does not make sense to forgive someone without there having been an offense, or at least a perceived one.[48] But as for the claim that suffering brings about greater understanding and mature wisdom, one could certainly ask how the death of kids by natural disasters accomplishes this, or the creation and deployment of flesh-eating bacteria. A greater understanding of what, exactly? You would think that God could find a less cruel way to teach somebody a lesson. Regarding the seemingly innate notion of justice and fairness, a critic could respond in three ways. First, if having an internal sense of what you "ought" to do is proof of God, then what about lust and aggression, also innate? If God planted a sense of fairness in humankind, did He also plant these as well? Second, how do you know that your internal sense of justice is empirically

---

Why Faith Matters (New York: HarperOne, 2008), 130, 139.

[47] Jonathan Wright, *Heretics: The Creation of Christianity from the Gnostics to the Modern Church* (Boston: Houghton Mifflin Harcourt, 2011), 25-28.

[48] Antony Flew, *How to Think Straight: An Introduction to Critical Reasoning* (Amherst, NY.: Prometheus Books, 1998), 19

and ethically right? Third, a sense of fairness does not have to be explained supernaturally. Fair play simply helps society function. It is a positive adaptation that helps human societies get along, resolve disputes, and move forward – more or less smoothly.[49]

In addition, the assertion that God chooses not to reveal the reasons for suffering is ridiculous. In the Old Testament, He reveals to the Israelites the specific measurements and accoutrements of priests' robes and temples, but is coy about revealing why one must endure a painful malady. One reader of this manuscript put it this way: "Apparently, then, God in His infinite wisdom thinks that wearing blue tassels on the corners of your cloak is an idea important enough to reveal to His children [in the Old Testament], but the purpose of schizophrenia isn't important enough to reveal." Finally, the Gnostic explanation of evil is clever, but if a demiurge created this world with all of its imperfections, could not the original, sovereign God have prevented this creation, foreseeing all of the suffering that would transpire? If he could not prevent it, then he evidently is not all-powerful. If he could not foresee all of the future evils, then he is not omniscient. If he could both foresee and prevent these evils or the original creation, then you have to explain why he did not. This puts us right back into the same situation with all of the explanations cited above.

Rejoinder: Pascal is whispering in your ear

Despite all the objections to Pascal's wager, which proposition are you willing to gamble your life-savings or eternal state on? Do you believe that you just happen to inhabit one or two of those many worlds that have the seemingly fine-tuned conditions for the flourishing of life, or would you place your money on the idea that God created and preserved the conditions of your universe and planet to enable your survival and potential felicity? Why is there something rather than nothing? This gamble is based on reason, though. Perhaps reason is not enough. Even Pascal noted that reason cannot explain everything, and that truth can also be known through our hearts.[50] Even if you still do not agree with Pascal's wager and the

---

[49] Mark D. Linville objects that even if it is true that morality has an evolutionary adaptive advantage for society over time, it shifts the proper focus from the *truth* of biblical morality to merely its social utility. See Mark D. Linville, "The Moral Poverty of Evolutionary Naturalism", in *Contending With Christianity's Critics*, 62.

appeal to emotion, then perhaps you can admit that his proposition at least provides an "incentive" to search and seek out God and the natural universe for meaning and explanation.[51]

THE BIBLE

For millions of Christians in the United States and around the world, the Bible is the literal Word of God. It does not simply *contain* the Word of God, but actually *is*. Under divine inspiration, God moved the hearts and minds of human authors to write down a record of his dealings with humankind. Those believers with a little more interpretive flexibility grant that God allowed each author's personality, background, and literary style to shape the essential message and record that God intended humans to hear. For fundamentalists and many evangelicals, not only is the Bible inspired, it is inerrant: it contains no scientific, historical, or scribal mistakes. It is perfect divine revelation. There are central themes that run through it, especially the deity and eventual return of Christ, and it should be viewed as a whole. One part of it cannot be understood without reference to other parts. Scripture should be interpreted in the light of Scripture.

For countless liberal and mainstream Christians, and certainly for secularists and nonbelievers, the Bible is simply the edited collection of different books with different authors from different time periods with different concerns and backgrounds. Each book and passage should be taken on its own merits and within its own historical context. The Bible is akin to an anthology of American literature: understanding a passage from Ralph Waldo Emerson does not necessarily have some hermeneutic connection to a portion of William Bradford's writing two centuries before. Rather than having a direct verbal conduit to God, biblical authors, critics claim, used written sources for information like any other writer – along with oral traditions that had been handed down. Even the author of Luke

---

[50] Paul Johnson, *A History of Christianity* (New York: Atheneum, 1976), 349.

[51] Peter Kreeft and Ronald K. Tacelli, 86. I can just hear a skeptic respond, "Where do I place my bet? I need to see or correspond with an actual person if I am going to wager such a hefty sum." A believer responds: "With God. You place your bet with God." The skeptic: "But his existence is the crux of the matter."

implied as much in the first chapter of his gospel.[52]   Some of these individuals maintain that the Bible, if not inspired or inerrant, is at least historically reliable in the broad sweep of things, and others pounce on what they see as historical inaccuracies, absurdities, contradictions, and discrepancies.[53] Some just seem to be implacable when it comes to the Bible and have an either veiled or open hostility. Others, despite pointing out perceived mistakes and shortcomings, still treasure the Bible as great literature and one of the main staples of our Western heritage. Let's look at some of their observations and responses by Christian intellectuals.

Bible Skeptics: The Bible is full of discrepancies, is historically unreliable, and has numerous translation and transmission problems

Okay, here are some standard discrepancies in no particular order:

- In the gospel of Mark, Jesus threw out the moneychangers from the Temple toward the end of his life. In the gospel of John, he performed this exact same action at the beginning of his ministry. Which is it, for neither gospel says that he did this twice during his earthly sojourn? And if you try and reconcile this by saying that Jesus indeed did this twice, then you are essentially writing your own scripture. The Book of Revelation itself prohibits that (Rev. 22: 18-19)

- In Genesis, the writing style and sequence of creation in chapter one is very different from that in chapter two, especially if read in Hebrew. Someone reading an English version would not catch it at first glance, or even subsequent glances

- Also in Genesis, if light was created on the first day in chapter one, where did it come from, since the moon, stars, and sun were not

---

[52] Luke 1: 1-4: "Since many have undertaken to set down [write] an orderly account of the events that have been fulfilled among us, just as they were handed on to us [orally] by those who from the beginning were eyewitnesses and servants of the word, I too decided, after investigating everything carefully from the very first, to write an orderly account for you, most excellent Theophilus, so that you may know the truth concerning the things about which you have been instructed." (NRSV)

[53] See Steve Wells, ed., *The Skeptic's Annotated Bible: The King James Version from a Skeptic's Point of View* (SAB Books, 2012).

created until the fourth day? Someone could say that this light emanated from God. "Let there be light" implies that it appeared at that instant. But if it was divine luminescence, then why wasn't that light emanating from God before that? Was God's natural light switch turned "off" for the eternity before creation?[54]

- A perennial favorite: Where did Cain's wife come from? There were only four people on earth at the time in Genesis – Adam, Eve, Cain, and Abel. In a pique of jealousy, Cain killed Abel because his sacrifice was favored in the eyes of God, and Cain's was not. God exiled Cain as punishment. In his exile, Genesis 4:17 says that "Cain knew his wife." Now, where did she come from? Perhaps this was an oversight by the author telling the story, or she was his sister, or God created other human beings but did not see fit to mention it, as the Baptists famously say. Chapter five in Genesis does indeed say that Adam "had other sons and daughters." I guess incest was okay in early biblical history, and at some point the expiration date for permissible, unforked family trees ran out. Besides, is not the birth of daughters important enough to mention, if not for being the 5th person born in the planet's history? In other places, Genesis makes clear the family relation between a man and his wife, like Abraham and Sarah and Isaac and Rebekah, but it is left unclear as to Cain's familial relation to his mate

- The book of Exodus: In chapter nine, one plague (the 5th) had killed "*all* the livestock of the Egyptians" [italics mine]. With the announcement of the advent of a later plague (the 7th) presumably very close in time after the above plague, God warns Egyptians to whisk away their livestock to protect them against this next plague. As Bart Ehrman asks, "What livestock?" Now, one can say that the Israelites felt sorry for the Egyptians and shared some of their livestock, which were divinely protected in the fifth plague. But that supposition would be an addition of a fact not in the Exodus narrative. Or, since the Israelites were slaves, perhaps the Egyptians seized their cattle once they had lost their own. That would be

---

[54] Patricia Reiff has an interesting way to reconcile this discrepancy. See " Three Heavens – Our Home" in Paul M. Anderson, ed., *Professors Who Believe: The Spiritual Journeys of Christian Faculty* (Downers Grove, Ill.: Intervarsity Press, 1998), 59-60.

another additional detail not mentioned in the biblical account, though.

- Who actually went to Jesus' tomb on the morning of his resurrection? All of the gospels mention different women in different combinations

- When Matthew explains in chapter twenty-seven of his gospel that Judas' betrayal of Jesus was a fulfillment of scripture, he attributes the prophecy to the book of Jeremiah, but it actually came from a loose rendering of the book of Zechariah.[55]

- Or perhaps some bizarre verses: Matthew 27.51-53 (NRSV). "At that moment the curtain of the temple was torn in two, from top to bottom. The earth shook, and the rocks were split. The tombs also were opened, and many bodies of the saints who had fallen asleep were raised. After [Jesus'] resurrection they came out of the tombs and entered the holy city and appeared to many." Okay, how is it that the Jews in Jerusalem, the Romans, and the three other Gospel writers did not mention this unusual occurrence? The living dead amble into Jerusalem and start talking to people. Nobody else noticed or took the time to record this zombie –fest (absent the eating of live humans that we know of)? Although not addressing this particular example, James Barr, a biblical scholar, is cited as saying "[t]hat there may well be no extra-biblical information to confirm this or that event referred to in the narrative. This in itself, however, does not seem to me to be in itself [sic] adequate ground for doubting the reality of the event." The star of Bethlehem is only mentioned in Matthew as well. Does that mean that we should disbelieve this too? You could apply this skepticism to lots of different areas of history, especially ancient history, where historical fact is often based on only one source. For instance, our only source for the mass suicide of Jews at Masada as the Romans laid siege was the Jewish historian Josephus. As David Henige has asserted, "Most of what we think we know about the past, we know from, or by way of, a single source."[56] Yes, the skeptic replies, but I doubt that scores

---

[55] Bart D. Ehrman, *Jesus Interrupted: Revealing the Hidden Contradictions in the Bible (and Why We Don't Know About Them)* (New York: HarperOne, 2009), 6-10, 19-60.
[56] Henige, 38, 49-50, 119-22.

of these single sources mention the living dead, astronomical anomalies, or other supernatural oddities, so we can ascribe more credibility to them if they mention things that are commonplace or plausible within everyday human experience

These examples can easily be multiplied. It makes a skeptic wonder why God did not ensure that his writers got it right, if the Bible indeed is inspired and inerrant. As for translation and transmission issues, a good book to read is Bart Ehrman's *Misquoting Jesus* (2005). He writes that Origen, one of the early church fathers, once complained that manuscripts were frustratingly different because copyists either made mistakes or knowingly cut and added material; that even the author of the book of Revelation had to threaten God's punishment for tampering with his text (Rev. 22:18-19), which implies that it was already a widespread problem before the last book of the New Testament was even completed; that early copyists were often not professionals, but simply "literate [and] willing;" that the famous scene of the woman taken in adultery in John and the last twelve verses in the gospel of Mark are not present in the "oldest and best manuscripts" we have, clearly implying that this content was added later on, and that even the literary style of those apparent add-ons is different from the rest of the gospels' writing; and that later scribes intentionally changed texts for theological reasons.[57] And, one could reasonably ask, if God inspired the original authors and prevented them from making mistakes, could he not have extended that same inspiration to amateur copyists and professional scribes, especially the former, since they would need assistance the most? Daniel B. Wallace has accused Ehrman of creating "Chicken Littles" in churches that "panic" when confronted with Ehrman's scholarship about the Bible's questionable transmission. He insists that none of the minor discrepancies even come close to altering significant Christian doctrine,[58] but, as stated below, Ehrman concedes that most of the irregularities are indeed very minor. Ehrman perhaps wishes to instill a healthy skepticism in Bible readers. Surely, a cautious reader of the Bible and a Chicken Little are not the same thing.

---

[57] Bart Ehrman, *Misquoting Jesus: The Story Behind Who Changed the Bible and Why* (New York: HarperSanFrancisco, 2005), 52, 54, 55, 63-67, 151-175.
[58] Daniel B. Wallace, "How Badly Did the Early Scribes Corrupt the New Testament? An Examination of Bart Ehrman's Claims" in *Contending With Christianity's Critics*, 148-66.

Response: Discrepancies can increase reliability and changes in transmission are only minor

If all the stories in the gospels were exactly the same, critics could charge that the authors colluded with each other to get their story straight, or that the accounts were all dependent on one source and a defender could then not claim the reliability that comes from multiple sources. Manufactured narratives tend to agree in every detail because of collaboration. Even a noted skeptic like Michael Shermer, in another context, has asserted that diverging details can strengthen the overall "veracity of the evidence."[59] Regarding the process of copying and recopying copies of the originals, textual and grammatical variations among manuscripts are insignificant and do not fundamentally alter any major Christian doctrine. The number of manuscripts (about 4700) and church father quotations (100,000) from copies of their letters and commentaries essentially certifies accurate transmission. In fact, you could almost reconstruct the entire New Testament by stringing together quotations of scripture from those church fathers. Even Ehrman concedes that "most" of the discrepancies between texts are minor and piddling. The Bible's track record compared to other ancient documents is very good. The time that elapsed between the original writing and the first extant copy is very competitive, if not superior. The difference between the originals and the earliest copies in the Bible's case is usually only a "couple of generations" – whereas centuries separate those of other ancient sources.[60] Skeptics, though, could easily retort that the above arguments only prove adequate transmission, not inspiration or inerrancy. Since we do not have the original copies, often called "autographs," we cannot say anything about divine inspiration or the lack of error. As Ehrman argues, the sheer number of manuscripts is not relevant to the historical credibility or truthfulness of the content: "It is true that we have far more manuscripts for the books of the New Testament than for Homer, Plato, Aristotle, Euripides, Cicero, Marcus Aurelius – name your ancient author.

---

[59] Michael Shermer, *Why People Believe Weird Things: Pseudoscience, Superstition, and Other Confusions of Our Time* (New York, 1997), 230-31; Strobel, *The Case for Christ*, 45-46.

[60] Johnson, *History of Christianity*, 26; Strobel, *Case for Christ*, 59-60, 64-65. Ehrman, writing several years later, places the estimate of manuscripts at 5700: Ehrman, *Misquoting Jesus*, 88, 207-08.

But that has absolutely no bearing on the question of whether the New Testament books can be trusted. It is relevant only to the question of whether we can know what the New Testament books originally said." Just because we have thousands of copies of Karl Marx's *Das Kapital* and Hitler's *Mein Kampf* that are very close in time to the writing of the original does not mean that we should trust the content of those works.[61] For those sensitive souls that might be outraged that he compared the content of the Bible with that of books by murderous communists and fascists, you might be missing the point: the impressive number of copies does not ensure the accuracy of transmission or the truth of the content. It's like burying in a cave 10,000 hard copies of a "fake news" article in preservation-friendly jars. Five hundred years later, someone discovers this cache and concludes that the story must be accurate because there are so many copies!

Secular Assertion: The Bible should be studied like any other ancient book or account

Historians, archeologists, and Biblical scholars insist that the Bible was composed like any other ancient document. Therefore, the same standards of rigor must be applied to its study. One of the first thinkers to insist upon and do this was the Jewish philosopher Baruch Spinoza. Later researchers would consider questions of authorship, literary genre, historical context, and the types of sources biblical authors used.[62]

Those are certainly conventional concerns for scholars, reply apologists. Christian philosophy professors Peter Kreeft and Ronald Tacelli assert that the Bible is indeed studied like other ancient works, but is unfairly subject to *extra* scrutiny. They do not fear rigorous analysis of biblical texts, but they insist that the same degree of adversarial, critical interrogation should be extended to all ancient documents. If it actually was, they argue that we would be unsure of many details and events from antiquity to the Middle Ages. In fact, it would be found that biblical documents hold up better under this scrutiny than secular or non-biblical texts.[63] Liberal biblical scholars

---

[61] Bart Ehrman, *Did Jesus Exist? The Historical Argument for Jesus of Nazareth* (New York: HarperOne, 2012), 178.

[62] Karen Armstrong, *The Battle for God* (New York: Alfred A. Knopf, 2000), 23; *The Bible: A Biography* (New York: Atlantic Monthly Press, 2007), 111, 196.

[63] Kreeft and Tacelli, 205

certainly adopt a very critical attitude toward the gospels, but they treat their pet Gnostic gospels and other writings with kid-gloves. These modernist scholars that reserve most of their doubt for the Bible are simply captives of the anti-supernatural Enlightenment mindset. Theological intent in a document does not mean that it is historically unreliable.[64] That is fair enough, reply secularists and scholars of ancient history, but the Bible deserves extra scrutiny because *it claims to be divine revelation*. If it is so accurate because of a Divine proofreader, then it should be able to stand up under rigorous textual analysis. Besides, other ancient documents do not claim to be inerrant or derived from God's own hand like the Bible does, so they get only slightly less rigorous treatment.

Critical assertion: We cannot be certain that Jesus spoke the words that are recorded in the gospels, or that other biblical narratives have not been redacted, that is, edited for theological purposes

According to John Dominic Crossan and Jonathan L. Reed, professors of religious studies and New Testament respectively, the gospels have literary layers within the received text much like archeological sites have ruins on top of older ruins. Scholars try to sift through the texts with analytical spades and literary tools and work their way back to the most primitive material that will reveal the original Jesus. Later authors and editors in the New Testament world constructed each layer to appeal to a new time and a new community with its own social and theological concerns. Jesus gets more "Christian" with each successive layer.[65] His followers shaped him into who they wanted him to be so that Jesus became more of a "literary character," according to famed Humanities critic, Harold Bloom. His words and actions were "mediated" by his disciples decades after his life, just as knowledge of Socrates comes filtered primarily through Plato.[66]

---

[64] Gregory A. Boyd, *Cynic Sage or Son of God? Recovering the Real Jesus in an Age of Revisionist Replies* (Wheaton, Ill.: BridgePoint/Victor Books, 1995), 23, 223; Craig A. Evans, "How Scholars Fabricate Jesus", in *Contending With Christianity's* Critics, 147; Strobel, *The Case for Christ*, 31.

[65] John Dominic Crossan and Jonathan L. Reed, *Excavating Jesus: Beneath the Stones, Behind the Texts* (New York:HarperSanFrancisco, 2001), 12-14, 37-39, 224.

[66] Harold Bloom, *Genius: A Mosaic of One Hundred Exemplary Creative Minds* (New York: Warner Books, 2002), 135.

One of the most well-known and established tenets of biblical criticism is the gospel writers' reliance upon "Q," a purported early source for the sayings of Jesus from these earliest layers of historical dirt and rock. The gospel of Mark is considered the earliest, having been completed by 70 AD. It seems that Matthew and Luke were heavily dependent on Markan material, for they both have substantially the same details that are in Mark's gospel, almost verbatim. So, scholars then extract similar material shared by Luke and Matthew that were *not* in the gospel of Mark and speculate that the evangelists secured this content from an earlier source than Mark, the gospel of Q, named after the German word for source, Quele.

Biblical Defense: Purported sources earlier than Mark are hypothetical, and eyewitnesses that were still alive could dispute creative editing

Gregory Boyd, both pastor and professor, argues that the case for Q and early Jesus traditions and sayings rests upon documents that do not exist. These hypothetical sources are reconstructed and imaginatively extracted from complete ones. Just imagine if historians of United States and European history cited primary sources that really do not exist. Besides that, eyewitnesses that were still alive when the first gospels were circulated would have objected to any false editing or omission of Jesus' actual words, or if sayings of Jesus were simply conjured for a developing theological trend.[67] Skeptics, though, could still ask this question: even if these eyewitnesses of Jesus were still around during the initial gospel circulation, what is the possibility that they were literate and would have come across, or heard recitations from, these gospels and the supposed untruths in them? Or the probability that they heard or read the portion of the manuscript that exactly corresponded to the only day they heard Christ address the topics in question? Further, if Herod's killing of the innocents would not have attracted attention due to the lack of modern media, as Christian apologists have maintained since the massacre is not mentioned in outside non-biblical sources, then how is it that gospel untruths would have been so easily noticed by eyewitnesses, with the same lack of newspapers, radio, and television?[68]

---

[67] Boyd, 80, 143, 216; Strobel, *Case for Christ*, 33.
[68] Strobel, *Case for Christ*, 104-05

Christian theologians are confident about the historical reliability of the New Testament and that Jesus was exactly who the texts say he was – the Son of God

Recent studies by scholars like Bart Ehrman point to a variety of different streams of Christian belief replete with their own favorite scriptures that coexisted with "orthodox" Christianity, some arguing that these traditions and communities existed before the crystallization of orthodox creeds and institutional structures.[69]   Christian apologists respond that diversity in early Christian thought and practice does not preclude a clear strain of conventional, true Christian doctrine.   In addition, the Christian creed existed very early, contained in Paul's letters to regional churches.   The apostle's letters were early (early to mid 50s) and were easily within the lifetime range of eyewitnesses that could confirm or dispute his assertions about Christ.   Even more incredibly, Paul asserted that he was merely passing on pre-existing doctrine about Jesus (1 Corinthians 15: 3-8), which takes us chronologically even closer to the time of Christ – possibly "the mid-AD 30s" – according to Gary R. Habermas.   Even though the gospels came after Paul's writings, enemies could have easily investigated the recorded stories because of the specific historical details in the gospels.   Besides, the extracanonical gospels and writings so treasured by liberal, modernist scholars were not cited by the church fathers, indicating that they were not taken seriously as authentic in representing the actions and sayings of Christ.   But detractors then counter that those who determined which books would be part of the New Testament were highly selective in their choices, even oppressive in their exclusion of certain books and communities. Apologists, though, then argue that the reluctance to admit certain books only proves the cautious deliberation of the church.[70]

How can we reconcile all of these conflicting claims? First, one interesting way is to assert that God had to dumb himself down in the Bible to

---

[69] See Bart Ehrman, *Lost Christianities: The Battles for Scripture and the Faiths We Never Knew* (New York: Oxford University Press, 2003).
[70] Boyd, 130; See Gary R. Habermas, "The Resurrection of Jesus Time Line: The Convergence of Eyewitnesses and Early Proclamation" in *Contending With Christianity's Critics*; Kreeft and Tacelli, 186, 191, 194; Strobel, *Case for Christ*, 69.

accommodate humans' limited capacity to understand deep theological things. Since God's thoughts so far exceed the human capacity to understand supernatural cognition, making it nearly impossible to communicate his message unvarnished and unmediated, He had to convey it through imperfect human language in the Bible. And with this imperfection came all the baggage: disputes over the meaning of words, the mistakes humans make, the inability of words to exactly correspond to things in the world as they are, etc. Second, maybe there are two levels of truth: one public and more literal/mundane and the other more secret, esoteric, mysterious and reserved for elites with proper understanding, training, or initiation. While the first group spends its time quibbling over contradictions, historical accuracy, and textual transmission, the second group recognizes the futility and even silliness of it all and, instead, focuses on higher, more liberating themes that emanate from the text if one sees it rightly. And third, in a similar vein, perhaps all of these disagreements will help participants to see what is essential to an understanding of the Bible – a bare bones theology, if you will – that brushes aside minor disputes that substantially have no effect on the really important things about biblical belief or appreciation. The Protestant era humanist, Erasmus, desired the emergence of such an orientation. [71]

GENERAL CRITICISMS OF RELIGION AND DEFENSES

In the following section, I will touch upon some major and interesting points made by writers, intellectuals, and nonbelievers about religion, monotheism, supernaturalism, and exclusive truth claims.

Critics: God is simply the creation of human minds with outsized human characteristics

One of the most persistent criticisms of monotheism throughout history is anthropomorphism, the attribution of traits to God that are clearly human but writ large. In other words, instead of God creating humans in His image, humans created God in their image. Like humans, God is spoken of as having eyes, hands, and a face (and obviously a butt since he sits on a throne), and

---

[71] Armstrong, *God,* 114, 288; *Bible,* 122; Johnson, 275, 278.

he also loves, creates, hates, and gets angry. Xenophanes once famously critiqued the existence or nature of God by pointing out that if an ox had a god, then that god would predictably have ox-like features. He replaced these conceptions with a god that was genderless, indescribable, aloof, and dignified. The famous Roman Skeptic, Sextus Empiricus, chimed in that if God's attributes are greatly magnified, perfect versions of human attributes, then it only makes sense that God should share our vices and shortcomings as well, also in outsized, perfect versions to maintain the kind of symmetry that appealed to a classical mind. Defenders of religion are well aware of such criticisms. As childish as it may seem, all religion must have some element of anthropomorphism to fashion a God that feels approachable, intimate, and appealing. A deistic god or one like Aristotle's seems too far removed from human affairs, being cold and distant. That kind of god does not evoke worship or adoration. God, to work as a concept and living reality, must be *both* different from and similar to us.[72]

Critics: Not only is God portrayed in human terms, but people postulate his existence as a means of comfort

A European atheist, Paul Heinrich, Baron of Holbach, argued that religion was simply a dishonest, cowardly attempt to cope with life's troubles. Unable to exert control in an unpredictable natural world, humans longed for an otherworldly force that would comfort them and diminish fear. Similarly, the famed psychoanalyst Sigmund Freud saw religion as infantile. God was a projection of insecurity and fulfilled the need for a protective father figure, a helicopter deity. And leave it to Richard Dawkins, a polemical atheist, to point out the obvious: Just because it comforts somebody does not make it true. [73] For absurd illustration, I find that my belief that the moon is made out of green macaroni greatly comforts me. But that does not prove that it is actually made out of green macaroni. Okay, granted, says Rabbi David J. Wolpe. But "Even if religion came solely from fear, that says nothing as to its truth."[74]

---

[72] Felipe Fernandez-Armesto, *Truth: A History and a Guide for the Perplexed* (New York: St Martin's Press, 1997), 142; Armstrong, *History of God*, 48; Hecht, 7, 167; Huston Smith, *Why Religion Matters: The Fate of the Human Spirit in An Age of Disbelief* (New York: HarperSanFrancisco, 2001), 222.

[73] Armstrong, *God*, 343, 357; Dawkins, 352.

[74] Wolpe, *Why Faith Matters*, 29.

If we have reached a point where the reader aspiring to be reasonable and well-balanced starts to settle for a watered-down version of God or a vague worship of nature, then apologists are ready to steer you back to a supernatural, conventional view of God. . .

Deism, or rational religious belief, is devoid of emotion; agnosticism has consequences for one's behavior and lifestyle; and materialism renders our own thinking unreliable

To begin with, deism is the theological view that God created the material world and placed its operation under natural laws, but He does not intervene in His creation. Traditional theists charge that deism is suffused with a bloodless chill; this remote God does not evoke warmth in the human heart. People need to surrender to a powerful, involved deity that cares for them, not a distant one fit only for theological speculation and a lukewarm admiration. Deists, to their credit, were partly motivated to conceive of God this way to combat fanaticism. Well, at least deists believe in God and uphold virtue and morality. We cannot be sure about agnostics, though. Traditional theists argue that those who do not know if there is a God, or claim that humans cannot know, often live *as if* there were no God, which leads to a selfish lifestyle. Pantheists, those that believe God is the sum total of all things in the universe, are no better, they say. Those who believe in a "Life Force" mistily pervading the ether are somewhat in the same boat. As C.S. Lewis has noted with some scorn, "The Life-Force is a sort of tame God. You can switch it on [or off] when you want, but it will not bother you. All the thrills of religion and none of the cost."

Also, materialists that regard nature with awe are suppressing or ignoring a serious philosophical objection. If the material world is all that there is, and everything is subject to deterministic cause and effect, how can materialists trust their own reasoning arising from a material entity (their brain), for their reasoning would have to be locked into certain natural patterns of physiological circuitry, making any judgment suspect? Mental results would ultimately be non-rational. Besides that, evil actions would simply be the result of materialistic forces that steer the body, and therefore are excusable; so, how can we uphold moral responsibility? This lack of responsibility seems just as much of a problem as secular objections to an omnipotent and good God allowing the existence of evil, according to C.

Stephen Layman. Apologists do not discount natural forces, but instead make room for free will: "Heredity plus environment *condition* our acts, but they do not *determine* them" assert Kreeft and Tacelli.[75] Clever distinction, that.

I am not so sure, though, that one can disentangle conditioning from determination that handily. In addition, the three assertions in bold above are not addressing the truth of those belief systems, but simply any undesirable consequences supposedly emanating from them. A supposedly "bad" result does not address the truth of the originating idea or belief system. As for the specific claim that agnosticism may lead to undesirable behavior, one could just as easily argue, with more and worse examples even, that theistic belief produces bad behavior as well: the Crusades, the Inquisition, the 100% Protestant Americanism of the KKK, Catholic priests sexually abusing young boys, the early aggression of Islamic expansion and conquest, and the Islamic attacks on 9/11. Now, as for the claim that materialistic thinking is unreliable, critics can offer a few rejoinders:

Let's concede the deterministic limits of a material organ, and that the subsequent thinking is unreliable. What are you going to replace it with? Do you prefer magic, secret rituals, or paranormal rites?

1. Methodological materialism/naturalism has proven pretty effective. Unless you are a Christian Scientist or a Scientologist, I doubt people would object to medicine and treatments that have been proven effective by those embodied material brains working in research laboratories. Do you often hesitate when driving over that bridge, for the people who built that are flesh-and-blood human beings caught up in the nexus of the natural world, and their thinking processes are therefore trapped within the limits and causation of the material world – or perhaps you will stop before driving over it because of a lack of government funding to maintain its upkeep (more about that in the next two chapters)?

---

[75] Johnson, 338, 343, 365; Kreeft and Tacelli, 66, 137; Moore, 97; C.S. Lewis, *Christian Reflections* (Grand Rapids, MI.: William B. Eerdmans Publishing Company, 1967), 89; *Mere Christianity*, 21; Edward Wilson, *Consilience: The Unity of Knowledge* (New York: Alfred A. Knopf, 1998), 33; Wolpe, 91-92.

2. Let's suppose that human thinking is subject to material forces. Our *awareness* of that would make us much more *cautious* – hence the controls often used in scientific studies. Not only are we more humble about what we can know, we also are less likely to impose our beliefs on others, or kill them if they do not share them, than religious extremists that have a monopoly on the truth

3. Even if one could clearly prove that materialist constraints make our thinking fundamentally unreliable, that does not therefore prove that supernatural essences beyond the material world exist or are superior in constructing knowledge

Well, speaking of a clash between naturalistic and non-naturalistic, or supernatural, causation and explanation, let's turn to our next subtopic.

EVOLUTION AND CREATIONISM

I have always been fascinated and entertained by the Scopes Trial (1925). It is one of my favorite topics during my lecture on the 1920s in my American history surveys. Tennessee had passed a law that forbade teaching any account of human origins that contradicted the creation narrative in Genesis. Born in response to the infamous Palmer raids of suspected radicals and subversives during the Red Scare right after World War One, the American Civil Liberties Union promised to pay the legal fees of anyone that violated the law. Meanwhile, a group of locals in Dayton, Tennessee plotted to put the little town in the foothills of the Appalachian Mountains on the map. They lured a young, idealistic school teacher into a test case. John Thomas Scopes agreed to teach evolution in class from a state-issued textbook. Scopes was arrested, and things had been set in motion for one of the greatest trials in American history. Two well-known individuals could not wait to get involved: the famed agnostic lawyer Clarence Darrow and three-time Democratic nominee for president William Jennings Bryan. Each headed up the defense and prosecution teams respectively. The town took on a circus-like atmosphere with banners all over town denouncing evolution.

During the trial, Darrow, less concerned about technically winning the case than defending academic freedom and science against fanaticism, tried to get scientific testimony into the court record by calling distinguished scientists to the stand to testify about the evidence for evolutionary theory. The judge ruled out the testimony because it had no bearing on the question of the case: Did Scopes teach evolution or not? Just bring students to the stand to recite what Scopes taught in class that day. After this letdown for Darrow, the numerous spectators started to drift away, thinking that the fireworks display was fizzling out rather than climaxing to a finale. They were about to miss the best part of the trial. In an unusual move, Darrow called Bryan to the stand to testify about his knowledge of the Bible. The judge amazingly allowed it because he thought the case could not possibly get any more bizarre. Bryan only agreed because he was assured that he would later be able to cross-examine Darrow in a role-reversal, which did not transpire. Darrow's interrogation of Bryan was withering and dripping with sarcasm. Darrow demonstrated Bryan's ignorance on the stand and Christian fundamentalism seemed vanquished at the feet of science – although Bryan got a few good jabs at Darrow, who probably could not answer his own questions if the tables were turned. Darrow actually instructed the jury to find Scopes guilty so that the decision could be appealed to a higher court to extend the exposure, and Bryan, being a Christian gentleman, offered to pay Scopes's fine.

Biblical literalists retreated from the national scene and waited to fight another day. They still continue to fight, either as literal creationists or the more sophisticated advocates of intelligent design, with all sorts of shades in between. Authors that advocate evolution recognize that creationism is not a monolithic movement or belief system. There are different types of creationists. Young earth creationists believe that God created the earth in six literal days and that it is no more than 10,000 years old. "Gap creationists" believe that there was a large gap of time between Genesis 1:1 and 1:2, during which God destroyed an older creation (for some reason) and recreated things in six literal days. The long expanse of time during this gap accounts for the Earth's extensive age. Some creationists believe that God, with divine foresight, created the earth with an *appearance* of age in an effort to reconcile belief in six literal days of creation with modern geological knowledge that would later unfold. Theistic evolutionists and intelligent design proponents, unlike traditional creationists, concede much of the findings of evolutionary science but believe that God's involvement accounts for the apparent design we see in nature.[76]

My discussion of evolution and creationism will frequently dovetail with conflicts between science and religion in general. Evolutionary scientists often fault creationism as not being scientific, and then take the opportunity to highlight the central elements of the scientific method that creationism lacks:

Method: Practitioners and philosophers of science never tire in reminding us that science is not just a body of data. Rather, it is a *method* of gathering and evaluating evidence about the natural world.

Causation: Science posits a natural world that operates by natural causation, and tries to uncover cause-and-effect relationships.

Experimentation: Scientists generate explanations (informed guesses) about the natural world and why things happen. They then set up experiments to test these hunches. For example, in the medical, biological, and social sciences, control and experimental groups are formed. The control group receives a placebo while the experimental group is exposed to the variable thought to have some effect on a speculated outcome. So that expectations do not influence how subjects behave during the experiment, double blind studies are conducted so that no one in either the control or experimental group knows what variable or treatment they received and neither do the researchers. Then they check the results and see if there were any differences between the groups that were statistically significant (not due to chance).

Replication: The results of an experiment like this need to be *replicated* under the same conditions and parameters in the original. The more times the experiment is replicated, with broadly the same results, the surer scientists can be about a cause-and-effect relationship between a variable and the outcome in the natural world, or the lack of one. After sufficient replication, a hypothesis moves into the realm of theory. A scientific theory has much confirmation and solidity behind it. Unlike the popular notion of

---

[76] Gardner, 15-16; Shermer, *Darwin Matters*, 166-67.

theory as little better than an hypothesis – like, "evolution is *just* a theory" – a theory is a well-established explanation, whether by observation or experiment, of a wide range of data concerning a particular set of phenomena in nature.[77]

Self-Correction: "Science is *self-correcting*." If scientists make mistakes or their experimental methodology is inadequate, other scientists discover this through *peer-review*, the process of submitting the results of your research by publishing in professional journals or other printed venues under some refereed oversight. Other researchers can be tough critics, but they are supposed to be. If a theory or hypothesis is inadequate, then it is either modified and retested, or abandoned.[78] This is one of the virtues of science, claims Richard Dawkins. Science books welcome criticism and modification, and holy books, which claim to have absolute truth, do not (even though, as we have seen, books and components of the holy books get modified to a certain extent, but not because of the intentional practice of falsification) . . . .[79]

Falsification: The famous philosopher of science, Karl Popper, argued that scientific explanations need to be subject to *falsification*. If you are so sure about your theory, you need to make it vulnerable to being proven wrong. For a simple example, my hunch that every person that walks through my office door over the next two years will be between the heights of 14 feet and 7 inches is so obvious to the point of uselessness. That one is going to be difficult to overturn. However, if between 6'7 and 2'3, now we have a theory that has specific, predictive power. If an NBA seven-footer stoops through the door, then we can modify the theory and make it more expansive.

Using the above criteria, evolutionary scientists claim that creationism is simply unscientific despite its claims to the contrary. Creationists and intelligent design proponents often retort that evolutionists are not open-

---

[77] Richard Dawkins, *The Greatest Show on Earth: The Evidence for Evolution* (New York: Free Press, 2009), 9-10.

[78] Robert Park, *Voodoo Science: The Road from Foolishness to Fraud* (New York: Oxford University Press, 2000), 9; Michael Shermer, *The Borderlands of Science: Where Sense Meets Nonsense* (New York: Oxford University Press, 2001), 317-318; *Why Darwin Matters: The Case Against Intelligent Design*), 85

[79] Dawkins, 282

minded about the possible emergence of new "paradigms." According to historian of science Thomas Kuhn, science operates under an accepted canon of procedures and methods that determine what questions are in and out of bounds, and what answers are acceptable within the same. When data or natural phenomena fall outside of those parameters, scientists explain them away or ignore them. Once these "outliers" reach a critical mass that breaks through scientific convention, a "paradigm shift" takes place that replaces or shakes up the previous parameters.[80] Evolutionists do not see enough, if any, data that fall outside the parameters that would cause them to overturn evolutionary theory. Evolutionary scientists are also not ready to accept explanations that involve supernatural oversight or intervention, for science, as defined, can only deal with natural causation. Despite creationist claims that Darwin is losing favor in the scientific world, I believe that it is safe to say that naturalistic evolution remains the dominant paradigm, so we will use their assertions and arguments as home plate with creationist runners trying to steal (of course, evolutionary scientists would not concede that creationists have even made it to first base, or even the batters' box. Or the stadium).

According to a recent poll, among nations in the world, Americans reject evolution the most, but know the least about it.[81] Given that ironic situation, a few words about evolution are in order. The idea that organisms have gradually changed over time under variable environmental and physical factors existed long before Darwin. What made Darwin unique was his explanation of how evolution happened: natural selection. Drawing upon the thought of Thomas Malthus, Darwin believed that organisms bred so much that the sheer number of offspring would outstrip available resources. So, starvation and predation played useful roles by weeding out the disadvantaged. Those organisms that happened to have useful traits and characteristics that better enabled them to survive the harsh competitive environment would have a greater chance of surviving, consuming, and mating. The survivors procreate and the process starts anew with the next generation. Breeders of livestock and other animals did this artificially by

---

[80] Theodore Schick, Jr. and Lewis Vaughn, *How to Think About Weird Things: Critical Thinking for a New Age*, 3rd ed. (Boston: McGraw Hill, 2002), 14-15.

[81] Kevin Phillips, *American Theocracy: The Peril and Politics of Radical Religion, Oil, and Borrowed Money in the 21st Century* (New York: Viking, 2006), 248.

systematically pairing superior animals to produce more of them. In like manner, Darwin postulated that nature does the same thing, but one big difference is that nature's execution of this grand process is *undirected*. Chance variations in the genetic lottery interacted with the shifting environment to give rise to a complicated, undirected stage upon which contact and response between species and environment, species and other species, predator and prey weeded out useless organs, individual animals, or entire species, and these factors recombined again, and kept changing the physical make-up of organisms. Species started to diverge from others and even changed into different species over time.[82]

Evolutionary thinking now pervades all scientific fields. A new (or old) explanation about how life emerged and fanned out over time must have extraordinary evidence to overturn decades of scientific orthodoxy. Like sentinels guarding the entrance to the citadel, scientists carefully screen any unusual claims before allowing entrance into the halls of scientific credibility. The explanatory nature of science has been a wonderful tool in improving human life. Science has proven itself time and time again, whether it be new medicines that cure debilitating diseases or the splitting of the atom for nuclear energy (with all due awareness of the destructive power of that discovery). Science's ability to harness or thwart nature and predict events is extraordinary. How is it that scientists can be consistently right about so many things in the universe but somehow are ultimately wrong about the age of the universe and the Earth as well as the course and history of biological development? Creationists need absolutely incredible reasons and evidence to overturn standard thought about evolution.

Let's first look at creationism and intelligent design.

---

[82] Shermer, *Why People* Believe, 140; It must be said, by the way, that many creationists also accept this scenario on a micro-level, but object to macroevolution, the view that species change into different species over time.

Creationists have traditionally argued that evolutionary thought is unbiblical, unscientific, and harmful in it effects

a) For Young Earth Creationists, the theory of evolution contradicts a plain reading of the six literal days of creation in Genesis

b) Evolutionary theory, with its attempt to explain everything in terms of material causation, reduces life to a cold, amoral materialism that renders human beings meaningless since they are just combinations of chemicals, molecules, and atoms no different than other configurations of the same elements pervading the universe

c) Given the previous point, evolutionary theory justifies immorality, self-centeredness, crime, homosexuality, abortion, and a whole host of other sins and atrocities, for self-assertion and coercion make more sense under the survival-of-the-fittest ethos of evolution as opposed to restraint and compassion

d) Scientifically, as laid out in the grandfather publication of young Earth creationism, *The Genesis Flood* (1961), dating rocks and fossils in relation to the other involves a circular argument, radiometric forms of dating are flawed, and contemporary layers of sediment and rock were deposited by the Great Flood, not uniformitarian processes

e) Other criticisms: the Miller-Urey experiment, in its attempt to duplicate the exact conditions on earth at the time of the formation of the first organic molecules, employed the use of the wrong elements; the lack of fossil evidence in the pre-Cambrian period does not demonstrate gradual descent from lower organisms; Ernst Haeckel, a German biologist, faked his drawings of vertebrate embryos to give the appearance of modification over time; and Darwin's famed finches played little to no role in his formulation of evolutionary theory.

f) Past events cannot be replicated experimentally with observation. Therefore, belief about past events, especially origins, is ultimately based on faith.[83]

---

[83] Michael Roberts, *Evangelicals and Science* in Greenwood Guides to Science and Religion (Westport, CT: 2008), 165-191; If we are unable to know about the past, evolutionists argue, then how do creationists know that Miller and Urey did not

The world appears designed; therefore, it must have a Designer

Intelligent design, or ID, is often distinguished from run-of-the-mill creationism, but has historical roots in earlier young earth creationism. Attempts to make equal time for creationism in the classroom have been thwarted as an attempt to introduce religion in the classroom, so the new tactic was to switch to "design" and/or "teach the controversy." Proponents like Bill Dembski, Phillip Johnson, and Michael Behe mainly argue that some organs, cellular structures, and other biological features and processes are so complex that they must have had a designer, for the complexity is irreducible and could not have evolved by natural selection. An irreducibly complex structure has at least three parts: if one aspect or part is removed, the biological feature will not work at all. Two important examples include the flagellum and the process of blood-clotting. ID advocates do not mention the Bible or the creation and flood stories in Genesis in laying out their case. They usually favor a very old age for the earth but do not discuss the issue, often alienating dyed-in-the-wool young earth creationists that proudly wave the banner of evangelical Christianity. They concede that microevolution has and does occur – that changes accrue within species – but they reject macroevolution, the idea that species change into different species. They are "sometimes coy" about the specific identity of this intelligent designer.[84]

There are many books and articles that address the specific objections that creationists have to evolution, and a full accounting here is beyond the scope of this chapter or book. Here are just a few of the broad critiques of creationism and intelligent design.

---

replicate the exact conditions and elements on earth at the time of the emergence of life? Were they there? Has God revealed to them the correct combo? As Michael Roberts has noted, this ironic line of thinking would even rule out the existence and teaching of Jesus Christ, the very core of their belief system. To be more specific, it would not rule out a belief based on faith, but one that is buttressed by historical evidence, for evangelicals like to rely upon both faith and evidence.

[84] Roberts, 191-99; Matt Young and Taner Edis, eds., *Why Intelligent Design Fails: A Scientific Critique of the New Creationism* (New Brunswick, NJ., 2005), 1-8.

Evolutionists: Disagreements among evolutionists about *how* evolution occurs does not mean that scientists are increasingly rejecting evolutionary theory

Creationists often point to significant gaps in the fossil record and the seeming explosion of life during the early Cambrian period. If evolution is true, then there should be evidence of a slow change in organisms spread out over successive layers of earth and rock but, instead, there is virtually no fossil record right before the Cambrian period, and then a huge burst of life in the fossil record. Evolutionists counter this by arguing that fossil preservation is sketchy at best, or they posit "punctuated equilibrium," a process of evolution that progresses in abrupt jumps and starts followed by stasis for long periods of time. So, did it occur gradually over time, or did it occur quickly in bursts? Creationists think that this fundamental disagreement over the process of evolution is a serious strike against the theory itself. Their argument, though, is akin to historians disagreeing over the basic causes of the Great Depression. Was it high tariffs, overproduction, tight Federal Reserve money policies, stock speculation, or a lack of credit? If historians disagree about the causes, does that mean that the Great Depression did not happen? Of course not. Although creationists would be offended with being compared to Holocaust deniers, Michael Shermer asserts that they share one thing in common. Both groups comb through the writings of their opponents and pounce on historical or scientific errors, and then claim that the whole narrative, either evolution or the Holocaust, is suspect.[85] The creationists and Holocaust deniers commit the fallacy of composition: if one part is entirely wrong or misleading, then the entire whole must be as well.

Evolutionists: "Irreducible Complexity," a touted concept of intelligent design proponents, is a basic bait-and-switch fallacy

As noted above, "Neo-Creationists" maintain that there are some organs or structures that are not functional if just one element is removed or does not materialize. A system or organ cannot be reduced any further by one single part without resulting in a total loss of function. God created and designed

---

[85] Shermer, *Why People Believe*, 132, 145; Jonathan Wells, *Icons of Evolution: Science or Myth? Why Much of What We Teach About Evolution is Wrong* (Washington, DC: Regnery Publishing, Inc, 2000), 37-38.

these complex structures with all of the parts intact and functional. Here's the fallacy: A bait-and-switch maneuver is when one says that something is true by definition and then reworks the definition when some variable is discovered that plays havoc with the original definition. For irreducible complexity, it is postulated by definition that when one part is removed, the whole thing will not work. But, when an example is found in nature of that same irreducibly complex system functioning *without* that essential part, then that new find becomes the new standard for an irreducibly complex system or organ.[86] Or, to use another sports analogy, when your field goal attempt strategy goes awry by one failed kick, just move the goal posts. One of creationists' favorite examples of irreducible complexity is the human eye. Shermer points out that the removal of one part does not result in complete blindness. Partial vision is better than none and those with this handicap have heroically coped. Even a primitive spot on the skin sensitive to light can warn an animal of an approaching predator. And Dawkins notes that creationists love to quote Darwin's apparent perplexity about the human eye resulting from natural selection. But they do not read further where Darwin goes on to give a plausible explanation consistent with natural selection – a classic example of taking a quote out of context.[87] And on top of that, the eye is very unintelligently designed: it is "built upside down and backwards," for light has to travel through and around all sorts of ocular clutter before it reaches the critical rods and cones for conversion and transmission.[88] Michael Behe's doubt over the functionality of half a flagellum is simply like the earlier, unfounded creationist doubts about the eye jazzed up with more terminology and impressive-sounding analogies.

Let's face it, evolutionists argue, ID is just a "Trojan horse" bearing creationist religious teachings. Promoters of ID "have an agenda: to *prove* that an intelligence guides evolution rather than *find out* whether an intelligence does so," the latter goal being more intellectually and scientifically honest and worthy. Again, "Looking for the footprints of the deity is not necessarily unscientific. What is unscientific is to decide ahead

---

[86] Michael Shermer, *How We Believe: The Search for God in an Age of Science* (New York: W. H. Freeman and Company, 2000), 110, 112, 113-15; *Darwin Matters*, 67; Schick and Vaughn, 190-91.
[87] Dawkins, 123.
[88] Shermer, *Darwin Matters*, 17; *How We Believe*, 112.

of time on the answer and search for God with the determination to come up with a positive result."[89] It's just one grand exercise in confirmation bias – finding the evidence that you think makes your case (and only that evidence). In fact, one could indict the entire industry of Christian apologetics of the same charge.   In closing this section, though, can creationists ask why natural selection has not done any better in crafting the human eye? And could they also accuse evolutionists that have joined the punctuated equilibrium bandwagon of a bait-and-switch maneuver? As for the former question, Jerry Coyne asserts, with some exasperation, that "bad design" is what we should expect from evolution, for the process of natural selection is not some teleological journey to perfection: "Perfect design would truly be the sign of a skilled and intelligent designer. *Imperfect* design is the mark of evolution; in fact, it's precisely what we *expect* from evolution." Furthermore, inadequate features and organs "make sense *only if they evolved from features of earlier ancestors*."[90]

Evidence against evolution is not evidence for creation

Creationists often pose a false dilemma: either the universe, earth, and life were created supernaturally or they evolved under natural processes. This either-or framing attempts to exclude other possible explanations.   For instance, the universe may be eternal or life was seeded from outer space. Creationists may reasonably ask, I think, if these possibilities are actually plausible. Even if they are not, there could still be explanations that are simply unknown until science uncovers them in the future. The present inability to explain another scenario of origins besides evolution or creation should not automatically get credited to supernatural causes on the cosmic balance sheet. Even if evolution is inadequate, evolutionary scientists ask creationists, what are you going to replace it with? Or, in the words of Martin Gardner, a famous foe of pseudoscience, "It's like writing a book denying that Earth is round but never indicating what shape you think it is." It isn't enough to debunk a notion, but one must replace it with a theory or explanation that accounts for all of the data that supported the former theory as well as any new data that supposedly called it into question. Creationists have not done that. In fact, their "research" is basically pulling

---

[89] Roberts, 195; Young and Perakh in *Why Intelligent Design Fails*, 23-25, 30, 185.
[90] Jerry Coyne, *Why Evolution Is True* (New York: Penguin Books, 2009), 81-85.

quotations out of context from scientific writings about evolution and presenting them as evidence that evolutionary theory is crumbling.[91]

The misuse of a theory does not invalidate it

Creationists have long maintained that evolutionary thinking causes a number of societal ills and harmful ideologies, from immorality and violence to relativism and communism. Defenders of evolutionary theory admit that it has been misinterpreted as justifying all sorts of undesirable actions and ideas. For instance, William Jennings Bryan misunderstood natural selection as a bloody conflict where the strong kill off the weak. Rather, it has more to do with "reproductive success" than superior fighting skills and bigger, sharper teeth and claws, which are obviously still important but not the only decisive factors. In addition, it is easily seen that many of the ills creationists include in their litany existed well *before* Darwin. Besides that, the competitive mentality associated with evolutionary thought was often cited as justification for a (cutthroat) free market economy in the United States, not just communism or Marxism. Creationists, who tend to be politically conservative, tend to leave that out of their list of evils.[92] Their probable response is that hefty economic competition without government interference is not evil – see the next chapter.

No matter what type of creationist, evolution proponents are certain that scientific evidence stands firm against creationist objections. Whether it is the inability of the Miller-Urey experiment to duplicate the exact conditions on earth at the time of the formation of the first organic molecules and its experimental use of the wrong elements; or the lack of fossil evidence in the pre-Cambrian period that would clearly demonstrate gradual descent from lower organisms; or that Ernst Haeckel faked his drawings of vertebrate embryos to give the appearance of modification over time; or that Darwin's

---

[91] Martin Gardner, *Did Adam and Eve Have Navels? Discourses on Reflexology, Numerology, Urine Therapy, and Other Dubious Subjects* (New York: W. W. Norton and Company, 2000), 19-20; Schick and Vaughn, 192; Shermer, *Darwin Matters*, 50.

[92] Stephen Jay Gould, *Rocks of Ages: Science and Religion in the Fullness of Life* (New York: The Ballantine Publishing Group, 1999), 162; Shermer, *Why People Believe*, 135, 144.

finches played little to no role in his development of the theory of evolution, all of these examples pale in comparison to the "convergence of evidence" from multiple fields from the entire scientific world that point to the evolution of species from a common ancestor.[93]

We'll let creationists have the last word. Probably one of the most fruitful avenues of challenging evolutionary theory is explaining the origin of life. Scientists still do not have a satisfactory answer. How is it that organic life emerged from inorganic matter and then self-replicated? How did the genetic code arise, and how was it encrypted *the very first time* so that genetic information would provide cellular structures a blueprint (or "recipe" if you are Richard Dawkins[94]) about how to replicate certain characteristics? The jury is still out.   There is no need, though, to jump to supernatural conclusions, argue unbelievers and believers alike.   Still, the probability that the correct sequence of amino acids with the proper peptide bonds folded to create a "functional protein," and that at least 250 of these functional proteins emerged at once to form a minimally complex cell, is astronomical: 10 to the 41,000th power. That's like finding one marked subatomic particle among all subatomic particles in the entire universe, and that analogy vastly underestimates the probability by "84 orders of magnitude" multiplied by 250.   Computer programs that try to mimic and demonstrate how this process works are themselves the product of intelligent minds. Showing how binary numbers or other random sets of digits interact until a functional sequence arises by chance ignores that the experimenters have pre-programmed the system with a target sequence that is functional, a target that the random digits work toward and are "rewarded" as they get closer, a type of computerized natural selection. One can show how the digits, standing in for molecules in the natural world,

---

[93] Shermer, *Darwin Matters*, 87; See Jonathan Wells, *Icons of Evolution*, for examples.
[94] Dawkins, *Greatest Show On Earth*, 221: "A recipe captures something of the truth, and it is an analogy that I sometimes use, to explain why 'blueprint' is not appropriate. Unlike a blueprint, a recipe is irreversible. If you follow a cake recipe step by step, you'll end up with a cake. But you can't take a cake and reconstruct the recipe – whereas . . . you could take a house and reconstruct something close to the original blueprint. This is because of the one-to-one mapping between bits of house and bits of blueprint. With conspicuous exceptions such as the cherry on top, there is no one-to-one mapping between bits of cake and the words, say, or sentences of its recipe."

seemingly self-organize, but a preexisting code with information is presupposed and ignored.

Detractors can only reply that with the possibility of any number of sequences of different variables or structures, "*any* result is going to be very improbable, and that we should not be able to infer back to say that anything other than chance is responsible for it." As Dawkins once put it, it's like seeing a license plate number on a busy freeway and then asking in amazement about the probability of seeing *that particular* license plate number.[95] Finally, this whole debate over abiogenesis is one giant red herring. The inability to explain the origin of life does not mean that evolution is untrue. It is a distraction from the overwhelming scientific evidence for evolution and its predictive, explanatory power. Creationists, however, can easily lob the red herring charge back at evolutionists: our inability to explain what caused the Designer does not mean that creation is untrue. IDers have been chided by evolutionary scientists for the same intellectual maneuver: just because they are unable to explain where the Designer came from does not refute the claim that things in nature appear to have design. It is a distraction from the overwhelming appearance of design in nature.

Evolutionists argue that one cannot claim that what is unknown right now will remain that way, for the history of science has clearly demonstrated plausible explanations for previously unknown phenomena – evolution being a great example. Suppose that intelligent design proponents

---

[95] A similar analogy comes from Bryan McGee. In one chapter of his book, *Confessions of a Philosopher*, he fondly recalled the intellectual engagement he found in graduate school at Yale. He recounts an interesting argument that he picked up from an influential professor – although about mathematical logic rather than the origin of life: Concerning the lottery, "Whatever ticket I pick out will have a number on it that is the only instance of that number in the whole pile. If at this point I clap my hand to my head and cry: 'My God, this is completely and utterly incredible! The odds against my picking this number were infinity to one against, and I've picked it. It's impossible!' – I might *feel* goggle-eyed with wonder, but in fact this sense of wonder is totally misplaced, because whatever ticket I picked I could say exactly the same thing . . . So here is something that *feels* amazing but is not in the slightest bit odd (127)." The license plate analogy can also be attributed to Richard Feynman. See Jordan Ellenberg, *How Not to Be Wrong: The Power of Mathematical Thinking* (New York: The Penguin Press, 2014), 182.

would concede that the inability to explain the origin of life does not necessarily mean that evolution is untrue, and that the origin of life could be eventually explained by natural processes. Would scientists concede, though, that appealing to the supernatural does not necessarily mean that the conclusion is unscientific? Yes, intelligent design advocates would still be at a disadvantage given the mysterious nature of the Designer, for the Designer's origin would be tied up with philosophical and theological notions of non-contingent existence. Invoking a supernatural cause, however, does not preclude scientific accuracy or respectability – just as biblical writers' theological purposes in penning their narratives in the New Testament do not preclude historical accuracy. Isaac Newton and Johannes Kepler at various points mentioned that the order in the universe must have been the product of an immense intelligence. Their invocation of something beyond nature did not make their findings unscientific at the time. Are you willing to say that Isaac Newton was unscientific, one of the bright lights of the Scientific Revolution (ah, an appeal to authority, I can hear the evolutionists respond)? And for the charge that creationists or intelligent design proponents do not actually conduct research, Steven Meyer has noted that neither did Einstein in 1905 when he re-imagined the world of physics from a humble patent office or Darwin himself during his famous voyage in the Galapagos Islands; neither thinker did laboratory research at those particular times, but simply reviewed what was known and offered up revolutionary new ways of looking at the world by relying upon observation and inference.[96] True, subsequent research has confirmed key aspects of Einstein's famous theory of relativity, for example, but he came to these conclusions without formal experimental evidence years earlier before substantial confirmation.

RECONCILIATION?

Countless theologians and scientific writers have tried to reconcile religion and science as well as religion and unbelief. I will not even pretend to have the formula for reconciliation. When it comes to religion and science, there are usually three approaches: science and religion will always conflict since

---

[96] Stephen C. Meyer, 136-49; 204-14, 269-295; Blackburn, 224-225.

they have different epistemological approaches; science and religion must necessarily harmonize since truth is unitary; and science and religion inhabit two different spheres, each superior in its own. Stephen Jay Gould embraced a form of this third relationship before his death. He rejected the conflict/harmonization scenarios, and instead argued that science deals with facts and theories about the natural world, whereas religion properly oversees questions concerning morality, meaning, values, and human relationships. Each is ill-equipped to address the concerns of the other.[97] There is precedent for this approach, for members of the Royal Society, a famous organization in England where scientists and researchers could share ideas and discoveries through presentation and publication, found religion divisive, so they intentionally kept institutional religion out of their proceedings, even though they were devout men and could pursue religious questions on their own.[98] Sir Isaac Newton, for instance, had an intense, bizarre interest in biblical prophecy.

Maybe there is a fourth way of recasting the relationship between science and religion, or another way of seeing Gould's argument. Arthur Herman, a professor of history, has suggested that the friction is not between religion and science, but between Plato and Aristotle. With his focus on a transcendent realm of perfect Forms, and the resultant view that material things are simply imperfect copies of these resplendent entities, Plato is "the spokesman for the theologian, the mystic, the poet, and the artist" while Aristotle, with his championing of observation and the celebration of the gritty material world, became "the father of modern science, logic, and technology." Aristotelian science focuses on this world and all of its beauty and complexity, using the senses to discern patterns and explanations, while Platonic approaches to reality point toward a realm of being that is beyond experience, understood only through pure reason or faith – rather than direct observation. Sometimes, the Aristotelian and Platonic approaches can be fused: "Galileo's science managed to fuse the Platonist's faith in mathematics with the Aristotelian faith in experience as the basis of discovery." [99]

---

[97] Gould, 4-5.

[98] Johnson, 328.

[99] Arthur Herman, *The Cave and the Light: Plato Versus Aristotle, and the Struggle for the Soul of Western Civilization* (New York: Random House, 2013), x, 327, 336.

As for unbelief, there are many instances of academics with an ingrained skepticism about religion, especially historic Christianity, who have worked their way toward confident Christian belief. The confidence and the extent of belief vary, though. Some can express belief in the traditional doctrines of the Christian faith while others can only adopt limited forms of it. William J. Wainwright, for instance, has serious doubts about the absolute truth of Christianity, but has calculated a probabilistic approach to ascertaining its truth. He does not believe that Christianity is more probable than not, but does believe that Christianity is more probable than other religions like Buddhism and has a better track record of making sense of human experience. Others, like Thomas Morris, cultivate the spiritual life to the extent that they can at least strongly sense, at moments, "growing suspicions of something more." For others, experiencing God does not come through reason or solitary dark nights of the soul, but through active involvement in the community of a church.[100]

Those with strong religious beliefs based on divine revelation do not abandon reason or empiricism, however. They are not sufficient for religious belief, certainly, but are definitely necessary to discipline religious thinking from descending into a muddled, incoherent emotionalism. Theologians could employ reason to clarify their language about, and conceptualization of, important doctrines like the Trinity and the Incarnation of Christ. Also, the study of philosophy hones your ability to make clever and useful distinctions for further clarity (or obfuscation, if you are a critic of religion). As Thomas Aquinas asserted, a greater understanding of natural processes operating in the world, aided by reason and empirical evidence, can only increase our awe about God's craftsmanship. Although secularists may scoff, one use of empiricism would be that of testing one's religious experience within a Christian community. In the same way that scientific findings are subject to the scrutiny of other scientists through peer review, a Christian geology professor has argued that belonging to a Christian community performs that same role, although with

---

[100] William P. Alston, "A Philosopher's Way Back to Faith" in *God and the Philosophers: The Reconciliation of Faith and Reason*, ed. Thomas V. Morris (New York: Oxford University Press, 1994), 19-30; Thomas V. Morris, "Suspicions of Something More" in *God and the Philosophers*, 8-18; William J. Wainwright, "Skepticism, Romanticism, and Faith" in *God and the Philosophers*, 77-87.

considerably less systematic rigor, by comparing and measuring his religious experiences with those of a local Christian community and that of past Christian saints.   Common religious experiences are affirmed, and unusual ones are lovingly questioned and, if need be, brought more in line with Christian traditions and collective experience through prayer and counseling.[101]

Secularists and nonbelievers, though, get irritated when believers, supposedly guided by faith, pounce upon evidence and reasoning that proves their case about the Bible or creation, often gleefully taking ammo from the realm of science and scholarship. Besides, if you have evidence and reasonable arguments, why do you need faith, a critic could ask? But one can almost as easily chide scientists that adhere to that wall of separation of science and religion: sometimes they come really close to scaling and peeping over that wall when they express an almost otherworldly wonderment about the workings of the universe.[102]   Albert Einstein has expressed this numinous gut feeling in a well-known snippet:

> The most beautiful and deepest experience a man can have is the sense of the mysterious. It is the underlying principle of religion as well as of all serious endeavor in art and science. He who never had this experience seems to me, if not dead, then at least blind. To sense that behind anything that can be experienced there is a something that our minds cannot grasp, whose beauty and sublimity reaches us only indirectly: this is religiousness. In this sense I am religious. To me it suffices to wonder at these secrets and to attempt humbly to grasp with my mind a mere image of the lofty structure of all there is.

Jerry Coyne, though, is quick to point out that Einstein's god was not a personal one, but a deity that Einstein himself implied was pantheistic –like Spinoza's.[103]

---

[101] John Suppe, "Ordinary Memoir" in *Professors Who Believe: The Spiritual Journeys of Christian Faculty* ed. Paul M. Anderson (Downers Grove, Ill.: Intervarsity Press, 1998), 65-73.

[102] Armstrong, *God*, 207; Dawkins, 59; Freeman, 330; Morris, 148; Rubenstein, 63.

[103] Quoted in Jerry A. Coyne, *Faith vs. Fact: Why Science and Religion Are Incompatible* (New York: Viking Penguin, 2015), 101.

Unabashed atheists would certainly reject any consideration of supernatural claims and a belief in God. How is it that they can be "moderate" in their consideration of religious claims? Peter Boghossian, a philosophy professor at Portland State University, has offered a powerfully simple redefinition of what atheism is. He asserts that an atheist should not be seen as a brash individual who does not believe in God – end of discussion – but someone who does not believe in God because there is "insufficient evidence" to verify such a belief. If "sufficient evidence" is offered, then an honest atheist would have to concede the validity of that belief: "I'm willing to change my mind if I'm presented with compelling evidence for the existence of a God or gods," he asserts in a footnote. He adds, though, that this type of atheism is superior to faith because the former should be, and is, willing to change its belief if there is enough verifiable evidence, but the latter "permit[s] no such revision."[104] I am certain, though, that Boghossian and other sportsmanlike atheists would set the bar pretty high in evaluating evidence and determining what is sufficient and compelling. As far as the author can remember, he never did spell out what would constitute convincing evidence that would incline him to reconsider a belief in God. Jerry Coyne has waded in, though:

> Suppose that a bright light appeared in the heavens, and, supported by winged angels, a being clad in a white robe and sandals descended onto my campus from the sky, accompanied by a pack of apostles bearing the names given in the Bible. Loud heavenly music, with the blaring of trumpets, is heard everywhere. The robed being, who identifies himself as Jesus, repairs to the nearby university hospital and instantly heals many severely afflicted people, including amputees. After a while Jesus and his minions, supported by angels, ascend back into the sky with another chorus of music. The heavens swiftly darken, there are flashes of lightening and peals of thunder, and in an instant the skies clear.

> If this were all witnessed by others and documented by video, and if the healings were unexplainable but supported by testimony from multiple doctors, and if all the apparitions and events conformed to Christian theology – then I'd have to start thinking seriously about the truth of Christianity.[105]

---

[104] Peter Boghossian, 27, 28, endnote # 8 on p. 38.
[105] Coyne, 119.

Consider the approach of Bryan Magee, a British commentator on philosophy and political matters. Like Boghossian, he is an atheist – or perhaps an agnostic. But, unlike Boghossian, Magee claims that any evidence from the empirical world that can be offered for the existence of God is simply unknowable. As a Kantian idealist, Magee is a superb doubter of empirical reality. He firmly asserts that true reality, the reality in and of itself "out there," is unknowable by human beings, for we come pre-equipped with mental equipment and "apparatus" that shapes our perception of what's out there outside our heads. We can only proceed with our *experience* of this reality out there, not as it actually *is*. This "part of our selves" that performs this processing, shaping, sorting, and categorizing is "outside the empirical world." Is he simply suggesting that there is a noumenal world that is inaccessible to us – but nothing "supernatural" about it – or that our perception-generating cognitive machinery makes up a nonmaterial order of things that resides outside of the material world? Or both? What is the difference between the latter and what Christians perceive as mind, spirit, and soul? Or are both unworldly and immaterial – the world as it actually is and the mental equipment we use to perceive it? This possible interface between the supernatural (as theists see it) and non-empirical, non-material entities (as Magee and other transcendentalist idealists see it) may be a fruitful avenue for discussion for theologians and philosophers. He even admits at one point that you could call this world-out-there and world-in-here as supernatural, but that there is "no evident foundation" for doing so. Magee does leave room for the possibility of God's existence and has "little intellectual patience with people who think they know there is no God, and no life other than this one, and no reality outside the empirical world." He feels in his bones that there is more than what we can inadequately perceive in this world. Magee seems to be invoking his own intuition, here:

> It just is as if the meaning and value of life have their roots in an order of being very different from this one, a realm to which we can never penetrate, which is destined permanently to remain mysterious to us . . . So I live my life *as if* there were a noumenal realm of meaning and value outside this phenomenal world, without knowing – indeed, knowing that I do not know – whether there is one or not.

But he will not cross the line between unknowability and religion: "Any talk about this opening up the way for faith is a dangerous playing with words. Ignorance is no justification for believing anything." It is not a justification for *not* believing, either. Magee asserts that Immanuel Kant's arguments spelled the demise of traditional Christian apologetics about the existence of God, but consistently noted that "*the same arguments demolishe[d] the intellectual foundations of atheism as well* [italics mine]." His position is intermediate – if that is the proper word – between "rationalistic humanists" that deny God and any other kind of order other than the empirical world and religious believers that assert the existence of God and the supernatural without any adequate grounds: "What I want very much to see are two mass migrations, one out of the shallows of rationalistic humanism to an appreciation of the mystery of things, the other out of religious faith to a true appreciation of our ignorance."[106]

Perhaps religion and doubt/unbelief need each other like two sides of the same coin. Chronicling the history of doubt, Anne Hecht observes that "religion has defined itself through doubt's questions" and certainly vice-versa. Not only doubt, but heresy also plays a similar role. Jonathan Wright has noted that heresy has played a "creative role" in shaping orthodox Christian belief. Responding to perceived deviations from the true faith forces adherents of the latter to deploy their best arguments and refine the meaning of doctrine. There must be an adversary to keep one wary, wise, and able, a counterpoint that forces one to reevaluate and more skillfully restate what one believes in. Or to put it another way, the Jerry Falwells of the world need the Larry Flynts.[107] One famous proverb tells of a preacher on a street corner warning sinners of the judgment to come. Since he is largely ignored, one sympathetic bystander asks him why he continues to

---

[106] MaGee, 9, 105, 157, 160 – 61, 397, 434, 440, 441, 447.
[107] Hecht, *Doubt*, xxi; Louis Menand, *American Studies*, 230: Larry Flynt is the publisher of *Hustler* magazine, a pornographic publication. He published an unflattering cartoon about Jerry Falwell, a prominent Baptist minister with a national following. The eventual court case revolved around free speech and expression and wound its way up to the Supreme Court. I realize this example/comparison is exaggerated for the purposes of illustration. Many unbelievers would object to being lumped together with Larry Flynt, and some believers with Falwell; see Jonathan Wright, *Heretics*.

preach if he has scant chance in changing them. He replies that if he stops preaching, the crowd will change *him*.   Certainly, opposition helps people cling to their own belief system or argument, but it does more. An opponent gives one the chance to approach his arguments with humility, sincerely enter into and understand the opposing viewpoint, and honestly consider the opponent's evidence before marshalling your own.

Chapter Three

Economics: The Free Market and Government Intervention

There's a true-believerism about the free-marketeers that is genuinely unsettling, as though it were a cult or a religion in which certain fundamental assumptions are never questioned. All you have to do to believe is ignore history and experience. Capitalism is a marvelous system for creating wealth. On the other hand, unregulated capitalism creates hideous social injustice and promptly destroys itself with greed. A marketplace needs rules.[108]

Molly Ivins

I think you all know that I've always felt the nine most terrifying words in the English language are: I'm from the Government, and I'm here to help.[109]

Ronald Reagan

One of the questions that I listed in the first chapter addressed how goods and services were to be produced and doled out in a manner that was both just and equal. Can the freedom of production and exchange ensure the relatively optimal distribution of things humans both need and value over time? Or do you need the guiding hand of government to ensure this fair distribution? Is equality of goods and living standards even a desirable or reachable goal? Perhaps it is enough to create conditions that increase the

---

[108] Molly Ivins and Lou Dubose, *Bushwacked: Life in George W. Bush's America* (New York: Random House, 2003), 15.

[109] http://www.presidency.ucsb.edu/ws/?pid=37733

probability that most everyone has a fair chance for a comfortable existence in terms of material goods and necessities. But how do you bring that about?

As I did in the previous chapter on religion, I will disclose my own leanings on this topic. The study of economics was not on my radar as an undergraduate. I did not become interested in economic issues until I went to graduate school and took a course with a free-market conservative. One of the books he assigned for the class was *Economics in One Lesson* by Henry Hazlitt. This book became the class bible for the rest of the semester. Each historical topic we scrutinized would almost invariably be run through Hazlitt's filter – or shredder. We cited chapter and verse when examining the flaws of FDR's New Deal, for instance. We will return to Hazlitt's gem-like postulates later, but it is enough to say at this point that a major critique of government intervention into a free market economy – according to Hazlitt and his supporters – is that the bureaucratic tinkering would unintentionally alter a myriad number of other economic variables that would have adverse consequences for the entire process of buying and selling, not to mention prices and wages.   Once I had mastered Hazlitt's principles and economic worldview, I took pride in knowing – or believing – that government intervention, despite the best of intentions, would turn things askew. With a mixture of resignation and glee, I could point out to any liberal the probable results of any government program or policy – or so I thought.

Then I went on to pursue a PhD at the University of Kentucky. During that first semester of seminars, I deployed Henry Hazlitt's principles whenever I could when faced with approving discussions of governmental action, labor unions, and the agency of oppressed people. My attempt to be the knowing conservative or libertarian gadfly fell flat. My process of analyzing historical issues and events through the lens of free-market principles ran up against a serious competitor: the Holy Trinity of class, race, and gender. Grad students and professors alike politely brushed aside or ably refuted my comments, focusing instead on how individuals, businesses, and even government treated Americans quite differently based on their class, race, or gender. For instance, in the 1830s, many businesses had signs that said "No Irish need apply," or factories would not hire black laborers, or women that did have a job were segregated into occupations just for women, or were paid less than men for the same job. Grudgingly over time, I came to agree that these situations were intolerable and needed some type of remedy: governmental regulation. But I still suspected that the remedy could have unintended ill consequences, so I held these contrasting approaches in an uneasy balance, and still do today. But I am grateful that my graduate education at two different institutions made me more aware of the complex relationship between economic issues and the role of government.

Before we continue, I think it is imperative to point out that my categorizations of "conservatives" and "liberals" or "free-market advocates" and "regulators" are broad ones for the purpose of comparison and convenience. There is a whole host of opinions and shades of gray in between those groups and outside of them. For instance, can one equate "free market" with extreme laissez faire economics, or can you easily assume that all conservatives reject any type of regulation or government program? Many conservatives that support the free market probably approve of such government-created entities like the Federal Deposit Insurance Corporation, which insures bank depositors up to $250,000, or the National Institutes of Health. Or perhaps a liberal that has a generally benign view of government will concede that too much regulation of the economy will hamper the spirit of enterprise. The *extent* of regulation is often the crux of the matter. But regulations are needed, contend liberals. The idea that buyers and sellers make rational choices and that the market magically brings about the greatest good for the greatest number is merely utilitarian rationalization. Instead, it's based on self-interest rather than data and reason.

DEFENDING THE FREE MARKET

Molly Ivins's characterization of those who believe in restraint-free capitalism as fundamentalist zealots is surely hyperbolic, but there is a certain elation animating those who advocate the relatively free operation of capitalism – and they point out the failures of government intervention with glee. They are certain that allowing human beings the freedom to choose who to work for and under what conditions, what products to buy, what price to sell at, who to hire, and how much to pay employees will, over time, bring about general prosperity much better than any other economic system, or capitalism restrained by excessive regulations. Competition in all economic spheres with minimal interference from the government will ultimately deliver a society with better consumers, producers, employees, and employers. The government's proper role in this free exchange is that of an umpire trying to ensure that the competition is fair (the relationship between government and business regarding competition is more complicated, as we will see later). Let's check out some of their most interesting truisms that they feel compelled to keep repeating until it sinks in.

Economics 101: Supply and demand determine the price of goods for sale

Since conservatives regard themselves as the defenders of the free market, I will place this principle in their column: the operation of supply and demand. The *natural price* is that lowest price that you can offer – after calculating and deducting the cost of production and labor – that does not result in any losses, but a price that can only be offered for a certain amount of time before you do start losing money. The *market price* is that price determined by how much product the seller provides (supply), and the willingness and ability of consumers to pay for it (demand). When the supply is plentiful and the demand is less so, prices will start to fall to attract customers. When demand is high and the supply is relatively low, the prices will rise. When the market price rises above the natural price, other competitors shift their resources into this more lucrative area to take advantage of the higher prices, creating more supply. The prices then fall. When the market price falls below the natural price, then producers and sellers will shift their resources to other products and services with a better return, and the supply of the former commodity then falls – prices start to inch back up. It is a delicate, complex dance and (largely) blind negotiation between buyers and sellers operating through their own self-interest, which abounds to everyone's benefit in the long run.[110] Granted, there are other things besides supply and demand that determine these market

---

[110] Jerry Z. Muller, *Adam Smith in His Time and Ours: Designing the Decent Society* (New York: The Free Press, 1993), 68-69, 74; Henry Hazlitt, *Economics in One Lesson*, (New York: Arlington House Publishers, 1979), 106-07.

adjustments. The design of a product, its quality, and its new technological features will also determine its price. But by saying that the market determines the price, what one really means is that millions of people exercise free choice, and their choices drive the fluctuation in prices, and that is far better than an elite corps of bureaucrats making centralized decisions about the operation of the economy.[111]

Most liberals concede basic economics 101. They think that conservatives have left a lot out of this picture, though. First of all, there is no perfect arena that ensures pure competition. That qualifying phrase the free-market economists love to use, "other things being equal," when postulating how the free market will operate in a given sector, is almost never true to reality. Besides that, in the era of large-scale corporations and a powerful financial sector, the emphasis has shifted from price competition to that of quality enhancement of products and more effective advertising. Also unmentioned is how often businesses in the past and present use the government to stifle competition, disrupting this ideal wonderland of supply and demand.[112]

Everything that the government must spend money on must be paid through taxation or borrowing

That's right, boys and girls! All those road projects, new bridges, make-work programs, new agencies for some emergency purpose, extended welfare and unemployment benefits, and bank and insurance industry bailouts must be financed somehow. Governments can continue to run up huge deficits, hoping that the spending will stimulate the economy. The rationale goes something like this: If more jobs are created, then these new incomes can be taxed, and more money will flow into the federal coffers. The gamble is that enough wealth and growth will be created so that the government can then take the increased revenue and apply it toward reducing the deficit. If that doesn't work, then the tax collector will emerge unsummoned with plans for a larger take. Thomas Sowell, a conservative economist, also points out that taxation is just a form of <u>wealth transfer</u>. Middle class families and small

---

[111] Thomas Sowell, *Basic Economics: A Citizen's Guide to the Economy* (New York: Basic Books, 2000), 308.

[112] Eugene O. Golob, *The ISMs: A History and Evaluation* (Freeport, NY: Books for Libraries Press, Inc., 1954, 1968), 36-53.

businesses, for instance, see an increase in their taxes. The revenue generated helps pay for new government programs that bring jobs to working class families, or save failing banks and sustain the living standards of banking CEOs. The government collects the money and then shifts it around to meet political promises or influence the outcome of the next election.[113] It is true that those working class families now have a paycheck and the CEO can continue to maintain his high living standard, which will have stimulative effects, but the beneficiaries and supportive politicians tend to forget that the money they are spending has been transferred to them, and that the middle class families have *less money to spend* because a portion of it has been siphoned off by higher taxes, which *could have* just as effectively stimulated the economy via increased consumption.

That certainly could happen, a liberal replies. But the projects that the tax increase funded do not just benefit the ones provided with jobs. Surely, new or repaired roads, bridges, and other infrastructure also benefit the same middle class that saw a tax increase. Lots of them drive to work, don't they? That new government building annex may serve citizens more efficiently or is more accessible, or that new computer modernization makes the processing of property and vehicle taxes faster and more reliable or accurate. Spending on education also benefits the offspring in middle-class households by making scholarships and loans more widely available. So, all of this tax money is not taken out of the private sector close to entirely, for it is "recycled back into the economy through the government programs it sustains, in the process funding institutions (like schools) that are absolutely vital to the long-term health of both the private economy and the wider society." Government deficit spending, if not immediately offset by taxation, does not rob future generations, for the outlays benefit them as well if lavished on public schools, hospitals, and better infrastructure.[114] Also, those workers that built that government-funded bridge, or those defense contractors that got billion dollar deals, get a paycheck: as a reader of this manuscript put it, "Government spending is not money that simply floats off into space. People get all that money and they buy stuff with it," which

---

[113] Henry Hazlitt, *Economics in One Lesson*, 31-32; Thomas Sowell, *Basic Economics: A Citizen's Guide to the Economy*, 325.
[114] David Coates, *Answering Back: Liberal Responses to Conservative Arguments* (New York: Continuum, 2010), 50, 261-62.

sparks local economies where they spend money. In addition to that, it should also be noted that the reshuffling of money from the private to the public sector is just one side of the story: "Governments *do* redistribute what people earn," concede political science professors Jacob S. Hacker and Paul Pierson, "But government policies also shape what people earn in the first place, as well as many other fundamental economic decisions that consumers, businesses, and workers make." The very notion of "redistribution" misleadingly implies an unnatural intervention into some perfect, raw state of market reality that existed well before governments and political solutions arose and intruded on this market Garden of Eden and dictated that the participants put on some clothes. The government and political leaders were in the garden at the outset setting up policy – like the serpent, conservatives would say. These policies that influence the distribution of income and consumption before taxes have been heavily tilted toward the top earners since the late 1970s.[115]

Taxation changes human behavior

In addition to funding government spending and the resulting transfer of wealth, Hazlitt also points out that taxation alters behavior and planned enterprise. If taxes are too high, that guy in South Florida who had a great idea for expanding his business may not pursue the idea. Expanding your business may mean hiring more people or building an additional facility. Building a new warehouse, for instance, stimulates demand in other economic sectors and keeps other people in active employment: you need to purchase those building materials from somewhere and hire people to build the warehouse. The taxes will inhibit the creation of jobs if the businessman does not pursue the idea just to avoid them. In addition to blunting the creation of jobs, the taxes may destroy them. For example, in 1990, a luxury tax was slapped on pricey automobiles, yachts, and private airplanes. Democratic politicians felt satisfaction that the wealthy would pay more taxes but, instead, yacht sales plummeted 77%, resulting in the loss of 25,000 jobs.[116] People will naturally try to reduce their tax burden by

---

[115] Jacob S. Hacker and Paul Pierson, *Winner-Take-All Politics: How Washington Made the Rich Richer – and Turned Its Back on the Middle Class* (New York: Simon and Schuster, 2010), 55-56.

[116] Walter Williams, *Liberty Versus the Tyranny of Socialism: Controversial Essays* (Stanford, CA: Hoover Institution Press, 2008), 371.

doing things differently, whether by reducing yacht purchases or shifting their money around. For example, if you raise taxes on the wealthy, which happened during the New Deal in FDR's second administration, the wealthy will follow the advice of their well-paid tax attorneys and divert their holdings offshore or into municipal bonds, locations or instruments that were both tax-free. As a result, a large bulk of the revenue intended to be extracted from the wealthy will simply be drawn from sales and excise taxes, which fall the heaviest on the middle and lower classes. Another example comes from Europe: high gasoline prices and taxes will incline drivers to purchase lighter vehicles for better gas mileage, but they will be trading more miles to the gallon for a "less safe" vehicle. [117] One final example is personal, charitable giving. When people are making more money, they tend to be more generous. When tax rates go up and income is siphoned off in other ways, giving to charitable causes goes down.[118]

Instead of raising taxes and increasing tax-avoidance reactions, one should reduce taxes. This is the familiar argument of the so-called "supply-side" economists. If you reduce taxes on everyone, especially on the wealthy, people will take that extra money and spend, save, invest, or donate it. If spent, this will have ripple effects throughout the economy and create jobs. If invested, this will create new enterprises that create jobs. If saved, this gives banks more money to lend to proposed business enterprises, which will create jobs. If donated, all the better for charity. All of those new jobs will produce new income taxes that bring in more federal revenue, which can be applied to the federal deficit. And guess what, conservatives gleefully ask? When people are making more money, they tend to give more to charity, as they did in the 1980s. In addition, by cutting the taxes of the wealthy, the government actually gets more money in income taxes from them because they are not hiding their money in tax shelters or municipal bonds anymore. The investment of the money generated from lower taxes results in more taxable income due to higher profits.[119]

---

[117] Burt Folsom, *The Myth of the Robber Barons: A New Look at the Rise of Big Business in America*, 5th ed. (Herndon, VA: Young America's Foundation, 2010), 117; Hazlitt, 38; David Henderson, *The Joy of Freedom: An Economist's Odyssey* (New York: Prentice Hall), 213, 224

[118] Henderson, 177-183.

[119] Rush Limbaugh, *See I Told You So* (New York: Pocket Books, 1993), 117, 121.

Liberals, though, could respond in a number of ways. For instance, concerning the shift to lighter, less safe vehicles due to higher gasoline taxes, one might point out that higher gasoline taxes would indeed deter one from driving a heavy gas-guzzler, but might prompt one to use public transportation more, if available. The demand for public transportation would increase – causing its expansion – and there might be a subsequent drop in air pollution. For sole commuters, the yearly cost of public transportation is lower than individual car ownership. Although planning your day around public transport schedules is admittedly less convenient, riders would save money because they no longer pay for gasoline or automotive maintenance (or purchasing the vehicle itself), and it would certainly make the roads safer if people are texting and chatting on their electronic devices on a bus or train rather than while driving. They may spend the savings and further stimulate the economy. And don't forget that building or extending public transportation will create jobs. As for tax cuts, especially for the wealthy, can you assume that the wealthy will invest that money into productive channels, benefiting lower tax brackets by trickling down, or would they simply spend that extra money on personal consumption and luxury goods – the demand for which would only benefit a local or regional economy, or certain industries? Maybe corporations would simply use the money to buy back stock, or they will simply accumulate it for a rainy day, like a recession.

Liberals may concede that taxes change human behavior but will object to the assertion that raising taxes on the wealthy will ruin the economy. If that is so, then why was there so much prosperity in the Cold War era when the tax rate on the very top of the income brackets was 91%? Place that question alongside this one: when has supply-side economics ever worked? The second Bush administration implemented tax cuts, but they "did *not* coincide with a spectacular leap in growth performance. On the contrary, the US economic cycle that began in March 2001 and ended in December 2007 registered the weakest jobs and incomes growth of any business cycle in the postwar period."[120] Well, conservatives counter, we were fighting in both Iraq and Afghanistan, both costly undertakings, which would put a damper on any economic growth. It is better to take a decade without major military operations: the 1920s. Tax rates were lowered on everyone, and

---

[120] Coates, 42.

that decade was exceptionally prosperous. Yes, on most everyone, the liberal grins, not just for the wealthy. But the prosperity was built to a large extent on installment buying and credit; wages, although on the rise, were far outpaced by productivity. And can you explain the onset of the Great Depression if supply side economics preceded it?

One must not look only at the short-term effects of a policy on one special group but the long-term effects on all groups

This nugget of wisdom is Henry Hazlitt's golden principle. When the government adopts a policy that favors one group in the immediate future, it will be at the expense of other groups once those ripples caused by government-tossed stones in the pond start emanating outward. Let's look at three examples: foreign steel imports restriction, the minimum wage, and agricultural price supports.

a) Steel producers often loudly complain that foreign companies dump cheap steel in the United States, putting domestic producers out of business and costing thousands of jobs. "By the way," quips conservative economist Walter Williams, "the real definition of dumping is when your competitor charges a price you think is too low." So, Congress places import restrictions or tariffs on cheap steel imports and saves – according to one study – nearly 17,000 jobs. Politicians that favored the bill can take photo ops with the steel workers that continue to get a paycheck. They love being seen with the "visible" beneficiaries of legislation, but overlook or ignore the "invisible and unseen victims of steel import restrictions": the 52,400 people that lost their jobs because they formerly worked for industries that had to pay higher domestic prices for steel.[121]

b) The minimum wage was adopted under the Fair Labor Standards Act during the New Deal in 1937, and it was raised periodically either from political pressure or a perceived rise in the cost of living, with the latter giving rise to the former. Conservative economists argue that employers, in order to afford greater labor costs, will simply raise the prices of their products, which takes more money out of the hands of consumers, or they cut back on other benefits that workers

---

[121] Walter E. Williams, 170, 209.

receive, like subsidized meals or health care plans. Or they simply dig in and will not hire more workers because they cannot afford it, which means an expanding workload for those already employed there. Thus, the minimum wage contributes to unemployment, especially for the unskilled, for employers *could have* hired them had it not been for the mandated rise in wages by the government. Businesses are not really that different than families. When the budget gets tight, you have to cut back somewhere. So, consumers pay more, current employees get less in other areas, and prospective employees do not even get a chance.

c) As for agriculture, the government has been trying to prop up crop prices since the Great Depression. Under the Agricultural Adjustment Act, the federal government paid farmers to leave part of their fields fallow and only till the rest of the acreage. The goal was to decrease supply artificially so that demand would go up along with prices, enabling farmers to make more money. But the government financed these checks to farmers by raising taxes on food processors, and they subsequently passed on the cost to consumers. Not only that, but if a farmer reduced his acreage by a third to qualify for a federal check, he would not need as many sharecroppers and wage workers. The program created more unemployment when, ironically, other New Deal programs were trying to create jobs. Farmers often would take their worst land out of production, and double up on their best acres; they then took the government checks and purchased tractors and fertilizer to increase their yield on the acres still under cultivation. Larger farmers won, but consumers and sharecroppers lost. The money consumers could have saved had they not had to purchase farm products with artificially higher prices could have been spent elsewhere, benefiting other sectors of the economy. Since sharecroppers and other farm workers no longer received compensation, their unemployment would affect the businesses where they usually spent money.[122] These agricultural price supports are still part of the economy today, to the tune of billions of dollars.

---

[122] Hazlitt, 15-17, 115; Henderson, 84, 114; Sowell, 154

d) Liberals would probably concede that the AAA caused unemployment in the short run but could argue that this regrettable outcome would have been cushioned somewhat if the welfare state of the New Deal had been expanded. Besides, conservatives are not the only ones that root for the advance of technology. Those AAA checks financed tractors and fertilizer. If these technological advances meant unemployment, then so be it: is the perpetuation of sharecropping really a good thing? As for the minimum wage, liberals could respond that a rise in unemployment, especially among the least skilled, sounds probable in theory, but they would ask conservatives if it actually happens. Nobel Prize – winning liberal economist Paul Krugman has cited a study by two Princeton economists that found that a raise in the minimum wage did not result in a loss of jobs, a study that has been confirmed by others.[123] First of all, Walter Williams parries that the study Krugman cited, according to peer-reviewed publications, suffered from "flawed statistical techniques;" secondly, he grumbled that Congress can mandate a rise in wages, but then asked if it also could mandate that the productivity levels of those low-wage workers that benefited would also rise "commensurate with the wage?" If those workers are given a boost by Congress, will they give their employer a boost as well with better work habits and more productivity?[124] If they do give their employers extra effort, it is usually employers that give their employees raises, not the government: One study found that before one full year of employment at the same establishment was over, 63% of those earning the minimum wage got a raise. Only 15% still made the minimum wage after three years. While toiling and waiting for that employer-derived raise, these workers, who tend to be between the ages of 16 and 24, are not suffering all that much since 40% of them live in households that pull in $60,000 or more as yearly income. Liberals may reasonably ask, though, how much was the raise? Thirty cents? Wow! One can just see that next tax bracket peeking over the horizon much like the mountains you can see in the distance out West, even though it takes hours of driving to get to

---

[123] Coates, 49; Paul Krugman, *The Conscience of a Liberal* (New York: W. W. Norton and Company, 2009), 261-62.

[124] Williams, 139, 141.

them.   Or at least that extra $12 a week might finance lunch for two at a fast food restaurant.

Profits get all the attention, but costs, outlays, and losses are largely ignored

A headline declares that a large oil company made $20 billion in fiscal year 2010. Those greedy bastards! What is often forgotten is the amount of money the company expended on overhead costs, wages and salaries, new drilling technology, and the additional costs of finding potentially lucrative oil fields. Regarding the last expense, companies often hunt for new locations only to find out that the money that was spent scoping them out was spent in vain – little to no oil. In addition, the money lost due to taxation on both the company's net profit and shareholders' stock should be subtracted from the ledger. The money flowing out amounted to $200 billion and the revenue streaming was $220 billion. After feeding the horses and canaries, the profit does not look so impressively, well, extractive anymore. Suppose the company had lost money. Those losses instruct company officials what *not* to do next year. If gasoline prices are low, for instance, then supply seems to be plentiful, so companies will cut back on pumping and certainly will not expend as much money locating new sources of oil. The public simply needs to understand the difference between selfishness and self-interest.[125]

Certainly the costs of doing business are immense, concedes the liberal, but missing in the above discussion is the huge tax breaks and subsidies that oil companies (and other corporations) get that soften the blow of anemic drilling operations and low prices. In 1995 alone, oil companies received billions of dollars of subsidies. Even after subtracting the special taxes that oil corporations pay, they pulled in "net subsidies" ranging from $5.2 to $11.9 billion in 1995, and that is not even mentioning the $10.5 to $23.3 billion spent by the US government in maintaining and protecting oil facilities and shipment, especially in the Persian Gulf. In addition, these companies also get subsidies for stockpiling reserve supplies, and tax breaks are triggered as the resource is depleted, often called an oil depletion

---

[125] Anthony Flew, 54, 104; Sowell, 8.

allowance. A subsidy is a grant of federal money, yes, a conservative oilman or politician concedes, but a tax break does not cost the government anything. Liberals counter that tax breaks are not "costless." The loss of potential revenue is simply pulled from other taxpayers: "Although tax breaks do not require outlays from the U.S. Treasury, they reduce baseline tax revenues, funds that must be raised in other ways, often from other economic sectors." And on top of that, these subsidies and tax breaks distort the market by not allowing natural prices to influence consumer and company behavior – the former to cut back consumption and the latter to explore more profitable alternative energies. [126]

Private businesses make better economic decisions than committees of government regulators since the former are risking their own money

Local business owners know what sells and what price allows a reasonable profit. They have a better knowledge of how much product to order or make based on the innumerable decisions freely made by consumers. A committee of government officials far removed from the industries they are regulating cannot come close to knowing all of the market variables, local oddities, and regional circumstances that inform the decisions of local people. There is too much (or not enough) economic information available to regulators to make good decisions about pricing and allocation of resources. Granted, local business owners are not omniscient and will very often miscalculate: certain sizes are not in stock or an item simply will not sell, or will get sold out more quickly than expected. But the market, operating freely, will do a better job compared to one hampered by centralized decision-making or intrusive oversight. It does this because private entrepreneurs have to risk their own money, not somebody else's: losses instruct them about what *not* to sell or make if they want to stay in business. They then shift their scarce resources and energy into more lucrative channels. Government officials, since they are spending taxpayers' money, i.e., somebody else's, are not so constrained by losses. In the same

---

[126] Douglas Koplow and Aaron Martin, "Fueling Global Warming: Federal Subsidies to Oil in the United States", http://archive.greenpeace.org/climate/oil/fdsuboil.pdf; http://www.mineralweb.com/owners-guide/leased-and-producing/royalty-taxes/depletion-allowance/

vein, private lenders are more cautious than government lenders because it is their own money at stake (or is it depositors' money?). Ownership leads people to take better care of their property, and they are more careful when risking it in a commercial exchange, whether it's money or merchandise.[127]

I can understand that position, a liberal could respond, but do those arguments apply to Wall Street, especially after the 2008 banking crisis? These banks are also private businesses, but they did not make wise decisions when it came to mortgage-backed bonds and all of the other complex financial instruments created in the years before the housing market slumped and started to drag down financial institutions with it, leading to a massive federal bailout of the major investment banks on Wall Street. Neil Barofsky, the former Special Inspector General of the Troubled Assets Relief Program (TARP) – which showered the banks with billions of dollars of capital injections – heard this argument (that only private bankers could understand properly their sector's operations) more times than he could stomach. Barofsky was tasked with overseeing and policing how the Treasury Department in both the Bush and Obama administrations dispensed the TARP money and especially how the banks used the money. When he found out that the banks often diverted the money into acquiring other banks or solidifying their bottom line – instead of lending the money out to grease the wheels of the economy, as intended – he blew the whistle many times. He noted that "Wall Street lobbyists" contended that "issues related to high finance are so hopelessly complex that it is nearly impossible for mere mortals to understand the unintended consequences of the legislation. The advocates of such regulation, the argument goes, just don't have the requisite experience to understand the complex markets and the negative unintended consequences that would supposedly flow from their proposals."[128]

It is certainly true that financiers probably know more about financial markets than their regulators – or are at least two steps ahead of them – but one also senses that the justification can be self-serving. And it has not been

---

[127] Anthony Flew, *Thinking About Social Thinking*, 2nd ed. (New York: Prometheus Books, 1995), 151-52; Hazlitt, 42, 45; Henderson, 33, 68-69, 190, 278, 330; Sowell, 70, 71, 133.
[128] Neil Barofsky, *Bailout: An Inside Account of How Washington Abandoned Main Street While Rescuing Wall Street* (New York: Free Press, 2012), 148.

lost on many commentators that the lords of finance are contradictory: on the one hand, they are suspicious of government oversight and intervention and denounce the meddling but, on the other hand, are willing to take billions of dollars from the government (or taxpayers) – a form of government intervention they do not have much objection to, unless there are too many strings attached.[129]   Conservatives, though, may offer a quizzical look. Doesn't the Wall Street example make our point, that private businesses are more careful with their own money than government regulatory agencies? Those Wall Street banks are taking risks with other people's money, right? Speaking of unintended consequences . . . .

Government intervention unconsciously conjures unintended problems, which brings on more government intervention, which then makes things even worse

When individuals or groups discern a "market failure" or some other economic injustice, or the government wishes to nurture a certain industry or technology, the government steps in with subsidies, tariffs, price-controls, and regulations – which distort the natural market. For instance, the Nixon administration imposed price-controls on oil prices in response to consumer anger over inflation in the early 1970s. But when OPEC raised their price per barrel of oil, regulators and fixers would not allow refiners and sellers of gasoline to pass on the extra costs to consumers. Since gasoline was priced far below what the market would normally dictate, the result was gasoline shortages. If gasoline was allowed to rise to its natural market-determined level, consumers would likely cut back on gasoline consumption. The same thing happens with rent-control. Having affordable housing is certainly a laudable goal, but if you set a maximum rent guaranteed not to rise during a mandated period of time, people will tend to use more housing than they need and will hold on to the properties. And the currently-occupied housing will decline in value since the landlord cannot charge what the market determines, so he cuts back on maintenance and upkeep because he cannot afford it, given artificially lower rents. On top of that, rent-control ruins the

---

[129] The big banks have paid the money back, though, but not without controversy. See Jonathan Weisman, "US Declares Bank And Auto Bailouts Over, and Profitable. *New York Times*, Dec. 19, 2014. https://www.nytimes.com/2014/12/20/business/us-signals-end-of-bailouts-of-automakers-and-wall-street.html

incentive to build new units because developers have no expectation of a reasonable profit. No new units are being built and people are holding on to the ones they have because of the low rent.

The bane of government intervention into the area of housing also extends to "urban renewal." Martin Anderson, in the classic conservative study, *The Federal Bulldozer*, showed how a federal program between 1949 and 1962 built only 28,000 units while destroying 126,000 homes. Urban renewal, instead of improving housing, had made it worse, and ended up destroying small businesses, hurting low-income persons, and shifting the slums to other locations. Here's an example from the 19th century: Railroad companies often sought federal subsidies to help fund railroad construction. With the famous transcontinental railroad slated to stretch from Nebraska to California, the two companies involved were paid by the mile by the federal government. Instead of finding the shortest, most efficient route, they built long, winding lines to scoop up as much federal money as possible; the construction was shoddy as well. Customers later complained, which brought on more government oversight, which only complicated things further. Those few that did not tie themselves to government purse strings fared better because they had to build their own railroads with their own money. The preeminent example is James J. Hill, the builder and financier of the Great Northern Railroad. He sought the quickest, shortest route that would finance itself. He even invested in the area on either side of the intended route by luring settlers west with enticing offers of free cattle.[130]

Some liberals may grant that excessive regulations and red-tape stifle economic activity and the entrepreneurial spirit, but the economy needs a certain level of regulation, they maintain. Reasonable people from both political parties and different ideological camps can disagree over the *extent* of regulation. The call for regulation can be self-interested or for the public good. As an example of self-interest, even businessmen and industries have argued for some level of regulation. For example, in the 1870s, American meat-packers grew very concerned when Europe began excluding American meat because of its poor quality. Shoddy meatpacking operations were

---

[130] Folsom, *Myth of the Robber Barons*, 18-19; Hazlitt, 119, 128; Henderson, 16-17; George Nash, *The Conservative Intellectual Movement in America Since 1945* (Wilmington, DE.: InterCollegiate Studies Institute, 2006), 430-431; Sowell, 24-25, 44.

making other American meatpackers look bad. So, they pressed Congress to adopt legislation that would require sub-standard meatpackers to meet a higher standard of good meat so as to win back European markets. This issue became even more urgent with the revelation that bad meat was dispensed to American soldiers in the Spanish-American War, and years later with the publication of Upton Sinclair's novel, *The Jungle*.[131] Sometimes, businesses want regulation that will eliminate competitors. Recently in 2010, the National Beer Wholesalers Association and the Wine and Spirits Wholesalers of America, after heavy lobbying, supported a bill in Congress that would foreclose consumer access to internet distributors of wine shipments and other "out-of-state retail operations" to maintain their dominance of the business. The bill was supported by both Democrats and Republicans.[132] A very recent example of needed re-regulation for the general welfare of the nation is the dismantling of the Glass-Steagall Act that separated commercial from investment banking. One of the goals of the legislation was to make sure that commercial banks, housing "ordinary people's money," did not engage in the same risk-taking financial maneuvers as investment banks. Many economists argue that the gutting of this needed New Deal–era regulation brought on the excesses in the banking world that led to the economic meltdown in late 2008.[133]

As to the overall assertion that government meddling creates unintended problems, yes, liberals concede, that certainly happens. Government bureaucrats cannot foresee everything, or even most, of what will happen from their policy-driven decisions. In all fairness, though, neither can private business owners and CEOs. Many of their decisions are driven by short-term results like higher profits next year, an increase in stock prices, or a bonus. These decisions may have long-term consequences

---

[131] James West Davidson and Mark Hamilton Lytle, *After the Fact: The Art of Historical Detection*, 5th ed. (New York: McGraw Hill, 2005), 241-43. Sinclair's intent for the book was to generate sympathy for America's working-classes by exposing their horrible working conditions, but the reading public instead focused on what was making it into the meat.

[132] Eric Asimov, "The Fate of Interstate Wine Shipments", http://dinersjournal.blogs.nytimes.com/2010/10/19/the-fate-of-interstate-wine-shipments/

[133] Joseph E. Stiglitz, *Freefall: America, Free Markets, and the Sinking of the World Economy* (New York: W.W. Norton and Company, 2010), 162-63.

for other players in the market, or employees in your own company with pension plans.   And can we admit that government regulations can have good consequences, too?   An important example is regulations about automobiles. From the mid -1940s to the early 1970s, other than outward additions and new styles, cars had not changed much. They still got basically the same gas mileage and lasted for about the same length of time. Once the federal government started mandating more miles-to-the-gallon and less pollution, car manufacturers had to create more efficient engines. Now, with requisite maintenance, cars last longer and have more fuel economy.

If we admit that regulations can have good results, we can also see that a lack of regulations can have bad results. For example, take the blow-out of the Deep Horizon oil rig in the Gulf of Mexico in 2010. Perhaps we needed a regulation that requires oil companies to let cement dry on its own. According to investigative reporter Greg Palast, it turns out that BP could not wait for the cement to dry, so they added nitrogen to the cement mix to speed up the drying process, but the jazzed-up cement mix made the platform less stable and more susceptible to gas/methane incursions. How could BP have known of the risk, you might ask? They should have been able to draw upon their own experience, for a similar – yet covered up – incident almost happened two years earlier on one of their Caspian Sea rigs. You see, waiting for "the Lord's own way of drying cement (evaporation)" is too expensive, so BP still chose to "[juice] the cement with nitrogen."[134] Perhaps Palast is confusing cause and effect, for I am not an expert on cement. But, anyway, I hope the point is more solid than BP oil platforms.

The income gap between the rich and the poor can be misleading

One of the frequent objections to unregulated free enterprise is that wealth becomes unevenly distributed. These statistics, however, only measure the percentage or share of income overall, not absolute wealth. A lower tax bracket may account for a smaller percentage of overall national income, but that statistic may obscure an absolute increase in income. To use easy numbers, let's say that a tax bracket comprises only 5% of the total national income, which amounts to 100. Perhaps its share of national income drops

---

[134] Greg Palast, *Vultures' Picnic: In Pursuit of Petroleum Pigs, Power Pirates, and High-Finance Carnivores* (New York: Dutton, 2011), 79-82.

to 4% two years later, but the total national income is now 200. The percentage has dropped, but the absolute number has increased from 5 to 8. And don't forget to factor in "public assistance dollars" that lower income groups receive as part of the income calculation, which would only increase the absolute total per person, family, or tax bracket. Besides, the income gap itself is not a stationary snapshot. Critics do not take into account that *people move in and out of tax brackets.* Young people are often in lower tax brackets, but years later, when their earning power has increased because of more education and work experience, they have climbed into a higher quintile. For example, less than 3% of those people in the bottom 20 percent of income-earners in 1975 were still there in 1991 and, on top of that, 39% of them had vaulted into the top 20 percent.[135] The trend continued throughout the 1990s and into the new millennium. According to a US Treasury study, close to 58% of people in the lowest income bracket in 1996 had moved up into a higher bracket by 2005. In addition, twenty-six percent of that same bottom bracket group was located along the middle class spectrum of tax brackets by 2005[136].

Liberals respond with their own numbers, leading to confusion and hesitancy about who's right: "As many as 77 percent of all low wage earners in the late 1980s (those in the bottom 40 percent of the wage distribution) were still there a decade later – and that decade was, after all, one of unprecedented prosperity and growth."[137] Does bracket mobility skip a generation, liberals query?

Conservatives reply in the face of such dueling statistics that the poor have never had it so good. In 1971, about 32% of Americans had the luxury of air conditioning, 43% owned a color TV, and only 1% had a microwave. By 2001, though, 76% of *poor* Americans had air conditioning, 97% had at least one TV, and 73% had a microwave. "The bottom line is, the richer are getting richer and the poor are getting richer." If one could choose which country to be poor in, it would be the United States. The poverty rate, though, is often lamented by liberals. Conservatives sigh and cite Jesus'

---

[135] Henderson, 138-140; Sowell, 137; Kevin Phillips, *Wealth and Democracy: A Political History of the American Rich* (New York: Broadway Books, 2002), 130.
[136] Williams, 133-34.
[137] Coates, 47.

observation that the poor you will always have with you, but the people that make up the poverty class will be different years later since, per the statistics above, people often move out of the cellar. Another thing that liberals do not mention is that people in the top brackets often fall out of them – there is mobility both ways. Among the top 1% of income earners in 1979, over half of them (52.7%) were no longer there by 1988.[138] This "new Fear of Falling" is more pronounced these days since wealth is increasingly tied up in paper, stocks, derivatives, and other less tangible instruments – which are much more vulnerable to major economic shocks to the system – than traditional wealth generators like land, real estate, and physical facilities. Besides that, don't envy those at the top, for many of them stay in debt to stay there: from 1989 to 2004, the amount of debt for the top 1% grew by 235% while their wealth only increased by roughly half that rate. From another angle, the top 5% of the rich account for 20% of the nation's private indebtedness.[139]   Liberals sniff in sympathy, for it is sad that the superrich have to cut back on a yacht or two because they fall a notch or two in the nose-bleed section of the tax brackets.

Conservatives, though, get a bit uneasy with these complaints. The hinted remedy is redistribution of income. The implication is that money should be diverted from the top to the bottom and middle. As Jacob S. Hacker and Paul Pierson point out, though, the solution to the increasing gap between the rich and the poor is not some "soak the rich" strategy like Huey Long's "Share Our Wealth" scheme in the 1930s, but only a course of action ensuring that levels of prosperity and income rise equally for all classes and tax brackets. There is certainly mobility in the tax brackets alright, but there is far more upward mobility in the upper tax brackets, especially the top 1 percent.[140] A rising tide should indeed lift all boats, allowing for a roughly equal rise in mobility in climbing the tax brackets.

More recent studies continue this graphs-and-charts face-off. Drawing upon US Census and IRS data, the Center on Budget and Policy Priorities argues that economic inequality marches on with a gallop. In 1989, the top

---

[138] Williams, 134, 143, 146.
[139] Robert Frank, *Richistan: A Journey Through The American Wealth Boom and the Lives of the New Rich* (New York: Three Rivers Press, 2007), 83-84, 153.
[140] Jacob S. Hacker and Paul Pierson, 24, 27-28.

1% of earners accounted for almost 30% of the wealth in the United States. By 2016, it was 49%. In 1989, the bottom 90% accounted for about 33% of the national wealth, but that had decreased to under 23% by 2016. Conservative sources continue to complain that such studies ignore "annual transfer payments" from the government to lower-income groups. If those are included in the calculations, then the gap between the top and bottom narrows noticeably. These transfer payments include, among other examples, the Earned Income Tax Credit, food stamps, and government-funded health care programs like Medicaid. As mentioned above, critics of the inequality doomsayers continue to point out that "for most people, poverty is a temporary condition," and those that are poor – while enduring their "transient" state – enjoy many more creature comforts than the poor of decades past. For example, from 2009 to 2012, only 2.7% lived in poverty for the entire four-year stretch.

How can we explain these contending sets of data? For those of us who are not economists and metrics experts, the safest generalization is that each camp claims that the other is not measuring correctly, often "underreporting" sources of income (for both the wealthy and the poor and lower classes) and excluding other factors that need to be incorporated.[141]

It sounds persuasive, doesn't it? The market is the natural order of things, and if you tinker with it, all sorts of factors and variables will get distorted. Many critics concede, as Molly Ivins partially did in the quotation at the beginning of the chapter, that capitalism is an efficient, powerful economic system that creates wealth and ably builds, moves, and sells goods and services. Now, Ivins is not a professional economist, so do not take her word for it. Try Paul Krugman: "Even liberal economists have a healthy respect

[141] Arloe Sherman, Chad Stone, Roderick Taylor and Danilo Trisi, "A Guide to Statistics on Historical Trends in Income Inequality", Center on Budget and Policy Priorities (May 15, 2018), https://www.cbpp.org/...inequality/a-guide-to-statistics-on-historical-trends-in-income; John F. Early, "Reassessing the Facts about Inequality, Poverty, and Redistribution", Cato Institute (April 24, 2018), https://www.cato.org/publications/policy-analysis/reassessing-facts-about-inequality-poverty-redistribution#full

for the effectiveness of markets as a way of organizing economic activity."[142] With that important admission, though, liberals can further respond that government intervention will indeed alter variables, but the risk of that is no excuse for "doing nothing" when economic downturns or commercial misdeeds demand some type of action: "Complex and interlocking social problems [and economic ones, presumably] are not solved by the quick fix of doing nothing. Interlocking social problems are only solved by joined-up policy initiatives that address each element of the conundrum simultaneously." [143] Let's hope the joiner-uppers know how to link each policy and element properly, warn conservatives.

The following section examines the basic objections of the critics of laissez-faire capitalism, and it is important to draw a distinction: some object to capitalism in theory and practice, and others to *unregulated* capitalism. The latter do not think that government regulations by themselves make markets un-free. Conservatives may grudgingly admit that the markets are still relatively free even with regulation, but would continue to doubt that politicians and bureaucrats can possibly foresee every economic effect, and plan "interlocking" policies that will properly manage every variable that will be impacted in the grand ripple effect.

CRITICIZING THE UNREGULATED MARKET

Conservative critics of regulation are hypocrites, for they denounce government intervention in one huff and inhale government favors in another

Liberal critics often point out that, despite all the rhetoric about how "rugged individualism" built the country, government has been involved in economic development since the early days of the Republic.

a) Railroads secured free land grants from federal, state, and local governments in the 19th century, certain industries successfully lobbied for tariff protection against cheaper foreign imports, banks

---

142 Krugman, 116.
143 Coates, 6.

have periodically received bailouts from federal agencies, high-tech industries mooch off taxpayer-funded government research, and companies have been given special charters and monopolies. Hey, what about all that talk about the benefits of good ole competition? Those foreign imports killing your industry? Tighten up your operation and cut costs. Dislike the strings attached to that federal money? Stop taking it. Throughout American history, businesses and corporations have not hesitated in grasping a helping hand from Uncle Sam. As a recent example, with the Telecommunications Act of 1996, the government gave away reams of additional electromagnetic spectrum for broadcasting in cable and digital, which critics see as a mass give-away of public property – not to mention that the bill eased restrictions on cross-ownership of different types of media, further contributing to corporate media consolidation. Private interests get these goodies and breaks through intensive lobbying. Also, let us not forget that businesses also benefit indirectly from government spending on infrastructure that facilitates the movement of goods and services.

a) Foreign countries notice this hypocrisy. American leaders in government and industry preach the free market to developing countries, encouraging them to lower or eliminate their tariff barriers against industrial imports, but those same cheerleaders support and maintain tariff barriers against the agricultural and textile exports of those same developing countries they are trying to crack open. On top of that, American agricultural products are propped up by federal subsidies, making it even more difficult for developing countries to sell their products in the U.S.[144] On the one hand, a conservative critic could then wonder why we have trade deficits if the United States is so discriminatory. We seem to be buying lots of things from abroad. On the other hand, really, one can discriminate and have a trade deficit, especially if you keep out the exports of a small South American country with tariffs but more than make up for it by buying goods from a large Asian country, say,

---

[144] Noam Chomsky, Peter R. Mitchell and John Schoeffel, eds., *Understanding Power: The Indispensable Chomsky* (New York: The New Press, 2002), 73, 240,255; Phillips, xiv, 248, 294; Joseph E. Stiglitz, *Globalization and its Discontents* (New York: W.W. Norton and Company, 2002), 60-61, 172, 240, 244.

China. And since the dollar continues to be the world's reserve currency, the United States can continue to pay with dollars for its imports, so we do not need a huge stock of foreign currencies earned by exports. Another example of hypocrisy is when the United States and the IMF lectured countries during the East Asian meltdown in the late 1990s to cut deficits, raise interest rates, and refrain from bailing out their banks. When financial trouble came to the United States in 2008, the government did the opposite of their earlier advice to countries like Thailand and Indonesia: it ran up deficits, lowered interest rates, and bailed out the troubled banks and institutions.[145]

b) Polls reveal that Americans in general are against "Big Government" but support government programs that benefit them. Americans are enthusiastic to slash spending on foreign aid, unemployment benefits, and welfare but insist on keeping or increasing current levels of spending for health care, education, infrastructure projects, and defense, etc. Speaking of defense, the Republican Party, vocal advocate of limited government, suspends fiscal frugality when it comes to fat defense contracts (and so do many Democratic politicians). Billions of dollars are transferred from the federal government to defense industries. To his credit, John McCain, a Republican senator from Arizona, criticized this wasteful spending, for the Pentagon complains that some of the new weapons systems don't work and that they are not needed. Congress, however, continues to heed the lobbying by defense industries for projects and weapons the Pentagon does not want. But, nonetheless, when it comes to stuff it does want, the Pentagon is still a "state-guaranteed market" for defense industries and other high-tech companies that get contracts and then develop new military hardware and sophisticated weapons. When the new equipment becomes obsolete in a few years, then those same companies get new contracts worth billions for even more advanced armaments that may not be used.[146]

---

[145] Stiglitz, *Freefall*, 221-222.

[146] Joe Conason, *Big Lies: The Right-Wing Propaganda Machine and How It Distorts the Truth* (New York: Thomas Dunne Books, 2003), 197; Jordan Ellenberg, *How Not To Be Wrong: The Power of Mathematical Thinking* (New York: The Penguin Press, 2014), 365-367; Robert Higgs, *Against Leviathan: Government Power and a Free Society* (Oakland,

Conservatives could then respond that defense contracts also pay for conventional social and military needs, like uniforms, ammo, salaries, lodging, training, etc. True, reply liberals, but we did not say that we were complaining about *that* – only expensive weapons systems that do not work or are not used, all for the benefit of defense contractors and the politicians whose campaigns they fund (more about this in the next chapter).

c) If you support free trade, then stop whining about illegal immigration. The North American Free Trade Agreement (NAFTA) enabled the United States to export "cheap subsidized" crops to Mexico. Mexican farmers could not compete with the artificially low prices, so thousands of them and their families were forced to migrate north across the border to find jobs. American corporations' and businesses' demand for cheap labor is handily met, for illegal migrants do not have the bargaining power to complain collectively about low wages.[147]

d) And another thing: conservative supporters of the free market argue that welfare causes laziness, but are silent about the possibility that inherited wealth does as well.[148] A conservative could rightly point out, though, that supporting the welfare state involves money taken from taxpayers, and inherited wealth does not. Which is worse, taxpayer-subsidized laziness or privately-funded laziness? Those lucky trust-funders infected by the latter virus can at least spend money trying to fill up their spare time, which maintains or creates new jobs. Liberals counter by saying that the tremendous gap in wealth is rife with social injustice, and that the gap itself is the result of political decisions that benefit the top income earners.

e) Conservatives often nostalgically invoke history, growing misty-eyed about those "rugged individualists" – especially those that migrated west – that built this country, not the government. Undoubtedly, the frontiersmen, ranchers, farmers, and cowboys were hardy types. But the West was certainly tamer because of the following things linked to or funded by government: the construction of dams, offering land

---

CA: The Independent Institute, 2004), 285; Chomsky, 240.

[147] Peter Phillips and Andrew Roth, eds., *Censored 2008: The Top 25 Censored Stories of 2006-07* (New York: Seven Stories Press, 2007), 85-88.

[148] Conason, 183-84.

under the Homestead Act of 1862, federal purchase of silver and gold, and let's not forget using the US Army to subdue those inconveniently located Indians and Mexicans that happened to be in the way of Manifest Destiny.

Free-market enthusiasts selectively read Adam Smith, if at all

Hailed as the prophet of free-trade, free-market capitalism, Adam Smith is often quoted as an authority by conservatives who wish to implement a pure version of his economic philosophy in the United States. What advocates of limited government often neglect to mention is that Smith himself was, ironically, a customs collector years after his publication of the *Wealth of Nations*. He supported free trade, but made a living collecting customs duties or tariffs on imported foreign goods. They agree with Smith that a government must provide national defense and an internal police force to maintain order, in addition to a legal system, but largely ignore Smith's call for the government to perform other functions: providing for an educational system and "even coerc[ing]" citizens and workers to utilize it, regulating public entertainment to protect against debasement, and constructing and maintaining a nation's infrastructure to facilitate the operation of commerce. That's a significant amount of government involvement. Smith did not believe that the market could operate in a vacuum, but needed an advantageous "social and political context" to bud properly. Presumably, the government helps nurture these conditions. He even implied that government helps maintain inequality: "Wherever there is great property," Smith wrote, "there is great inequality . . . Civil government , so far as it is instituted for the security of property, is in reality, instituted for the defense of the rich against the poor, or of those who have some property against those who have none at all."[149]

Another thinker that holds an endowed chair in the conservative pantheon is an Austrian economist, Friedrich Hayek, but even he saw that the government played an important role in several areas of the economy, an acknowledgment that goes unrecognized or ignored in conservative circles:

---

[149] Muller, 8, 186; Stiglitz, 219; Hacker and Pierson, 82.

Effective market competition "requires a good deal of government activity directed toward making it effective and toward supplementing it where it cannot be made effective. . . . I am not an anarchist. I do not suggest that a competitive system can work without an effectively enforced and intelligently drawn up legal system.

Again,

The successful use of competition as the principle of social organization precludes certain types of coercive interference with economic life, but it admits of others which sometimes may very considerably assist its work and even requires certain kinds of government action.

He even believed that "some minimum of food, shelter, and clothing, sufficient to preserve health and the capacity to work . . . . be assured to everybody," and that the government should step in to assist "victims of such 'acts of God' as earthquakes and floods."

In case the point has not sunk in:

To prohibit the use of certain poisonous substances or to require special precautions in their use, to limit working hours or to require certain sanitary arrangements, is fully compatible with the preservation of competition. . . . Nor is the preservation of competition incompatible with an extensive system of social services – so long as the organization of these services is not designed in such a way as to make competition ineffective over wide fields. [150]

If you think the above quotes were taken out of context by some liberal economist, think again, for they were taken from a conservative author recommending the ten books conservatives should read (one of which was F. Hayek's *The Road to Serfdom*).

Pursue market reforms or else

---

[150] Stiglitz, *Freefall*, 273; Quoted in Benjamin Wiker, *Ten Books Every Conservative Must Read: Plus Four Not to Miss and One Imposter* (Washington, D.C.: Regnery Publishing, Inc., 2010), 194-95, 204.

A largely unregulated market is often an unquestioned requirement when it comes to helping other struggling countries. The prescription for their economic calamities calls for large doses of market capitalism coupled with a severe reduction in government programs and assistance. The capitalism cure has to be "pure" in order to work. This absolutist approach ignores the complexities of national and regional economies around the world, argue liberals. The International Monetary Fund (IMF) and the World Bank were created after World War II to help ensure regularity in exchange rates by "pegging" other currencies to the US dollar and by extending loans to developing or struggling countries around the world. Accepting financial help from these mega-institutions, though, came with conditions: the countries receiving the loans had to agree to cut government social spending, privatize industry formerly owned by the government, and deregulate industries. You're damned if you don't, and damned if you do. If you do not accept the conditions, you get cut off from the IMF money, which might actually be less painful. But if you do take the deal, it comes with lots of suffering, discontent, and protest. Many people in these developing countries have always depended on government assistance, and when it is diminished or cut off, they are thrown back onto their own resources, which are very little. There isn't a big box store or fast food joint just down the street hiring in an impoverished village. How do you survive? When the IMF takes the wheel and pauperizes the government, incomes start to fall; illiteracy increases; government workers lose their jobs through privatization; foreign corporations sweep in to take over resources once under government control; and the commercial borders are thrown open to allow currency speculation and capital to flow in and out without regulation. The IMF takes a "one size fits all" approach. Each country must implement this formula in order to continue receiving financial assistance.

It must be added, though, that there is some evidence that the IMF has lightened up a bit in recent years, at least for a few favored countries. Iceland, for instance, was allowed to run a deficit for a limited time and pursue Keynesian solutions to unemployment. For unfavored nations, though, the medicine remained as bitter as always. In a strange twist of irony, free market advocates love to point out that committees of bureaucrats do not have enough knowledge about market conditions on local and regional levels to manage them efficiently, but those that work at the IMF are ignorant of the conditions in each of their client countries, and run the same playbook step-by-step. When their free-market nostrums did not work, they insisted even more that a purer version should be implemented and given time to work.[151]

Enthusiasts for an unregulated free market are akin to religious fundamentalists

Coined in the 1920s, fundamentalism merely referred to conservative Protestants who adhered to what they considered were the "fundamentals" of the Christian faith[152]. Over the decades, a "fundamentalist" has come to mean anyone that has an unquestioned belief in certain principles or doctrines, and fiercely resists any dilution of them. Some liberals compare those who champion an unregulated free market to fundamentalists. Like fundamentalist religious believers, free-market advocates maintain an unswerving belief that allowing individuals to pursue their self-interest by making free choices in a free market economy will redound to the benefit of everyone in the long run. If unimpeded capitalism is not working properly, then it's because the country is still practicing a less-than-pure version of it, so the economy must be purged of the interventionist impurities so that it will function as it should. Just as religious fundamentalists may have grudging respect for atheists and contempt for moderates, "market fundamentalists" actually half-way respect someone who is openly a socialist because they were honest about it, and castigate those who favor "mix-and-match economies" that are a strange hybrid of the free market and government intervention.[153] Besides, conservatives could also ask, are not many interventionists, and outright socialists, just as fundamentalist in their own ideology? Socialists often explain away the fall of communism by asserting that a state-run economy would have worked if it had been

---

[151] Greg Palast, *The Best Democracy Money Can Buy: The Truth About Corporate Cons, Globalization, and High-Finance Fraudsters* (New York: Plume, 2003), 144-158; Stiglitz, *Freefall*, 215 & *Globalization*, 20, 34.

[152] The fundamental beliefs included the inerrancy of the Bible, the Virgin Birth of Christ, His blood atonement on the cross, and His physical resurrection. Fundamentalists did not concede an inch of ground in defending these doctrines and strictly warned or denounced others that made compromises with modernism.

[153] Naomi Klein, *The Shock Doctrine: The Rise of Disaster Capitalism* (New York: Picador, 2007); 62, 64.

implemented better, or if "real" socialism had been tried. The irony is evident, though, when conservatives adopt the same excuse when it appears that capitalism has failed – that it would have succeeded if only a pure version of it had been tried.

Buccaneer capitalists think that disasters are good, for they wipe the slate clean and allow the imposition of a free-market utopia before the dazed populace can resist

Sometimes, democracy just gets in the way of implementing a purist version of market reforms. A few brave liberals charge that some unscrupulous capitalists have to wait for a disaster to implement what would, in normal times, be resisted. In her best-selling book, *The Shock Doctrine*, Naomi Klein argues that free-market reform cannot approach its purest form in a true democracy because there are so many competing interests jockeying for advantage. A natural disaster like a hurricane or tsunami, or a political upheaval like a revolution or coup-assisted change in government, leaves an ideal laboratory for implementing free-market reforms. In the same way that a prisoner is broken down by loud noises and shock therapy, local inhabitants are so overwhelmed and stunned by meteorological or political events that they are powerless to resist a free-ranging market whirlwind that usually would evoke opposition in normal times. What little government is left can then mimic a corporation and outsource some of its duties to private contractors. Some of Klein's examples of where this has been attempted include New Orleans after Hurricane Katrina, Sri Lanka after the devastating tsunami in 2004, and Russia after the fall of the Soviet Union.

What is really outrageous and frightening is that a few capitalist provocateurs have speculated that a crisis needs to be *intentionally created* in order to achieve their dream of unregulated capitalism. [154]

Mobility within tax brackets cannot be true if wages continue to fall, and taxes on the wealthy and corporations continue to decline as a percentage of overall taxation

Conservatives often claim that the rich pay the most taxes. In 1998, the top 1% earned 18.5 percent of all "adjusted gross income" and paid out 34.8% of

---

[154] Klein, 8, 13, 20, 175, 323, 363.

total federal income taxes. The top 5% earned 32.9% of the same and paid out 53.8% that same year. How about 2005?[155]

Percentage of All Federal Income Taxes Paid: 2005

Percentile of Income Earners	Percentage Paid
Top 1%: An annual adjusted gross income of $365,000 and higher	39%
Top 5%: $145,000 and higher	60%
Top 10%: over $103,000	70%
Top 25%: over $62,000	86%
Top 50%: over $31,000	97%

The wealthy benefit from tax cuts more because they pay more taxes, says David Henderson. Liberal critics counter that conservatives only focus on the income tax and leave out a whole host of other taxes: sales, excise, property, and payroll taxes. Yes, the rich are paying more because they are earning more, liberals admit, but they are paying a *lesser tax rate* as compared to decades earlier. So are corporations, for that matter. According to Molly Ivins, corporations in the 1950s paid on average 25% of federal taxes, but it has dropped to 10% in 2000 and 7% in 2001. "Working people" (left undefined) contribute three times more money in payroll taxes alone to the federal treasury as compared to all taxes for corporations. In addition, the treasury is losing about $70 billion a year because corporations move assets to tax-free offshore accounts. Corporations and other wealthy individuals basically buy these perks with lobbying operations and contributions to political campaigns. Only one-tenth of one percent of Americans contributed 83% of all campaign contributions in the 2002 elections and then reaped the rewards. Yeah, there's some mobility alright – in the upper echelons of the tax brackets. In addition to political advantages, CEO pay is skyrocketing compared to their employees. From roughly 1978 to 2008, that ratio of CEO pay to those that work for them went from 70:1 to around 300:1.[156]

---

[155] Williams, 215.
[156] Coates, 251; Hacker and Pierson, 47.

While these corporate elites are buying politicians with campaign contributions and riding their compensation into the stratosphere, the working class is floating downward toward terra firma. Real wages have fallen from 1973 to 1996. Although they went up again in the late 1990s, they slid back again by the millennium, and keep sliding. Meanwhile, the income of the wealthy continues to grow with exuberance, while that of the super-wealthy exponentially more. "This is not the function of [free market capitalism]. It's the result of a series of political decisions made by politicians who are increasingly owned by their rich donors" through periodic campaign contributions, according to Ivins.[157] How can wages keep falling with our creature comforts continuing to increase, conservatives parry? A liberal could answer with four possibilities: 1) Two-income families are necessary to keep up with the cost of living, allowing for more purchases, 2) that individual Americans are simply working more hours a week to stay afloat,[158] 3) that Americans simply go more into debt to maintain a culturally-determined standard of living, and 4) that Americans took advantage of rising home equity – at least until 2008 when the housing market crashed due to lenient lending policies and toxic, complex financial instruments.

Unregulated capitalism can undermine sovereignty and democracy

Multinational corporations are not moved much by patriotism. With operations in many countries, their loyalty is to profits. Did you know that projected, future profits are actually property? For instance, under Chapter Eleven of the North American Free Trade Agreement (NAFTA), a corporation can sue a national government if that particular country has labor or environmental laws that can deny or reduce the *potential* profits that could have been made absent such regulation. Here's one example: In 2000, the Metaclad Corporation won a lawsuit against Mexico because that country refused to allow it to build toxic waste dumps in Mexico. Taxpayers south of the border paid out $16.7 million dollars in the settlement. This kind of power is dangerous because unelected business leaders can override the

---

[157] Henderson, 225; Ivins, 40-41, 45-47. Is Ivans hinting that, absent these political decisions, the free market may have resulted in wages going up, a pesky capitalist could ask?

[158] Coates, 46.

laws passed by elected representatives. Just the threat of corporate lawsuits will make a country think twice about considering future regulatory legislation, even if really necessary. As we have seen, the IMF and the World Bank basically do the same thing. On the positive side, it is the resistance to capitalism, not just in its corporate form, which drives forward democratic development in countries, according to many on the Left. [159] This resistance draws the attention of the superrich in the United States. As Nancy MacLean has argued, an extremely wealthy elite in the United States has been funding think tanks and conservative intellectuals for decades. Their goal is to protect capitalism from too much democracy. In the name of economic liberty, they want to chip away at government programs, limit workers' rights, destroy unions, dismantle public education, and strip away entitlements. In order to do this, they have to put shackles on democracy – like appointing conservative judges at all levels of the judiciary, for instance, and changing the public narrative about the relationship between liberty and property.[160]

Outsourcing is not free trade

Although a conservative in the Reagan administration as assistant secretary of the treasury, Paul Craig Roberts has many objections to "free trade," the main one concerning the adverse effects of outsourcing on the American economy and worker. Large corporations increasingly move their operations to other countries to take advantage of cheaper labor costs, which contributes to unemployment in the United States. The main motive for offshoring operations and production is certainly cheaper labor costs, but companies also take this route because other countries do not have the same costly environmental and labor regulations that the United States does. Not only that, but foreign countries offer subsidies and tax breaks to companies to relocate, not to mention that many of these countries have workers with better aptitudes for science and mathematics.

---

[159] Harvey J. Kaye, *"Why Do Ruling Classes Fear History?" and Other Questions* (New York: St. Martin's Griffen, 1997), 45; Peter Phillips, ed., *Censored 2003: The Top 25 Censored Stories* (New York: Seven Stories Press, 2002), 72-75, 89.
[160] See Nancy MacLean, *Democracy in Chains: The Deep History of the Radical Right's Stealth Plan for America* (New York: Penguin Books, 2017).

Apologists of outsourcing argue that these lower costs and higher benefits give businesses a competitive advantage, and thus is a natural component of free trade. Roberts heatedly disagrees. First of all, outsourcing is not only not free trade, but not even trade. Trade is the exchange of physical goods and services. Countries exchange goods and services based on what they are good at producing. They export wine if they are really good at producing it, and they import wool because they comparatively are not as efficient in wool's production like one of their trading partners, a trading relationship often known as "comparative advantage." Seeking the cheapest labor possible outside one's own country is not searching for comparative advantage, but "absolute advantage." Not only does this practice cause unemployment, but it also reduces the productive performance of the United States. All of the production that takes place outside of the United States due to outsourcing reduces the GDP by the amount produced offshore. It further contributes to the trade deficit when Americans buy these same goods, for offshored production comes back to the United States as *imports*.

Defenders of outsourcing often counter the unemployment accusation by asserting that the savings in labor costs allow companies to hire more educated, skilled workers, or that those laid off soon find jobs elsewhere at the same or higher pay. Walter Williams argues that the "creative destruction" of manufacturing jobs due to technological innovation brings savings and benefits, and, "In the process, U.S. workers are reallocated to more competitive, mostly better-paying jobs." After all, look at what innovation did to farming. In 1900, of all American workers, 40% were farmers. By the first decade of the 21st century, due to astronomical advances in productivity, that percentage is now under 2%. Over time the displaced farmers were absorbed by manufacturing and other economic sectors. In the same way, our manufacturing output is soaring while the number of jobs in manufacturing keeps declining, but the workers are absorbed elsewhere.[161] Roberts answers with data from the Bureau of Labor Statistics that indicates that the bulk of new jobs are created in lower-paid domestic work and services, not higher-paying jobs in heavy manufacturing or professional services like engineering. And these

---

[161] Williams, 136-37, 194.

domestic service jobs do not produce things that can be exported to bolster America's GDP.[162]

Regulation and redistributive policies are not synonymous with socialism

One familiar cry from the right-wing is that government initiatives, regulation, and growth are, if not outright socialism, putting the United States on the road to it, often referred to as "creeping socialism." More specifically, any attempt to raise taxes, especially on the wealthy, or reduce economic inequality is quickly labeled by free market conservatives as socialism or "socialistic." These statist attempts to redistribute economic and social benefits through taxation or some other policy or program is a fundamental assault on the freedom of Americans. Putting an exaggerated label on some governmental action or program is a typical conservative gambit, liberals complain.[163]

A THIRD WAY AND ALL THAT

The expression "third way" or "middle way" is not a new idea or innovative path. Economists and intellectuals have been debating these concepts for decades. How does a country position itself between unregulated capitalism and over-reaching government intervention? Perhaps the choice between unregulated capitalism and statist solutions is a false dichotomy. Maybe there are other pathways. Politicians and economic reformers have tried to conjure some combination of the two or pinpoint some midway buoy between the two poles, subject to periodic repositioning, that best preserves both freedom and security. Dwight Eisenhower, our moderate Republican president from 1953-1961, called for something like it when he advocated "the middle way." On the one hand, capitalism is by far the most efficient system for producing, distributing, and selling goods – even liberals and critics concede that – but its short-term effects are often fraught with

---

[162] Paul Craig Roberts, *How the Economy Was Lost: The War of the Worlds* (Oakland, CA.: CounterPunch and AK Press, 2010), esp. 237-238; The Week, "Where America's Jobs Went", March 25, 2011.
[163] Coates, 17.

displacement and pain. Defenders point out that we should focus on the beneficial long-term effects of a market economy, to which John Maynard Keynes famously retorted, "In the long run, we are all dead."[164] In other words, it is cold comfort to tell someone displaced by market competition (whose living standard is deteriorating) that it will all work out to the benefit of most everyone over the long haul. Utilitarian thinking and policies will always leave someone out.

On the other hand, extensive government involvement in society seems more compassionate by offering aid during bad times and entitlements during good, but suffers from a cumbersome, rigid response at both the macro- and microeconomic levels. Experienced private groups and businesses are best positioned to make choices about buying, selling, and transporting goods, and these activities work best without excessive compulsion or constraints. Historian Douglas Brinkley, for instance, provided a great example: Wal-Mart in the aftermath of Hurricane Katrina while FEMA fumbled about. The much-maligned retail giant set up warehouses full of necessary clean-up equipment, made donations of food and clothing, opened up their stores to emergency personnel and provided them with what they needed, and gave cash advances to employees washed out by the storm in addition to guaranteeing many of their jobs. "The Red Cross and FEMA," Bay St. Louis Mayor Eddie Favre suggested, "should take classes on logistics, mobilization and compassion from Wal-Mart. They opened up their Waveland store and gave us whatever they needed. It was awesome."[165] Liberals would then probably grumble that, after the crisis and favorable news coverage of Wal-Mart was over, Sam's company simply reverted to their usual practices – like low wages that force many of its full-time employees to rely upon food stamps.

Some type of synthesis of the two will result in a partial loss of both freedom and security on both ends. Politically, it is difficult to hold the free market and substantial government intervention in an ideal alchemical mixture without being pulled in one or the other direction. If you swing too far toward the free market, those on the left of the political spectrum will

---

[164] Stiglitz, 249.

[165] Douglas Brinkley, *The Great Deluge: Hurricane Katrina, New Orleans, and the Mississippi Gulf Coast* (New York: William Morrow, 2006), 251-52.

decry the seeming devotion to greed and impersonal market forces. And if you swing too far to the side of governmental centralization, those on the right of the spectrum will warn of creeping socialism and never tire of reminding us that the full-blown version of it failed. The balancing act continues.

Ever since the New Deal, a substantial number of Americans continue to support some type of regulation of the economy and a "safety net" to smooth out the booms and busts of the normal operation of the market. This safety net includes, among other things, unemployment insurance, pensions for the retired, and disability payments.[166] These state benefits and extensive governmental regulations exist uneasily alongside an economy that is purportedly capitalist. Paul Krugman has argued that we can maintain this balance, and have done so in the past: the golden age of the late 1940s up until around the early 1970s. During the so-called Gilded Age from the 1870s until the Great Depression, there was massive inequality in the United States with only spotty government involvement. From the early 1970s on, inequality returned in the United States with the incomes and share of wealth of the richest citizens increasing – with political help – and the income and share of wealth for the poorest and the middle class barely rising, stagnating, or declining. But in between those two long eras of inequality was a time of prosperity for America's middle classes. Beginning with the Great Depression (ironically) and accelerating with World War Two, progressive taxation policies and government spending decreased the huge gap between the top and bottom tax brackets, often dubbed the "Great Compression." Not only was income inequality muted during this era, but political feuds were not as polarized as recently, for Republicans and Democrats often overlapped into a consensus, especially when Republicans stopped trying to dismantle the New Deal. He cited a study that examined the ideological differences between the two political parties based on roll-call votes, with the legislation and the representatives ranked along an ideological spectrum: "What stands out from the results is just how modest the differences between Republicans and Democrats were in the fifties and sixties, compared with a huge gulf before the New Deal, and an even larger gap today." [167]

---

[166] William C. Berman, *America's Right Turn: From Nixon to Bush* (Baltimore, MD: The Johns Hopkins University Press, 1994), 72, 89; Higgs, 285.

In the political climate of the 21st century, conservative Republicans have recently taken to labelling their more center-right comrades in the party as RINOs – Republicans In Name Only. In other words, these centrist but right-leaning colleagues don't lean far enough to the right. They might as well give up their party identity and declare themselves Democrats. Krugman's above analysis aligns with a comment by David Brown: "It is easy to forget today that from 1936 to 1976, moderate Republicans controlled the GOP. . . ."[168] Instead of RINOS, why don't more centrist Republicans, if there are any left, and more conservative Democrats, decry the disappearance of Republicans The Way They Used to Be? Granted, the acronym would not be very catchy; RINO does have an efficient snap to it.

Ideologues on both the left and the right continue to protest that Americans cannot have it both ways, especially on the right. The free-market economy and the preferences of liberal regulators are not buffet tables where you can pick and choose what you want and ignore and discard what you do not. Conservatives, for instance, often have an all-or-nothing kind of mentality that characterizes their approach to religion and political economy, despite actions and policies that belie it, as covered above. With the Bible, you cannot choose which parts to believe and which to dismiss. Either Jesus said all those things in the four gospels or he did not. You cannot embrace the Sermon on the Mount but cast away those portions that hint at or assert his divinity or that demonstrate his supernatural power.[169] Their economic beliefs are much the same way. You cannot simultaneously hold that a supermarket can charge what the market determines for bacon and then advocate rent control for inner-city high-rise apartments. One has to admire the consistency in principle, if not in action.

Rather than an all-or-nothing mentality, liberal thinking is disconnected when comparing their orientations in two separate categories: the environment and the economy. Ironically, liberals have an attitude toward the environment that is inconsistent with their position on the economy and

---

[167] Krugman, *The Conscience of a Liberal*, 3-7, 73.

[168] Brown, 8.

[169] Awkwardly for conservatives, that is exactly what one of our Founding Fathers did. Thomas Jefferson took the Gospels and snipped away the supernatural acts of Christ and any portions that alluded to his divinity. His edited Gospels kept Jesus's moral teachings front and center.

government intervention. Concerning the environment, it is a standard belief that all natural things are interconnected, and that human activity often alters natural variables for the worse. For example, if pollution destroys one seemingly dispensable species, it turns out that that species played some vital role in the local ecosystem, and when it is removed, other variables are altered in the surrounding natural world with a ripple effect. Liberals strive to minimize human activity that might upset this natural, delicate balance. Could you not argue that the economy is roughly comparable? Compare human activity in the environment to government involvement in the economy. When the implementation of a policy alters some economic variable, it will eventually reverberate throughout a local or regional economy and, if serious enough, will have national repercussions. Liberals should acknowledge that any governmental policy should be implemented with as little disruption to the natural flow of the economy as possible. If a policy wonk or economist knows how to do that, a job is surely waiting for him. A critic, though, could deride my comparison of ecosystems with economies as a false analogy. The analogy imputes an organic nature to the operation of an economy that just isn't there. The delicate balance and interplay between species and resources in the environment is not the same as supposed rational actors making choices in an economy.

And speaking of the environment and the history of the natural world, shouldn't conservatives embrace natural selection, asks Michael Shermer? If liberals' orientation toward the environment and the economy is somewhat contradictory, so is conservatives' rejection of evolution operating by natural selection and their embrace of the free market. Charles Darwin's principle of natural selection is akin to Adam Smith's invisible hand. Both have "unintended consequences" that come about by unimpeded competition, but in a good way. In the natural world, the complex interaction between organisms allows nature to sort out the best adaptations for survival and ensures the long term upward advance of favored species while, in the economy, free competition among buyers and sellers keeps an optimal balance of supply and demand that benefits everyone over time, creating "national wealth and social harmony."[170] If there is anyone who should cheerlead for natural selection, it is

---

[170] Michael Shermer, *Why Darwin Matters: The Case Against Intelligent Design* (New York, 2006), 136-138.

conservatives; if there is anyone that should decry natural selection, it is liberals, who usually see Darwinian evolution as the best explanation for the course of natural history but denounce cutthroat competition as hurtful and wasteful. Actually, conservatives do embrace forms of Social Darwinism, an ideological derivative of biological natural selection that advocates a "sink or swim" mentality in business and life – exchanging "the survival of the fittest" for "the success of the fittest," if you will. This form of Darwinism is okay, but the biological parent of this social offspring, oddly, is not.

Outside of the United States, struggling countries have had a tough time finding a nice balance between unregulated capitalism and socialist governmental structures, especially when the latter were already firmly embedded for years. Swallowing the medicine of the IMF and World Bank is often the only choice they have. Joseph Stiglitz, a former economist for the World Bank and now a critic of the policies of his former employer and the IMF, knows all too well the consequences of thrusting a pure version of capitalism on developing countries with a recent socialist past. Dismantling socialistic government structures overnight and allowing the aggressive forces of capitalism to flood the country brings a world of trouble: unemployment for public sector employees, high prices for staple goods, and possibly foreign control of national resources. But globalization in a broadly capitalist framework has also brought benefits: it has opened up new markets for developing countries and has provided jobs. Indeed, peasants working in a Nike factory, for instance, get paid low wages, but they are probably better off there than practicing agriculture in a local village, which might be the reason they took the jobs in the first place. A Cambodian making 75 cents a day digging through trash cans for usable, sellable junk is surely not being exploited if she chooses to work in a factory for $2 a day. Stiglitz, although supportive of economic reforms that move toward a healthy market economy, cautions that market reforms need to be introduced with cautious "sequencing," which simply means putting "safety nets" and a "regulatory framework" in place before the steady tide of privatization and market liberalization comes in. Stable banks and other financial institutions, for instance, should be up, ready, and running to direct properly this transition to a new, competitive economic system. Agencies should be established that generate, gather, and provide market information that allows private business and the government to make informed decisions about production and sales. This useful information should not only be provided to business and government, but to private individuals as well. Citizens, whether in the United States or around the world, need "open access to information" so they can make good financial decisions, which will only enhance the operation of the market. [171]

In addition to reasonable governmental oversight and provision, historian Jerry Muller has noted that Adam Smith advocated restraints on the economy that did not come from government, but from the moral influence of families, communities, churches, and other private social organizations. Far from advocating pure self-interest, argues Muller, Smith thought that one's self-interest should be tempered by the cohesive restraints embodied in these different communities. Liberty was not the ability and prerogative to do almost anything one wished, but the freedom to control one's passions and constrain one's vices to bring about a litany of choices that serve the best interests of oneself and society at large.[172] I think many conservatives and liberals would agree with this assessment, especially social conservatives and more traditional Democrats.

Issues that revolve around the extent of the government's involvement in the economy and society are usually the bread and butter of politics. The following choices, by no means exhaustive, give politicians and other leaders a framework of principles to defend and talking points on which to run for office.

1. An unregulated free market economy
2. A regulated market economy
3. An unregulated free market economy with redistributive safety nets
4. A regulated market economy with redistributive safety nets
5. An unregulated market economy informally restrained by the moral influence of family, society, and religion with redistributive safety nets
6. A regulated market economy informally restrained by the moral influence of family, society, and religion with redistributive safety nets

---

[171] Stiglitz, xxii, xx, 18, 73; Williams, 203-4.
[172] Muller, 2, 98.

7. A mixed, non-Marxian socialist economy and welfare state where the government owns, controls, and runs large national industries, like oil, gas, and other municipal entities, in addition to transportation and communications operations, while a majority of the economic enterprises remain in private hands, although heavily regulated
8. A Marxian socialist economy where the government owns, controls, and runs most industries
9. One third way not mentioned yet is the revival of strong unions in the United States to either augment or lessen the role of government in restraining the civilized pirates of the business world. If you believe in a free market where employees, employers, buyers, and sellers freely choose, then we should support – in theory – workers that freely choose to walk off the job collectively and bargain for higher wages and benefits. It is no different than a bunch of businesses that get together in a trust or trade association that promotes their interests and products. Strong unions, though, need the support of a strong government and a legal infrastructure that protects collective bargaining from business attempts to gut union activity. But an anti-union conservative could wonder, then, if the striking employees would allow the same freedom of choice to their employer who chooses to hire new workers to replace them.

These combinations can be further complicated and altered – willingly or unwillingly – by events, circumstances, and political considerations. Politicians maneuver among these options and often modify their views and positions when the political winds change direction. By having the defenses and criticisms summed up and listed, perhaps the skeptical moderate can make better choices or judgments.

Before we move on, it must be noted that **20th and 21st century** American history is truly unique. The operation of our markets and government has not been disrupted within the continental US by the damage of major wars, unstable governments, large-scale refugee problems, civil wars, foreign occupation, the death of millions of people, or the flight of intelligent scientists and engineers (who came to the US right before and after World War II and only increased US intellectual, cultural, and economic heft). Yes, we eventually fought in both world wars, but major damage to government operation centers and industrial capacity was confined to

Europe. Sure, the British sacked Washington, DC in the War of 1812, Americans fought amongst themselves in a deadly civil war, the Japanese attacked Pearl Harbor, and terrorists launched assaults on 9/11, all of which caused death and destruction, but they still do not compare to the monumental devastation of World Wars One and Two. It must be noted that the total number of men killed in the Civil War –anywhere between 620,000 to 850,000 – still tops the death totals of all other American wars combined, but the two world wars killed millions, leveled cities, and obliterated infrastructures. The tangled operation of the above economic arrangements could have been far more complex if the United States had experienced just some of the crappy conditions that Europe and Asia have had to put up with. But, alas, those two continents, one could argue, brought it on themselves. As one reader of this manuscript has stated, "During the 20th century, maybe the United States should have periodically thanked other countries for consistently, spectacularly" inflicting the continent of Europe with political instability, mayhem, aggression, and violence, culminating into major confrontations that left large swaths of physical and economic destruction. "Perhaps American wealth and dominance were partly products of other countries' self-inflicted failures." Or we should thank the Pacific and Atlantic Oceans for giving us at least partial insulation for all of these years. American historians of a conservative bent often point to American exceptionalism. Indeed.

Chapter Four
Politics: Conservatives and Liberals

Conservatives are fond of observing that there are some problems that cannot be solved by throwing money at them. There are even more that cannot be solved by dropping bombs on them.[173]

Molly Ivins

The defining characteristics of modern liberalism are radical egalitarianism (the equality of outcomes rather than of opportunities) and radical individualism (the drastic reduction on limits to personal gratification). These may seem an odd pair, for individualism means liberty and liberty produces inequality, while equality of outcomes means coercion and coercion destroys liberty.[174]

Robert H. Bork

Conservatives and those on the right are usually willing to settle for thinking themselves correct on political issues; those on the left have always needed to feel not so much that they are correct but that they are also good. Disagree with someone on the right and he is likely to think you obtuse, wrong, sentimental, foolish, a dope; disagree with someone on the left and he is more likely to think you selfish, cold-hearted, a sellout, evil . . . .[175]

Joseph Epstein

For the entire twentieth century and into the twenty-first, politics has been a tug of war between conservatives and liberals in the United States. Their

---

[173] Molly Ivins and Lou Dubose, *Bushwacked: Life in George W. Bush's America* (New York: Random House, 2003), 266.

[174] Robert H. Bork, *Slouching Towards Gomorrah: Modern Liberalism and American Decline* (New York: Regan Books, 1996), 5.

[175] Joseph Epstein, *Snobbery: The American Version* (Boston: Houghton Mifflin Company, 2002), 157.

ideology is well-known.[176] Conservatives favor limited government, the free market, morality in social life, and law and order. Liberals advocate a legitimate role for government in the nation's economic life but do not wish that government get entangled with certain moral decisions concerning, for instance, abortion or drug use – and libertarian conservatives would often agree. Liberals would also respect law and order, but tilt toward an egalitarian ethic that upholds civil rights to the point of making amends for discrimination in the past.

These generalizations are not comprehensive, certainly, and do not hold for every single conservative or liberal. There are different subgroups within both camps. Conservatives, for instance, often can be divided into free-market conservatives and traditional, social conservatives. Drawing inspiration from the anti-statism of Austrian economists Frederick Hayek and Ludwig von Mises, market conservatives wish to see a very limited form of government, especially in relation to economic affairs. They champion individual liberty and freedom. Social conservatives – who can trace themselves to Russell Kirk and Wilmore Kendall – support these emphases to a certain degree, but the pursuit of rugged individualism, they think, often violates historic values and community norms. They tend to side with what they think is moral rather than licentious. For them, freedom is wonderful, but should have limits. Historian Eugene Genovese has gone further and identified this strain as a special brand of southern conservatism. Taking a dim view of human nature, southern conservatives uphold individualism, but insist that it be tethered in a community with historic roots and restrained by civic values and moral standards. They are suspicious of egalitarianism and recognize the need for a social hierarchy – ideally not based on race – for good order. Furthermore, they are distrustful of consolidated forms of finance capitalism and rampant consumerism tied to a worship of economic expansion and unreflective technological innovation. Such market-driven changes, they recognize, have eroded traditional community ties and long-standing social relationships.[177] These two camps

---

[176] A useful definition of ideology is found in David Henige, *Historical Evidence and Argument* (Madison, Wis: The University of Wisconsin Press, 2005), 6: ". . . a quasi-systematic ensemble of beliefs, attitudes, and aims that underpin the way we argue, the evidence we use and how we use it, and the ways we hope to influence others."

[177] Eugene D. Genovese, *The Southern Tradition: The Achievement and Limitations of an American Conservatism* (Cambridge, MA.: Harvard University Press, 1994), x, 2, 14, 22,

within conservatism have often coexisted uneasily. There is often an unsettled relationship between individualists and communitarian moralists: one group attempts to enlarge freedom and individual liberty while the other faction tries to ensure virtue and a belief in – and adherence to – a transcendent moral order. Complicating this split is also a considerable divide between high-brow conservatism, replete with those that do not trust the masses, and a more populist variety that casts a wary eye toward elites, experts, and intellectuals – with the latter gaining ascendency in the past couple of decades.

The different camps have been united by solid commonalities, though: anti-communist sentiment; liberalism as the common enemy; a spirited defense of private property; a desire for decentralization and individual responsibility; subscription to the idea of social mobility and self-improvement; suspicion, if not outright hostility, toward "social engineering;" a strong military; a broad defense of Christianity, especially pertaining to an absolute moral code; and a generally positive view of the United States and the virtues of the Founding Fathers.[178]

I'm not sure if you can divide liberals into two or three groups, but some like to refer to themselves as "progressives." They recognize the dangers of an overly intrusive government, but still wish to "reinvent" it so that it plays a helpful role alongside business by funding and channeling new technology and forward-looking initiatives. Eric Alterman has asserted that liberals recognize that "liberty and equality . . . must always coexist in tension with each other," and that the government should play a role in tempering inequality and crafting a collective solution to problems that individuals cannot surmount on their own.[179] More distinctive traits about liberalism will emerge as we proceed.

34, 83, 98-99; Genovese fears that this brand of conservatism is being diluted by the increasing corporatization of American life and the ascendency of market values and consumer culture, which exalt free choice and affluence without moral considerations, that "filth" is just another commodity available from a broad menu of products and services bought and sold.

[178] An excellent discussion of the history of conservative thought is George Nash's *The Conservative Intellectual Movement in America Since 1945* (Wilmington, DE.: Intercollegiate Studies Institute, 2006), 16, 123, 269-272, 276-278, 547-48. More broadly, Nash divides conservatives into five different camps: free market libertarians, morally-minded traditionalists, anti-communists, neoconservatives (former Leftists that have moved Right), and the new, Radical Right (conservative evangelical Protestants).

My own ideological path has mirrored the intellectual course that I sketched in the last chapter about economics. During my undergraduate days, I cannot say that I had a firm political ideology. If someone had asked me if I was a conservative or liberal, or why I was a Republican or Democrat, I would not have been able to give a coherent answer, not even an answer that hit the buzz words that summed up the ideology or party platform in some sporadic fashion. By the time I went to graduate school, I became quite conservative under the influence of some professors and, yes, I listened to Rush Limbaugh for a while. When I entered the doctoral program at the University of Kentucky, I clung to that conservatism as best I could. But graduate school does make one more liberal over time, even though I did not consider myself a card-carrying liberal. My immersion in the study of history and the process of straining out a dissertation gave me an appreciation of how knowledge is generated and how multi-faceted it can be. Complexity often does not merge well with set principles. So, today, I consider myself a moderate independent. It seemed like a good career move – not seeming like too much of an ideologue or radical in either the conservative or liberal direction. If you had to pin me down even further, I like to think of myself as an evidence-based, case-by-case Eisenhower Republican.

It is obvious at this point in our political universe to recognize that both conservatives and liberals have their own newspapers, foundations, think tanks, sets of statistics, talking points, media platforms, websites, and pundits. Each side is able to assemble an array of facts, analyses, and arguments, and then skillfully (and selectively) picks and chooses from this information to vanquish their opponent. Recipients of this information then focus on the evidence that backs up their own opinions, and largely ignore or marginalize evidence that challenges or contradicts their beliefs. Although in a book about science, skeptic Michael Shermer notes that the process of confirmation bias is pervasive in the political world as well:

> Liberals read the paper and see greedy Republicans trying to rig the system so that the rich can become richer. Conservatives read the same paper and see bleeding-heart liberals robbing the rich of their hard-earned dollars to support welfare queens on crack. Context is everything and the

---

[179] Eric Alterman and Kevin Mattson, *The Cause: The Fight for American Liberalism from Franklin Roosevelt to Barack Obama* (New York: Viking, 2012), 472-73.

confirmation bias makes it very difficult for any of us to take an objective perspective on our own beliefs.[180]

I still try to make sense of it all. Once again, I have assembled some pertinent guidelines and observations about liberals and conservatives that may help a reader see a larger landscape, an overhead perspective that may at least bring some understanding. A bird's eye view of both sides of the battlefield may aid us in diminishing our propensity for favoring evidence and arguments that support our viewpoint and discounting those that do not. First up are the liberals. They generally support capitalism but insist that there should be rules; that equality of opportunity, while preached from the rooftops, often has to be fostered by government help; that mass culture is certainly what the masses choose, but the finer things of life must be preserved and supported; that there are limits to economic growth and the resources of the planet; and that inequality augmented by governmental policies is simply immoral.

LIBERALS TAKE AIM AT CONSERVATIVES

The attempt by conservatives to portray themselves as the defenders of common people against the liberal elites is a laughable sham

Populist conservatives tout and align themselves with the values, interests, and folkways of America's working and middle classes, and decry the attempt by liberal intellectuals and academics to impose their egalitarian, relativistic values on everyone else. They really resent the condescension that liberal elites supposedly have toward less educated, less sophisticated Americans. Castigating liberals for historically fomenting class warfare, conservatives play the same game when they denounce "limousine liberals" that support government actions that aid the lower classes. Liberals themselves do not buy the rhetoric. On one hand, conservative elites pump up the pride of the working and middle classes, proclaiming that they are the real, authentic Americans. With a sleight of the other hand, they undermine

---

[180] Michael Shermer, *The Borderlands of Science: Where Sense Meets Nonsense* (New York: Oxford University Press, 2001), 89.

the economic interests of the very group of people they exalt with policies that benefit the wealthy. As Thomas Frank puts it, "From Fox News and the Hoover Institute [a conservative think tank] and every newspaper in the land they sing the praises of the working man's red-state virtues even while they pummel the working man's economic chances with outsourcing, new overtime rules, lousy [or no] health insurance, and coercive management techniques." Indeed, Frank's book, *What's the Matter with Kansas* (2004), centers on how conservative Republicans have whipped up the support of small town and suburban America by focusing on hot-button cultural issues – like gays in the military, the wanton display of sexualized images, and abortion – while quietly pursuing economic policies that do not benefit, and even harm, that same demographic. As Jefferson Cowie has noted, the attempt to lure blue-collar workers away from the old New Deal coalition and channel them into the Republican fold is first noticeable with Nixon's 1972 re-election campaign against George McGovern. Pitching appeals to white ethnic workers, his team fast-tracked cultural issues to the forefront of political conversation – the themes included denouncing the excess of permissiveness and the dearth of patriotism, for instance. These were not the bread-and-butter issues of yesteryear: "Roosevelt's famous 'Forgotten Man' was becoming a Republican, his enemy less the 'economic royalists', the class *elites*, against which Roosevelt inveighed in his landslide 1936 victory, than the cultural *elitists* who would look down on the politics and culture of blue-collar America." This campaign fell flat after Watergate but emerged again with the ascendency of Ronald Reagan.

Not only are these cultural issues supplanting real economic ones in the minds of ordinary Americans, but the crusade seems hopeless and unattainable, for the entertainment culture reflected in movies and on TV continues its slide into vulgarity, and gay Americans are making strides toward more acceptance.[181] Conservatives could interject, though, that their

---

[181] As an example of getting in a jab at the highly educated, see Martin Anderson, *Imposters in the Temple: American Intellectuals Are Destroying Our Universities and Cheating Our Students of Their Future* (New York: Simon and Schuster, 1992), 125: "Those who have earned doctorates get to "add the three little letters 'Ph. D.' after their names, and 'Professor' or 'Dr' in front. Most of them know they were pretty intelligent to begin with, but the act of being formally certified smarter than most, and then being addressed daily as 'professor' or 'doctor', getting to tag 'Ph.D' every time they sign their names, can prove to be an intoxication from which some of them never recover"; Conason, 13, 17, 24-25; Jefferson Cowie, *Stayin' Alive: The 1970s and the Last Days of*

present inability to clean up the culture does not provide an excuse to stop trying, and that they are not denouncing "limousine liberals" for their wealth, but their hypocrisy. Fair enough. But the charge of hypocrisy does not cancel out the ruinous economic policies that conservatives support to the detriment of the working class, one could point out. Besides that, the spectacle of multi-millionaires and billionaires parading around as populists denouncing the cultural and media elites is just that – a spectacle, and a phony one at that. They are part of the uber-elite in the financial and business world.

The military–industrial complex and other revolving door relationships are money merry-go-rounds for mostly conservative Republicans

In his farewell speech in 1961, the outgoing moderate Republican President Dwight D. Eisenhower warned of an establishment that was unprecedented in American history, the "military-industrial complex." This behemoth hybrid of defense contractors and the Pentagon could be traced to World War II, when a handful of corporations got the lion's share of contracts for wartime production. It grew in size and influence, and became a permanent fixture on the landscape during the Cold War with the Soviet Union. To combat the communist threat, the United States had to build what historians call "a national security state" to ensure our security. Building advanced weapons systems, delivery mechanisms for nuclear warheads, and increasingly sophisticated aircraft was good business for defense industries: they received billions of dollars from contracts with the Pentagon. Those of a conspiratorial bent claimed that it was secret policy to make sure that the United States always had an enemy to combat to continue justification for such expensive weaponry and a massive military. After communism in Eastern Europe fell and the Soviet Union disbanded in the late 1980s and

the Working Class (New York: The New Press, 2010), 228; Thomas Frank, What's the Matter with Kansas? How Conservatives Won the Heart of America (New York: Metropolitan Books, 2004), 121, 151, 239; Paul Krugman partially agrees with Frank, but thinks he has left out an important issue: race. "Movement conservatives" use race to scare working-class white voters, whether it is lazy blacks on welfare or criminal blacks roaming the streets, while pursing economic policies that increase inequality. See Krugman, The Conscience of a Liberal, 176-183.

early 1990s respectively, defense contractors were worried that the money tree would shrivel up. So, a new enemy fortunately arose: Islamic terrorism. As for the money merry-go-round part of the above truism, its operation goes something like this: defense contractors like Halliburton, Eastman Kodak, and Bechtel make campaign contributions to conservative Republican politicians. Once elected – and having secured a strategic position on some really important congressional committee – they make sure that these same defense contractors continue to get more contracts worth billions from the Pentagon. The benefactors once again donate more money to Republican incumbents or candidates, and the whole cycle of contributions-election-contracts-contributions goes for another swing around the circle. One can almost hear a square-dance leader on a microphone yelling out, "Swing your partner . . . turn around," etc.

And that is not the only thing swirling. There is a revolving door linking defense industries, government agencies, foundations, think tanks, and even banks. For instance, an elected or appointed government official channels lucrative defense contracts to a defense company while in office. If he leaves or loses office, the same company hires him, or he finds a cushy position at a think tank or foundation that issues position papers that advocate an aggressive foreign policy, which further justifies more defense spending, which keeps the revenue coming in for defense contractors. These revolving door relationships are not just confined to the military-industrial complex; they also extend to intelligence and security services (discussed later) and the world of banking. As an example of the latter, Travelers Group – an investment company – took over Citibank in 1998. The only problem is that this merger was illegal (at the time) under the Glass-Steagall Act, which prohibited the combination of commercial and investment banking. A government official with clout, like Moses, had to part the Red Sea so that this illegal deal could be justified. Enter Secretary of the Treasury Robert Rubin. He helped dismantle this crusty ole New Deal legislation, and a bill finished it off in late 1999 months after he left the post; he took up a position at Citibank just two weeks before the bill was passed. He netted $126 million for his government service work. Of course, with such a cozy relationship between government and the world of banking, why not take some risks that will be covered – read: bailouts – by the government if they do not pan out: "They were cranking out new derivatives 'products' faster than bedsheets from a whorehouse," as Greg Palast colorfully describes it.[182]

Republicans, though, would rightfully point out that Rubin was treasury secretary under Bill Clinton, a Democrat. No matter who or which party one pins this on, these "incestuous," "interlocking relationships" among government officials and defense contractors and other private entities are a dangerous thing that only puts confirmation bias into overdrive, like looking for evidence to support a certain foreign policy decision – for instance, invading Iraq.[183]   Conservative Republicans would probably shrug their shoulders and say: a) liberal Democrats play the same game on a scale that approaches ours and b) what are you going to replace the military-industrial complex with?   This close affiliation with the military also allows conservatives to mooch off some of the machismo . . . .

Conservatives like to portray themselves as hyper-masculine and sneeringly deride liberals as effeminate

Perhaps these characterizations spring from conservatives' championing of traditional gender roles where men are men and women are women. Liberals, by contrast, uphold women's rights outside the home, gay marriage and civil unions, curbs on high-powered rifles, and policies against bullying. And they wonder if football and lacrosse incline men to violence or, recently, cause serious long-term brain impairment.   These liberal positions and suspicions all seem to blur gender roles and dampen the natural outlet of male testosterone. What a whining group of Nancy boys! Just as status quo politicians in the past have denounced reformers as effete – or just lacking any gender – and consequently having neither "fecundity [nor] virility," conservatives cannot resist labeling liberal intellectuals as unmanly snobs. Even conservatives are not immune within their own camp. If conservatives are not tough enough, they are often called out by one of their own. *National Review*, a respected conservative periodical started by William F. Buckley, Jr., fired Ann Coulter several years ago for her comments about fighting terrorism.   To cure Middle Eastern terrorism, she advocated invasion, assassination, and conversion to Christianity. Not wanting to be associated with such comments, *NR* no longer continued her column.   In response,

---

[182] Greg Palast, *Vulture's Picnic*, 322-23.

[183] Chomsky, 240; Sheldon Rampton and John Stauber, *Banana Republicans: How the Right Wing Is Turning America into a One-Party State* (New York: Jeremy P. Tarcher/Penguin, 2004), 112 – 115.

Coulter denounced the editors as "girly-boys" for not having the "spine" to stand behind her remarks.[184] One feels like we are back on the playground: "You don't want to swing on the military-industrial complex Jungle Jim? Ah, come on, sissy!"

Liberals acknowledge that the free market is the most efficient economic arrangement in theory, but a pure version of it will harm certain people and destroy valuable things

We touched upon this line of thinking in the last chapter. I can only defer here to an excellent, concise summary of this position by Bryan Magee, a British "popularizer" of philosophy. He has conducted interviews with important people in the world of philosophy for the BBC, and is often considered a master of explicating philosophical issues in an easy-to-understand manner without dumbing down the serious content. We earlier encountered his stance on religious belief. His comments largely pertain to British political economy, but could just as easily apply to the United States. In his debates with those of the "radical-right," he readily admits that their position was the most coherent, not to mention its "intellectual honesty." He judged their critiques of socialism "dauntingly impressive." Praise aside, Magee could not bring himself to accept a "free-for-all," a purely competitive economy and society without any kind of cushion to soften the blows of life. A utilitarian economic system, one that brings about the most good for the most people, will always leave many people out of the prosperity loop: the physically disabled, those of marginal intelligence but otherwise decent folk, and those who simply had a string of bad luck. The highest forms of culture will not survive for long in an economy where people freely choose their entertainments and diversions. Independent bookstores, theater, opera, and other artistic venues cannot compete with radio, television, video games, gadgets, movies, and social media on the Internet. To preserve unique communities and culture itself from lowest-common denominator trends and protect people not equipped to compete through no fault of their own, government must provide support and help. Magee admits that reconciling this free market mentality with government assistance is no easy balancing

---

[184] Frank, 130; Hofstadter, *Anti-Intellectualism in American Life*, 188, 90; Anthony York, "*National Review* Fires Anne Coulter", *Salon* (October 2, 2001), http://www.salon.com/news/politics/red/2001/10/02/blue

act and has no suggestions for a proper ratio.[185] Protecting hoity-toity theatre groups and poetry readings, conservatives would ask? Subsidizing such dainty, cultural entities because the mass of consumers do not attend or support them is basically elite contempt for the vulgar, unwashed masses that are too ignorant to pick what is best or good for them. The charge of elitism plays out well politically, as we've seen.

Liberalism is actually a mainstream ideology (and Rush Limbaugh claims the same thing about his brand of conservatism)

Instead of talking points and shouting down opponents, liberalism is an ideology that embraces an engaged public concerned about exploring different points of view, exercising rationality, humbly acknowledging our own presuppositions and prejudices, and confidently believing in the possibility of objectivity, all of which are intellectual pursuits that take place in a "democratic civic culture and public sphere built on trust and respect." According to Kevin Mattson, a history professor at Ohio University, "Liberalism, no matter how much conservatives have ignored this point, has historically stood in the middle of the political spectrum."[186] I will assume that the middle of the political spectrum is synonymous with the mainstream. It is unclear, however, if the above virtues are currently practiced by the mainstream, or if Mattson was simply outlining what he hoped that all Americans would try to attain – characteristics that the mainstream does not currently possess, but might with effort. If the latter, then liberalism is not the mainstream, but is instead a hope that the mainstream will move toward this ideal liberalism. Conservatives, on the other hand, think that they represent what mainstream America thinks and does: right-wing radio talk-show host Rush Limbaugh believes that he owes his "success in great measure to the reality that mainstream Americans are in fact conservative," and has frequently asserted on his radio program that he is not brainwashing Americans, for they simply agree already with his message.[187] One can only ask, will the real mainstream stand up?

---

[185] Bryan Magee, *Confessions of a Philosopher: A Journey Through Western Philosophy* (New York: Random House, 1997), 324-26.

[186] Kevin Mattson, *Rebels All! A Short History of The Conservative Mind* (New Brunswick, NJ: Rutgers University Press, 2008), 139-140.

[187] Rush Limbaugh, *The Way Things Ought to Be* (New York: Pocket Books, 1992), 28; *See*

Conservatives exalt freedom, but their view of freedom is narrowly defined and contradictory

When it comes to endlessly chanting words like "freedom," "liberty," and "individualism," conservatives certainly excel in this rhetorical areana. But their notion of freedom is usually negative, meaning they focus on *freedom from things*, like the federal government and any other type of bureaucratic meddling in their business operations or the use of private property. But freedom from those things does not translate into the freedom to do what one pleases. Limbaugh, for instance, argues for "the establishment of limits on behavior. Laws are the tools we use to build an orderly society. An orderly society cannot be achieved or maintained if we allow people to do whatever they want to do, with no regard for anything but their own pleasure." If everyone lives as they desire without any restraints, then "anarchy" results. Liberals point out, though, that the rhetoric is inconsistent. Conservatives shout to the high heavens about government interference in the operation of private business through regulation, prohibitions, and taxation, but certainly wish the government would prevent or punish that educated, middle-class couple from smoking marijuana in the privacy of their home. Conservatives themselves are often divided on these issues as well[188]. More libertarian conservatives wish that the government would stay out of economic affairs *and* private lives, while more traditional conservatives wish to police drug use, pornography, and other purportedly immoral actions. Ex-conservative David Brock has longed for the good ole days when conservatives were not as intrusive, when they stood for "classically liberal political values," like "respect for the Constitution, skepticism about government power, defense of privacy and individual liberty, pluralist discourse, civility, and restraint."[189] Classically liberal? One should use that phrase with care. Do not point out to a contemporary conservative that many of the modern-day principles that conservatives

---

I Told You So (New York: Pocket Books, 1993), xiv.

[188] Eric Foner, *Who Owns History? Rethinking the Past in a Changing World* (New York: Hill and Wang, 2002), 70; Limbaugh, *The Way Things Ought to Be*, 174, 276; Rampton and Stauber, 33.

[189] David Brock, *Blinded by The Right: The Conscience of an Ex-Conservative* (New York: Crown Publishers, 2002), 311.

embrace were once known as "classical liberalism" in the nineteenth century. Conservatives grudgingly acknowledge that history lesson with an impatient huff.

Conservatives are anti-intellectual

There are many liberal charges that raise conservatives' dander, and this has to be one of the most epidermis-invasive (it gets under their skin). "People who read and think often arouse suspicion on the far right," asserts Joe Conason, a liberal antagonist. Those people who luxuriate in ideas and the life of the mind, that is, intellectuals, are often seen as elitist liberals with their extensive bookshelves, National Public Radio purring in the background, and a steaming cup of coffee coupled with a croissant before them on a desk with stacks of books and annotated papers. Conservatives charge that these people try to tell us how to run our lives and what to believe, especially those with a lofty sinecure in government or a high perch in academia with an easy teaching load. It seems to be a truism today, liberals lament, that people want politicians and a president they can sit down and have a beer with, like George Bush.[190]   Critics love to quote an observation usually attributed to H. L. Mencken regarding conservative Americans' desire for a president like themselves:

> All the odds are on the man who is, intrinsically, the most devious and mediocre — the man who can most adeptly [propagate] the notion that his mind is a virtual vacuum. The Presidency tends, year by year, to go to such men. As democracy is perfected, the office represents, more and more closely, the inner soul of the people. We move toward a lofty ideal. On some great and glorious day the plain folks of the land will reach their heart's desire at last, and the White House will be adorned by a downright moron.

For all of their reverence for the Founding Fathers and their principles of government, conservatives do not seem to want a president or any other elected official like them, liberals charge.   Thomas Jefferson, Benjamin

---

[190] Liberals do try to siphon off some of this appeal: Barack Obama's beer summit with an African-American Harvard professor arrested for trying to get into his house and one of the white police officers at the scene. In defense of George Bush, he is an avid reader of biographies, an activity that does not support the charge of anti-intellectualism.

Franklin, James Madison, John Adams? These men were well-read, sophisticated, and cosmopolitan. If they were not intellectuals, then who is? Since when did intellect become a disqualifying factor for high office, asks Richard Hofstadter? Partisan hyperbole aside, Hofstadter, a famous historian that is hard to pin down ideologically, says that it is difficult to say that a person that is occasionally hostile to intellect is "constitutionally anti-intellectual," for they often esteem their own ideas and hold anti-intellectual opinions strategically and only at times for a certain purpose. But there is certainly something to be critically said about conservatives' suspicion of the overly-educated, scientists, and experts, especially if the latter's findings or policy recommendations interfere with their business and lifestyle, or undermine important tenets of their cultural and political beliefs.[191] To be fair, though, there is nothing wrong with healthy skepticism of authority as long as it is not primarily driven by ideological or religious reasons, but by a sincere desire to know the actual state of affairs or cause of something.

Liberal bias in the news media is less significant than corporate ownership and self-censorship

Eric Alterman and other critical voices have argued that conservatives have plenty of presence in the news media; that liberal opinion diminishes farther up the media totem pole; and that reporters must walk carefully so as to preserve their press passes to the corridors of power.

a) First, he shows that conservative voices are more than adequately represented in the media. William Bennett, Anne Coulter, and Robert Novak are, or have been, frequently in front of the camera on news shows, and Jonah Goldberg of *National Review* and columnist George Will get plenty of opportunities to fill the nation's newspapers with conservative opinion. And that is just a sampling of those voices. Besides, ask anyone in Western Europe under governments that practice a form of social democracy, and they will

---

[191] Conason, 19; Hofstadter, 22, 145-46; Susan Jacoby, *The Age of Unreason* (New York: Pantheon, 2008), xviii-xix; Limbaugh, *Way Things Ought to Be*, 162-64; Charles P. Pierce, *Idiot America: How Stupidity Became A Virtue in the Land of the Free* (New York: Doubleday, 2009), 27-51. Pierce was finally driven over the edge when he saw a saddle on a dinosaur in a creationist museum, which prompted him to write this book.

see American media, not just Fox News[192], as conservative compared to their countries' news coverage.

b) Second, the liberal media is not so liberal. Even smart conservatives in the loop concede the ruse: "I admit it," Bill Kristol told the *New Yorker*. "The liberal media were never that powerful, and the whole thing was often used as an excuse by conservatives for conservative failures." Sure, Alterman admits, "most journalists" are pretty liberal about social issues like gun-control and abortion, and certainly support social welfare and regulation, but the ideological tide starts to turn once you move up into strata with higher-paid journalists and editors. Producers and other higher-level news officials must remember that they work for a huge corporation that owns many other different companies and has a host of advertisers, and one must also keep in mind that those owners and publishers usually are conservative and vote for Republicans. Those who decide what to "run with" in a newspaper, online forum, or TV news program had better pick topics, angles, and facts that do not offend any of the companies or advertisers to which the mother ship has ties, or anything that would prompt the owner or publisher to make a phone call complaining about a proposed story. If one does, those advertisers might take their business elsewhere, and the editor or producer that allowed the story to run may be on the unemployment line. The result is that, in the words of Noam Chomsky, "dissident perspectives are weeded out, or marginalized" by a "complex system of filters." Smaller newspapers and TV stations will follow the lead of the heavy-hitters since they usually do not have the resources to send someone overseas or do in-depth analytical reporting.[193]

c) And then there's the Big House. When it comes to getting information at the White House or other centers of government, reporters and investigators must bite their tongues. They must

---

[192] Rampton and Stauber, 70: "Fox claims to be 'fair and balanced', but by 'balanced' what it really means is that its conservative tone offsets the alleged liberal bias of other networks" like CNBC.

[193] Eric Alterman, *What Liberal Media: The Truth About BIAS and the News* (New York: Basic Books, 2003), 11, 17, 20-24; Chomsky, 13-14; Conason, 34, 39; Frank, 132-33; Greg Palast, *The Best Democracy Money Can Buy: The Truth About Corporate Cons, Globalization, and High-Finance Fraudsters* (New York: Plume, 2003), 192.

practice self-censorship to preserve their access to "official" sources.[194] If your stories or questions are too prosecutorial, you might not get invited back for that intimate interview with the high-ranking official or the president. Better replace those curve balls with some underhanded softball pitches so the elected official can slug some into the outfield. Liberals and conservatives, though, see this caution only when it restrains their own reporters. Liberal reporters must monitor their questions when interviewing a Republican president, and conservative ones a Democratic president.

Conservatives love to target government programs that do not work, but fear and denounce even more intensely those that actually do, or can

The best example is Social Security. Despite the dire warnings about collapse in the near future, Social Security continues to be one of the most solid achievements of the New Deal. The US government may be in debt, but Social Security is not – for the time being. In 2007, the money flowing into the program exceeded benefits paid out by $200 billion, and had an overall surplus of $2.2 trillion. Liberals certainly concede that the fund will eventually be in trouble as the ratio between those drawing upon the benefits and those working and paying into it through taxation starts to narrow appreciably. The moment of trouble, though, may be farther off if one uses more "realistic" estimates of national economic growth and productivity. Conservative fears about the solvency of the program are based on their estimate of an economic growth rate of 1.5% annually – and that of productivity, 1.3% - for the next 75 years. The US economy, though, has easily exceeded those rates many times in the latter half of the 20th century. If you use numbers more in line with past US performance, like 3% and 2.5% respectively, the Fund will be solvent, and maybe even healthy, "well past 2040 and on." Conservatives are so intent on privatizing parts of Social Security, if not all of it, because it is a successful program that shows that their statist fears are unfounded. And, for the record, it is private corporations that have a more dismal track record when it comes to reneging on their employees' pensions – sometimes by raiding them – not

---

[194] Morris Berman, *Dark Ages America: The Final Phase of Empire* (New York: W.W. Norton and Company, 2006), 222.

the federal government. These same fears drive the hysteria over state-supervised universal health coverage, for liberals believe that it would work if tried, just as it does in other modern, industrialized countries.[195]

Regarding the claim that robust economic growth will save Social Security, conservative authors counter that such optimistic estimates of GDP growth rates between 3 and 4.5% are wishful thinking. We haven't consistently seen those rates of growth since the 1960s. Besides, the Social Security fund started running a deficit in 2009. The federal government has been siphoning from the fund for decades – applying the money toward other needs or paying interest on the debt – while replacing the withdrawn funds with what amount to IOUs.[196] Do you seriously think politicians will replace those funds at some future point, even granting that economic growth between 3 and 4% will bring in more federal revenue? Democrats, seeing that kind of money roll in, will start dreaming of making deals in congressional committees to redirect that federal money to their home districts for special projects, and Republicans will argue that the surplus needs to be returned to taxpayers with a tax cut, always politically popular with their base. Furthermore, here is what the president of the National Center for Policy Analysis (NCPA) said in 2005: "By 2030, about the midpoint of the baby boomer retirement years, federal guarantees to Social Security and Medicare will require one in every two income tax dollars. By 2050, they will require three in every four." All federal revenue will go toward these two entitlement programs by 2070.[197] The NCPA, grunt liberals, is a suspect source. Here is how its website describes its identity: "The National Center for Policy Analysis is a nonprofit, nonpartisan public policy research organization, established in 1983. Our goal is to develop and promote private, free-market alternatives to government regulation and control, solving problems by relying on the strength of the competitive, entrepreneurial private sector."[198] It may claim to be nonpartisan, but its exaltation of the market and castigation of regulation clearly indicates that it is a conservative organization, which means that its numbers – according to

---

[195] Coates, 91-92, 94; Krugman, 228.

[196] James Piereson, *Shattered Consensus: The Rise and Decline of America's Postwar Political Order* (New York: Encounter Books, 2015), 94-97.

[197] Williams, 272-73.

[198] http://www.ncpa.org/about/

liberal skeptics – may be suspect, selective, or spun. Conservatives could respond that such an objection is a form of the *ad hominem* strategy known as "poisoning the well" – attacking someone's argument and numerical evidence by questioning his motive.[199]

This list of liberal observations, assertions, and refutations is certainly not even close to being comprehensive, but simply reflects both my interest and those comments that I find most frequently. Now, let's look at the conservative side of the ledger. The economic arguments laid out in the last chapter will certainly overlap with these. Conservatives firmly believe that people should be self-reliant, rather than dependent on the government; that, as reflected in Robert Bork's comment leading off the chapter, giving people an equal chance to succeed does not mean that all will or should; that human ingenuity can overcome perceived limits to growth and world resources; that government serves useful functions but often simply tries to perpetuate itself; and that inequality is simply natural due to different levels of hard work, intelligence, and abilities.

CONSERVATIVES TAKE AIM AT LIBERALS

The Constitution should be interpreted according to its historical, textual meaning rather than in an unwarranted, flexible manner that reflects current social ideology

In the last half of the nineteenth century, law was strictly interpreted by adhering to the text and following clear, accepted rules of legal reasoning. If practiced correctly, judges could determine a legally correct verdict, a school of legal thought known as "legal formalism." By the 20th century, legal formalism had to confront new legal philosophies: "legal realism" and, later, its more radical progeny, "critical legal studies." Both schools injected uncertainty and relativity into the law, the former arguing that other things beside the law decided cases and the latter suggesting that all law was

---

[199] Patrick Grim, *The Philosopher's Toolkit: How to Be the Most Rational Person in Any Room*, The Great Courses (Chantilly, VA.: The Teaching Company, 2013), Lecture 14.

rigged to protect the interests of the powers that be.[200] Scholarship in law schools eventually has an influence on the practice of law at all levels of the court system. Liberal judges and lawyers were influenced by these legal trends in their decision-making and arguments before the bench. By the 1970s and 1980s, conservative jurists and law students began challenging these judicial schools of thought. One of the most influential of these jurists was Robert Bork, a Supreme Court nominee voted down by the Senate after nomination by Ronald Reagan. Bork believes that the Constitution should be interpreted according to the "original intent" of the authors. If it is not, then it simply becomes a subjective text that allows judges to read their own values into it, and these values usually reflect liberal preoccupations with "egalitarian and socially permissive" decisions and outcomes (although he admits that conservatives are guilty as well and opposes their eisegesis too). It opens up the possibility that burning the US flag or operating a striptease joint is freedom of expression protected by the first amendment. Liberal detractors often point out that determining the original intent of the framers of the Constitution is almost impossible. Bork retorts that the assertion that we cannot know the original understanding would undermine all historical study. Undoubtedly you can understand the historical context and meaning of a written document; historians practice this all the time.

When injecting their own meaning into the Constitution, the due process clause in the 14th amendment is a favorite route that liberal judges take. Bork argues that due process should not license a treasure hunt for new rights and equalities but was simply meant to ensure neutral procedures in a court of law. If you want to create new rights, that is certainly fine, says Bork: Congress can pass new amendments and states can ratify them, for instance. Judges, however, are supposed to judge laws – not create, pass, and ratify them.[201] Another adherent of this view was Associate Justice of the Supreme Court Antonin Scalia, an Italian-American jurist appointed to the court by Reagan and confirmed by the Senate. He was considered brash and combative, but even his opponents conceded that his written opinions were

---

[200] Chad Gregory, "Judges, Lawyers, and Historians: Parallel Developments in Historical Interpretation and Legal Thought", unpublished manuscript, 2009.

[201] Robert H. Bork, *The Tempting of America: The Political Seduction of the Law* (New York: Touchstone, 1990), 2, 6, 67, 131, 164-65, 171, 180.

models in style and verve, and he was certainly entertaining to listen to on the bench during arguments before the court.[202]

Liberals and other legal commentators have offered several criticisms of originalism.

- The text is not an artifact waiting to be discovered full of self-evident meaning. The text has to be interpreted.

- Even if one could determine the original intent, the Constitutional wording may not be able to address current issues that the founders could not have envisioned. Even if you could agree on the meaning of the words, the application of the text to modern situations and circumstances may still be unclear.[203]

- Not only is the original intent difficult to decipher, but you also need to clarify the precise identity of the founders and framers. Are we referring to the actual drafters, the delegates at the conventions, the members of Congress that provided legal commentary, or those in each state that voted for (or against) ratification? All of those groups were important interpretive stakeholders in deciding what the text meant.[204]

- Also, questioning original intent does not undermine historical study; employing skepticism when reading historical sources is just a normal part of historical scholarship. Historians scrutinize primary historical documents and come to different conclusions about the impact of a document, the meaning of the words, and how the audience or the purpose of the document influenced the author's reasoning and outlook.

- And since when are liberal judges the only ones that are activist? David Coates, a political science professor, proclaims that "We need a war on adjectives," especially those misused by conservatives. Just as they misuse the word "socialism" when describing government involvement in the economy and society, they exclusively label liberal or progressive judges as "activist," but not conservative ones.[205]

---

[202] Joan Biskupic, *American Original: The Life and Constitution of Supreme Court Justice Antonin Scalia* (New York: Sara Crichton Books, 2009).

[203] Joel P. Trachtman, *The Tools of Argument: How The Best Lawyers Think, Argue, and Win* (North Charleston, S.C.: CreateSpace Independent Publishing Platform, 2013): 75.

[204] Jay M. Feinman, *Law 101: Everything You Need to Know About American Law*, 4th ed. (Oxford University Press, 2014): 22.

One example would be Scalia. His opinions almost invariably come down on the side of states' rights, unless the issue is personal morality, like drug use. In one case, he went against states' rights when it came to drug use, a moral position that could have possibly stemmed from his Roman Catholic background. In the 2005 case of *Gonzales v. Raich*, he sided with a federal law that overturned a California law that allowed the use of medical marijuana. The most divisive case where he contradicted his own judicial principles was *Bush v. Gore*, where all five conservatives on the court decided in favor of George Bush after votes for the candidates were disputed in several counties in Florida in the 2000 presidential election. The justices, including Scalia, invoked the equal protection clause of the 14th amendment, going against their standard practice of deferring to state authorities – in this case, the Florida Supreme Court – which directed an extension of the deadline for the recounts. Critics wondered if Scalia stood by his "originalism" doctrine only if it delivered the political or moral outcomes he found acceptable.[206] The safest generalization to make about judicial activism is that the charge is made when one's ideological antagonists dominate the bench. Throughout the 1960s when liberal judges were expanding the notion of rights during the Warren Court era, conservatives decried liberal judicial activism. When conservative judges sat on the bench after the 1980s and into the new millennium and cast decisions that usually limited the scope of the federal government, liberal voices pointed to conservative judicial activism.[207]

Let democracy decide

As we have seen, conservatives rail against activist judges that impose their values on the rest of Americans through their court decisions. Judges can impose minority values and opinions – claiming they are legally derived from the Constitution – because they have the luxury of not having to stand for reelection. Congressmen and state legislators do not have that kind of

[205] Coates, 22.
[206] Biskupic, 9, 231-251.
[207] David J. Bodenhamer, *The Revolutionary Constitution* (New York: Oxford University Press, 2012): 111.

tenure: they can be kicked out of office in the next election. The most contentious laws and issues concern morality. Bork argues that moral questions should be left to the people through their state representatives, not the Supreme Court. The ultimate issue that centers on morality is abortion and the case that made it legal – *Roe vs. Wade* (1973). Bork asserts that abortion was left up to the states to decide for the entirety of United States history until 1973. The judges read a right to privacy and abortion into the Constitution when a simple, literal reading of the text does not reveal those rights. Besides, most people that support this right to privacy do not see the implications: the right to do *what* in privacy? Molest your offspring or step-offspring? Smoke pot? Plot revolution? Entertain prostitutes? Furthermore, forbidding state legislatures from enforcing morality is hypocritical, for the judges are often imposing their own standards of right and wrong. They are enforcing morality, too. Moral questions are almost impossible to determine because antagonists have different moral presuppositions and ultimate concerns. What is the solution? Let citizens vote on it.[208] If you do not like the outcome, you can vote in the next election or vote with your feet (leave the state). Nancy MacLean, though, as noted earlier, would heavily qualify this maxim: let democracy decide (unless that democratic decision might undermine economic liberty or is a threat to private property rights).

Government agencies that exist to correct injustices have self-interest in finding, or even perpetuating through redefinition, more of the same wrongs to justify their continued existence

Anthony Flew once commented on this process: "Employees of agencies established to combat perceived evils, for instance, cannot but have strong job-preservation interests in the continuation of at least sufficient of those evils to justify the preservation of the agency which employs them." So, in other words, an agency that combats flying donkeys[209] and employs 100 people must continue to find flying donkeys to be nuisances. If the number

---

[208] Bork, *Tempting*, 8-9, 17, 90, 112, 126, 256; Biskupic, 216; Limbaugh, *Way Things Ought to Be*, 56.

[209] I am not making a reference to the Democratic Party and its historical mascot. Remember Flo from the TV sitcom *Alice*? When she expressed skepticism, she predictably bellowed "When donkeys fly!"

of flying donkeys drops off or they start behaving, people will eventually lose their government jobs. To protect their jobs, these clever employees start redefining annoying behavior to catch more flying donkeys in their net so as to give everyone enough to do to justify their employment at the agency. These new annoying behaviors were not as egregious during an earlier regime at the agency, but they have been upgraded. Flew gives the Equal Employment Opportunities Commission in the United States as an example. If overt discrimination based on race, gender, or ethnicity has been combated to manageable levels, the agency may be tempted to move on to "indirect discrimination," the charge that a certain business does not have enough employees of a certain group that equals that group's percentage of the overall population. To put it another way, Limbaugh claims that self-reliance in combating discrimination or some other social evil would put liberals out of a job and on the streets. They need people to be dependent, for liberals are dependent on that dependence.[210] I can just hear a liberal gadfly respond: so, according to that argument, police officers actually want to maintain the current level of crime, or increase it, to keep their jobs. Is that right?

Affirmative action ensures reverse discrimination and perpetuates racism

It is simply not rational or fair to favor a member of a minority group that presumably has not experienced discrimination, and fail to hire someone just as qualified that presumably has not discriminated against someone on the basis of race, gender, sexual orientation, etc. With race, for instance, such practices only cause more racial suspicion and hostility. Under affirmative action, not only are you hiring someone because they are a member of a minority group, and another applicant may be equally (or more) qualified, the practice actually harms those groups it is designed to help. If employers have to hire a member of a minority group to stay in compliance with the law, a person that may in fact not be qualified, society may be tempted to think that *all or most* of the members of that group get their positions through affirmative action because they are not qualified if judged on their own talents and work history. Thus, people wrongly

---

[210] Anthony Flew, *How to Think Straight,* 67-68; Limbaugh, *Way Things Ought to Be,* 249.

conclude that all or most minority hires are "tokens" or "quota hires," and therefore inferior, which only promotes *more* discrimination. Besides that, it does not make any economic sense for employers to discriminate. If you do not hire someone because of their race, for instance, you may suffer a loss because that individual may have had the potential for high productivity. Employers hire the best employees that promise superior performance. Employers can only discriminate in a noncompetitive environment; on the contrary, in a highly competitive environment, they must hire the best people, regardless of race, gender, or other factors.

In a competitive environment, employers are reluctant to discriminate against customers as well. A famous example is the case of Rosa Parks in Montgomery, Alabama in 1955. City buses had been divided into three sections designated as black, white, and "as needed." She was actually sitting in the as needed section of the bus when a white man got onboard, and there were no seats left in any of the sections. When she refused to give up her seat, she was arrested. Local bus companies did not want to segregate their buses, but they were required to by local governments. They often refused to enforce racial segregation for years before being compelled to comply. Blacks made up the bulk of their customers, so they did not want to jeopardize the biggest source of fares by offending customers. It simply costs money to discriminate. Thomas Sowell, a conservative African-American economist, concludes that government has historically exceeded private business in discrimination. The private sector has historically hired blacks at greater rates than the public sector in certain instances: in 1936, there were only three black chemists with PhDs employed in white universities, but 300 were employed in private businesses.[211]

Well, I agree that the government has played an important role in perpetuating discrimination, the liberal replies. Segregation in Washington, DC during the administration of Woodrow Wilson is widely known. And affirmative action may make whites, for instance, see minority hires as inferior but favored – which perpetuates racism. However, it is even truer

---

[211] Reid Buckley, *Speaking in Public: Buckley's Techniques for Winning Arguments and Getting Your Point Across* (New York: National Review Books, 1988), 84; Biskupic, 70, 174, 182; Robert H Bork, *Slouching Towards Gomorrah: Modern Liberalism and American Decline* (New York, 1996), 237-38; Tempting, 106, 109; David R. Henderson, *The Joy of Freedom: An Economist's Odyssey* (Upper Saddle River, NJ, 2002), 115-116, 123, 127, 174; Thomas Sowell, *Basic Economics: A Citizens' Guide*, 143; Williams, 230.

that ending affirmative action is not going to end racism either. When African-Americans, for instance, and whites start the race in life with different starting lines due to economic inequality, the results will continue to be unequal.[212] Besides that, diversity in the workplace, the halls of government, and on campus is a positive good, for people are enriched when they interact with people of different backgrounds and ethnicities. Affirmative action does not mean hiring persons from a minority group that have inferior qualifications, but simply that race, gender, etc. is an important factor considered equally along with other criteria for the job. Conservatives get anxious, though, when liberals point out that nonwhite families and white families often start out their lives from different starting points, meaning that white families tend to have more economic and educational advantages, or males have an advantage in the marketplace. What is the solution for erasing the difference and ensuring the same starting line? Liberals are hinting at another government program – and this program needs to be funded with taxpayer money. This is just another instance of redistribution, the conservative sighs.

Environmentalism is basically an attack on private property rights and a cover for socialist measures

When Eastern European and Soviet communism fell in the late 1980s and early 1990s, conservatives claim that dispirited socialists simply reinvented themselves and tried to achieve some measure of socialism under a new guise: concern for and protection of the environment and animals. Many environmentalists, some conservatives argue, certainly are sincere in their efforts to preserve the environment, but their remedies require federal regulation, ownership and control. One publication from a conservative think tank described environmentalists as "green on the outside and red on the inside." Colorful, that. In fact, animal rights activists have the same goal as environmentalists. According to Rush Limbaugh, the People for the Ethical Treatment of Animals also have a (well-treated) Trojan horse concealing the same agenda: along with protecting animals from abuse, they really wish to dismantle the capitalist system and undermine "the American way of life." They aspire to achieve these goals through "central planning"

---

[212] Coates, 68-69.

and government interference with how private individuals use their property.[213]   According to Walter Williams, the environmentalists' "true agenda is to find a means to control our lives. The kind of repressive human control, not to mention government-sanctioned mass murder, seen under communism, has lost any measure of intellectual respectability. So people who want that kind of control must come up with a new name; that name is environmentalism."   The fear of global warming is just the latest environmentalist crusade full of tree-hugging warriors pursuing "their dream of controlling our lives."   They are usually unable to achieve this goal through state legislatures or Congress, so their only viable hope is obstructing the use of property rights through liberal activist judges and the myriad rules and regulations of a host of government agencies.[214] Wow, a liberal may respond, don't you see the irony? Surely the environmentalists, if this is their real goal, have realized that socialist governments do not ensure the protection of the environment. Chernobyl? Massive pollution in China? Precisely, the conservative grins, for protecting the environment is not their real goal. The liberal would greet such question-begging with an eye-roll.

Advocacy of limited government does not mean that conservatives favor no government at all

Conservatives believe that government is needed to ensure law and order (police forces and a court system) and to protect the country from foreign attack (a military). There is clearly a need for an executive, legislative, and judicial branch, with supporting personnel, as outlined in the United States Constitution. Beyond that, it is a matter of debate among conservatives and libertarians about what else the government should perform. Even Rush Limbaugh, in his attempt to refute the inflated numbers of homeless people in the United States, says that the 25% of actual homeless people that are mentally ill should be institutionalized.[215]   He does not say how these institutions should be funded. Presumably, these institutions would be state-funded. And as noted in the last chapter, free-market gods like Adam Smith and Frederick Hayek believed that there should be necessary regulations to ensure fair competition and security.

---

[213] Limbaugh, *Way Things Ought To Be*, 107, 166, 167; Rampton and Stauber, 37.
[214] Williams, 47, 51, 55, 246.
[215] Limbaugh, *Way Things Ought To Be*, 2, 252.

We are happier than you

In *Gross National Happiness* (2008), business and economics professor Arthur C. Brooks lays out statistics that show that conservatives are significantly happier than liberals and that religious people are much happier than secularists. Interestingly, extremists on the left and right are actually the happiest, perhaps because they *absolutely know* that they are right, secure in their worldview safe from any contrary evidence. Brooks notes that political extremism, though, tends to lower average national happiness by making other people unhappy. But a run-of-the-mill conservative is happier than his ideological counterpart: In a survey of happiness from 1974 to 2004, with fluctuations, conservatives outdistance liberals. In 2004, for instance, 44% of those who regarded themselves as conservative or extremely conservative said that they were "very happy" while only 25% of those that identified as liberal or extremely liberal rated themselves in that charmed category. The only years in which the percentages were dead even or separated by one percentage point were 1975 and 1985 respectively. In a similar comparison, those that advocated government intervention into economic affairs were less happy than those who wished to limit government interference, and those that believed in social mobility through hard work and perseverance were happier than those who were more pessimistic about their chances of success. Brooks is well aware that correlation does not imply causation – other factors can be the cause of the happiness – but he often cited studies that controlled for other variables such as income, gender, education, and church attendance.

Liberals could respond in at least two ways, as Brooks briefly noted. First, feeling happier because of one's political or religious beliefs does not imply or prove that those particular beliefs are *correct*. A happy individual may assert that the government has no authority to tax incomes, but his happiness arising from that position – and related beliefs about limited government – does not prove that the government shouldn't do those things. As related in the chapter on religion, one's belief in the benevolence of the Green Goblin in the Sky because it brings happiness and comfort does not confirm the existence of such an atmospheric entity. A second response is more dismissive: Ignorance is bliss. Even though Brooks cites a study that shows that religious individuals tend to be more knowledgeable and better educated than secularists or non-churchgoers, liberals gleefully note that it is odd that illiteracy rates are higher than the national average in the former Confederate states, the very beating heart of the conservative "red states" and Bible Belt. In addition, the percentage of people earning a bachelor's degree or higher is lower in those same states than the national average. To cap all of this off, violent crime and divorce rates are higher in the red states than the national average – strange side effects for a conservative region that is comparatively happier than the rest of us.[216]

TOOLS OF THE TRADE

These ideological groups compete with each other in the realm of ideas, yes, but they also have a few nifty political maneuvers to inflict body blows on the other side or maintain power and office, sometimes out of a sense of consistency and often for reasons of national security.

To discover the source of political support and how a politician will vote on a bill, follow the money

It is no secret that politicians' votes on bills will be influenced by who contributed campaign money. They will almost invariably vote for or against a bill that has a direct bearing on the companies or individuals that gave money to their campaign. Or if a politician uses his influence to curry favor with a foreign government, say, Kuwait, on the behalf of an oil company, you can bet that he or his party will get a nice hefty contribution from the same company.[217]

---

[216] See Arthur C. Brooks, *Gross National Happiness: Why Happiness Matters for America- and How We Can Get More of It* (New York: Basic Books, 2008). For statistics on violent crime, divorce, illiteracy, and college degrees, see Federal Bureau of Investigation; the Division of Vital Statistics, National Center for Health Statistics, Centers for Disease Control, U.S. Department of Health and Human Services; the National Assessment of Adult Literacy, National Center for Education Statistics, U.S. Department of Education; and the *Digest of Education Statistics*, National Center for Education Statistics, U.S. Department of Education.

[217] Palast, 89.

The ole "If this had been" tactic

When your party or one of its members is heavily criticized for words or actions, then watch and wait for the other party or one of its members to make a similar mistake. If they are not criticized by the press, then scream bloody hell: "If this had been a Republican that said or did that . . . !" For example, President George W. Bush was roundly denounced for his clumsy, delayed response to the devastating destruction of Hurricane Katrina in New Orleans and the adjoining areas of the Gulf Coast in 2005. Years later President Barak Obama, a Democrat, did not respond quickly enough to a catastrophic oil spill in the Gulf in 2010 and seemed to ignore massive flooding in downtown Nashville in the same year. When the press did not go after Obama aggressively enough, Republicans were quick to assert, "If this had been George W. Bush . . ." In addition, the Obama administration had continued to give scores of "environmental waivers" and "drilling permits" even after the explosion on the oil rig that developed into this disaster. Mary Kate Cary of USNews.com exclaimed that if these permissions had occurred under a Republican administration, "the screams from the Left would be deafening." Democrats can play the same game. In this instance, it was reversed: outcry against our guy but not for yours. When the White House announced a planned speech by Obama to school children across the country, conservatives issued dire warnings of socialist brainwashing. It turns out that the speech stressed basic conservative themes about staying in school, working hard, and making no excuses for failure. "If this had been Ronald Reagan . . ." presenting these same exhortations, cried the Democrats, Republicans would have had no problem with so-called presidential indoctrination. In fact, Ronald Reagan, as well as George H.W. Bush, did give a similar speech to kids in school with little to no outcry.[218]

Defund, or threaten to defund, the government agency that produces information that contradicts the official policy or raises too many questions

---

[218] "A Growing Environmental Disaster", *The Week*, June 4, 2010; "Conservatives on Obama's stay-in-school speech: "Indoctrination," "brainwashing," Communist China, Hitler Youth", http://mediamatters.org/research/200909020012, Sept. 02, 2009.

The Future of Iraq project: David Phillips was a consultant for a group within the State Department, the Future of Iraq project. He wanted to rebuild Iraq into a stable country, but his advice was ignored by those that had already decided what they wanted to do, and had assumed that it would take a short period of time to do it. His project was marginalized by the Department of Defense and the Office of the Vice-President. His group was issuing reports and information that did not support the mission, so it seems that his project was defunded: Phillips noted that "When information surfaces that contradicts [their] firmly entrenched views, [they] dismantle the institution that brought [them] the information."

The Government Accountability Office (GAO): This agency, a supposedly nonpartisan arm of Congress that oversees fiscal responsibility, requested official documents from Dick Cheney, vice-president under the Bush administration, about a top-secret meeting regarding energy policy in 2003, the Energy Task Force. When denied those documents, the GAO threatened a lawsuit. The chairman of the Appropriations Committee presumably threatened the GAO with significant budget cuts for the agency if they did not back off the lawsuit.[219]

The Securities and Exchange Commission (SEC): When the chair of the Securities and Exchange Commission wished to adopt tighter, more transparent accounting methods that would help prevent "conflicts of interest" in the corporate world, like the ones that led to the famous Enron collapse and similar mishaps, Senator Phil Gramm "threatened to cut the SEC's budget."[220] By the way, Gramm was notorious for advocating the repeal of the Glass-Steagall Act and championing the Commodity Futures Modernization Act, which gutted regulation of the derivatives and other complex financial instruments that played such a central role in the economic freefall of 2008.

Just outsource what you legally cannot do

---

[219] "GAO Authority Undermined", http://www.ombwatch.org/node/1244 March 10, 2003; Pierce, 244.
[220] Hacker and Pierson, 197.

The FBI, according to investigative reporter Greg Palast, would love to snoop on you even more than they already do. But there are certain lines they cannot cross in acquiring this information. The solution is to subcontract the job to a private agency, like ChoicePoint (CP). Under the USA Patriot Act, passed in response to the horrific 9/11 attacks on America, the FBI can ask private agencies like ChoicePoint to provide sensitive electronic data that they cannot legally generate themselves. As Palast puts it, "Congress has outsourced the snooping." It was CP, by the way, that produced the list of some 94,000 voters to be scrubbed from the Florida voting rolls before the 2000 presidential election because they were felons. Thing is, "at least 91,000" of them were innocent of felony or even misdemeanors, and tended to be black, which means Al Gore lost a lot of votes, not just from the indeterminate hanging chads.

The FBI is not the only intelligence agency that doles out assignments and contracts, for it is joined by the National Security Agency (NSA). What the agency can and cannot eavesdrop on is still murky and disputed, and they are supposed to get clearance to eavesdrop by the Foreign Intelligence Surveillance Court with an official warrant. But there are ways to get around that. In what author James Bamford describes as a "surveillance-industrial complex," the NSA receives all sorts of information from private contractors, many of whom are located in buildings stretched out in an industrial park very near the NSA's headquarters. This cozy relationship is facilitated by a "quick-turning revolving door" that sees high profile contractor employees accept jobs in the NSA, and when NSA employees call it quits, they are quickly hired by the private contractors. They send information and business each other's way. Another possible avenue for snooping is allowing one of NSA's "partners" in Britain or Canada to do the eavesdropping for the agency and then forward the information.[221] One cannot help but wonder if all these fly-on-the-wall capabilities are not utilized in some way in the world of politics.

Just rename it

---

[221] James Bamford, *The Shadow Factory: The Ultra-Secret NSA from 9/11 to the Eavesdropping on America* (New York: Doubleday, 2008), 37-38, 197-206; Greg Palast, *Armed Madhouse: Who's Afraid of Osama Wolf?, China Floats, Bush Sinks, The Scheme to Steal '08, No Child's Left Behind, and Other Dispatches from the Front Lines of the Class War* (New York: Dutton, 2006), 39-40.

With a knowing grin and cynical chuckle, most of us are familiar with how corporations use euphemisms about firing employees: downsizing, rightsizing, restructuring, carrying out normal involuntary attrition, effectuating a workforce adjustment, eliminating redundancies in the human resources arena, implementing a skills-mix adjustment, rebalancing one's workforce, etc. It is almost as if public relations departments have hired euphemism-generating consulting agencies. Government, especially at the federal level, adopts these clever tactics as well:

Prisoners of war are supposed to be treated in a humane manner as prescribed by the Geneva Convention. In a post-911 world, to avoid those restrictions, just call them "enemy combatants" or detainees, who are not covered by the Geneva Convention.

"Rendition" is the controversial policy of nabbing suspected terrorists in one country and transporting them to another country for interrogation. The Obama administration quickly moved to dismantle many of the anti-terrorist programs of the Bush administration – for instance, the seemingly indefinite detention of suspected terrorists at the military base at Guantanamo Bay, Cuba. However, the newly incoming administration chose to continue the practice of rendition. Knowing that the term was infamous, renditions were renamed "short-term transfers." John Rizzo, a career lawyer at the CIA, wryly conceded that the term "does sound much more pleasant."[222]

Torture is difficult to sugarcoat. When at these detention centers around the world – often called "black sites" – these detainees were often subject to creative methods of questioning, which critics bluntly described as torture. For years before these methods were (supposedly) discontinued, they were known as "enhanced interrogation techniques" or "repetitive administration of legitimate force." [223]

---

[222] John Rizzo, *Company Man: Thirty Years of Controversy and Crisis in the CIA* (New York: Scribner, 2014), 260.
[223] Ibid; Henry Beard and Christopher Cerf, *Spinglish: The Definitive Dictionary of Deliberately Deceptive Language* (New York: Blue Rider Press, 2015), 214, 225, 232.

Some words may not be euphemisms but are "loaded" with politically intentional meaning. For instance, instead of referring to "government officials" or "civil servants," conservatives contemptuously say "bureaucrats," for the latter designation implies a bunch of red-tape-toting, pocket-protector-clad employees that take pleasure in citing the rules and regulations that business owners must abide by.

Just lie

Commercial advertisers cannot make false claims about their products without legal action, but politicians can. As Brooks Jackson and Kathleen Hall Jamieson have noted, "There is no federal law requiring truth in political ads at all," so politicians can continue to lie or misrepresent political reality or their opponents, and if the ruse works, they can get elected. If found out later, it does not matter because most people will have forgotten, and the politician employing the falsehoods is safely ensconced in office.[224]

Just keep repeating it

If a political party or a politician wants to embed an idea, image, or connection into the minds of American voters, even if untrue or shaky, repetition is the key. Just ask Lyndon Johnson. He was running in Texas for senator in a Democratic primary in 1948. His opponent was Coke Stephenson, a widely-beloved Texas attorney and former governor of the state. Stephenson, often dubbed "Mr. Texas," had a sterling record of personal integrity, honesty, and economy in government, and remained unbeaten in political contests. When he received the *unsolicited* endorsement of the American Federation of Labor (AFL), Johnson leaped at the connection and kept charging that Stephenson, in a secret deal with the AFL, would, if elected, work toward repealing the Taft-Hartley Act, a law widely regarded as anti-labor. Although the accusation was untrue, Stephenson felt that it was beneath his honor as a pro-business Texan to respond to such a ridiculous assertion and would not deny the secret agreement until it was too late. Johnson continued to make the charge,

---

[224] Jackson and Jamieson, *Unspun: Finding Facts in a World of Disinformation* (New York: Random House, 2007), 22-23.

among others, and burrowed into Stephenson's heretofore large lead in the polls. Johnson eventually won the primary – with the help of 201 votes added to the poll list in Alice, Texas (in alphabetical order) and a clever, risky legal maneuver to prevent the opening of the ballot box in question. Although reluctant to admit the voter fraud, Johnson's aides later openly offered a bit of political advice: "Repeat the same thing over and over – jumping on Coke Stevenson's having secret dealings with labor. You knew it was a damned lie [but] you just repeated it and repeated it and repeated it. Repetition – that was the thing."[225] More recently, the Bush administration, in the days after 9/11, was determined to link Iraq and Saddam Hussein to the terrorist attacks – and repeatedly made the connection. Despite any substantial evidence of a link or the possession of weapons of mass destruction, many Americans continued to believe that Iraq either attacked the United States or had some covert relationship with Al Qaeda: ten years after the attacks, "Forty-six percent thought Iraq gave Al Qaeda substantial support (31%) or thought it was directly involved in 9/11 (15%).[226]

The tradition continues. Within the past year at this writing, Donald Trump repeatedly denounces journalistic coverage and news stories critical of him as "fake news," crudely but cleverly appropriating the concept from the 2016 presidential election when his opponent, Hillary Clinton, was dogged by false stories that circulated online that were actually, and easily, determined to be fake. In addition, he repeatedly asserts that there was no collusion between his campaign and Russia during the election despite several instances of his family members and campaign officials meeting with Russian officials or individuals with ties to Russia looking into Russian promises of useful dirt on Clinton – meetings that were not disclosed to federal authorities or the FBI. Trump is a master of inversion and repetition, though. He throws the same charge right back: his opponents keep repeating dubious claims, trying to cement the connection in Americans' minds. Continually repeating charges of collusion between his 2016 campaign and Russia does not make them true, Trump asserts. In addition to the Russian connection, he has also been accused of pressuring

---

[225] For the 1948 contest, see Robert Caro, *The Years of Lyndon Johnson: Means of Ascent* (New York: Vintage Books, 1990), 224-25, 227, 275, 287, 295, 328, 334. Quote on p. 275.

[226] http://themoderatevoice.com/121921/ten-years-later-belief-in-iraq-connection-with-911-attack-persists/; http://www.sadat.umd.edu/911Anniversary_Sep11_rpt.pdf

Ukraine to announce investigations of Joe Biden, a possible contender in the 2020 election and his son – who sat on the board of a Ukrainian gas company – in exchange for releasing military aid. Once again using his go-to tactic, he turns the charges around by claiming that it was Ukraine that interfered with the 2016 election. Facing impeachment charges stemming from a fear that his corrupt behavior is undermining democracy, Trump counters by charging that impeachment itself undermines democracy by overturning an election – a charge he keeps repeating by constantly tweeting "Witch Hunt!"

A WAY FORWARD?

Can't we all just get along? Rodney King asked this famous question during a press conference days after riots erupted in Los Angles when a jury acquitted white police officers who forcefully subdued King, an African-American, after a high-speed chase in 1992. When it comes to principles and cherished beliefs among conservatives and liberals, it is difficult to compromise. So the answer is probably no. But politics is about compromise, and ideological purity is difficult to maintain. This may sound trite, but sometimes the only way to get along and accomplish things is to find common ground.

Believe it or not, liberals and conservatives, especially those on the far ends of each spectrum, actually share some things in common – as do those close to the middle on either side of the center. For instance, in the 1960s, both radical protestors on the Left and conservative intellectuals on the Right were alienated by the growing bureaucracy on college campuses. Students were no longer seen as individuals, but part of the mass of students only known by their social security numbers and tuition checks. The Left should have given more credit to Barry Goldwater, who voiced some of their same critiques of a bureaucratized university and society. Old Right thinkers like Russell Kirk certainly did not agree with the solutions offered by student radicals, but sympathized with their rebellious mood. Although probably intended as a cynical parody, conservative students adopted tactics practiced by "the Movement" – like staging sit-ins at the offices of Students for A Democratic Society, a leftist student organization that protested the Vietnam War, racism and, well, almost everything else. Other conservative groups and corporations mimicked the tactics of the student and civil rights movements in the 1960s by adopting a conservative version of "grassroots organizing." Conservative columnist and author David Brooks notes that the radicals of the 1960s and the bourgeois market advocates of the 1980s have two things in common – "liberty and freedom." Granted, when liberals think of freedom, they have personal and behavioral freedom in mind while conservatives stress political and economic freedom.[227] Freedom has always been a contested concept, but at least the two sides can understand each other to a point.

Maybe we are just hard-wired to be partisan. One study examined the brain activity of supporters of George Bush and John Kerry during the 2004 presidential election. When presented with evidence that their candidate had flip-flopped on an issue, the emotional centers in the brain lit up first while the reasoning centers showed little activity. When they finished the experiment by coming to reassuring opinions of their candidate, the reward centers in their brains lit up in the same manner that a drug addict's brain flares in those same centers when getting his fix.[228] Our emotions react to certain ideas, persons, or events much more quickly than our thoughts about the same things. If confronted with contrary evidence that is substantial, after the initial emotional reaction, partisans and believers of all stripes simply jump through all sorts of hoops and concoct rationalizations – "motivated reasoning" – to explain away the evidence that undermines their positions and belief systems. When it comes to evolution or global warming, for instance, people – usually conservatives – say that they do not reject science, but then make subjective judgments about what "true" science is, usually the views of a few dissenting scientists that support their political or environmental beliefs. Those on the left react in a similar manner when credible evidence demonstrates that autism is not caused by childhood vaccinations, or that genetically modified food is deemed safe by most researchers. [229] Those who embrace "true" science and reject findings that undermine a passionately-held position can be seen as deploying the No

---

[227] David Brooks, *Bobos in Paradise: The New Upper Class and How They Got There* (New York: Simon and Schuster, 2000), 260; Mattson, 60, 73-74, 76-77; Rampton and Stauber, 208.

[228] Jackson and Jamieson, 75.

[229] *The Week*, "Made-Up Minds", May 20, 2011: The article is based on a longer version written by Chris Mooney in *Mother Jones*.

True Scotsman fallacy. In these cases, if a conservative or liberal confronts scientific findings that they don't like, they simply redefine science so as to exclude the inconvenient studies: "True science would not support those conclusions!"[230]

I am unsure if the above studies have been replicated, but one online fact-checking and urban legend-debunking website thinks that presenting facts to partisans is futile. Snopes.com had this to say when they continued to get grief after its report that showed that Barak Obama did not appoint Elena Kagan to the Supreme Court because of her legal efforts to stymie unsubstantiated rumors about Obama's lack of eligibility for the presidency:

> When reporters interview us about our work, they often ask us to comment on the notion that we're engaged in a great public service, making the world a better place by "striking a blow for the truth" and stamping out rumor and misinformation by replacing them with facts. Those reporters usually seem to be taken aback or disappointed when I tell them that I don't really believe our site makes much of a difference in the greater scheme of things; that the responses we get tend to indicate *a good many people are determined to believe whatever they want to believe* [italics mine], and no collection of contradictory factual information, no matter how large or authoritative or impressive it might be, is ever going to dissuade them from their beliefs.[231]

British authors have noted with astonishment how devoted people in the United States can be to their political principles and parties. Bryan McGee was taken aback by otherwise bright people that were captive to "the football-fan attitude to party affiliation – the assumption that what is required of one is to cheer one's own side, and to boo their opponents. . . ."[232] Why is this partisanship greater among Americans? Another British author finds Americans' preference for one political extreme or another both puzzling and amusing. First, he acknowledges that finding the midway point of some issue can be difficult: "What is the middle way between racism and antiracism, or tickling someone as opposed to torturing them," for instance?

---

[230] For a discussion of the No True Scotsman fallacy, see Anthony Flew, *How to Think Straight*, 49-52.

[231] http://www.snopes.com/info/notes/kagan.asp

[232] MaGee, 219.

But he then affirms the British predisposition toward practical moderation: "The British believe that life is mixed and muddled, a view of the world that is exemplified by their weather. . . .The British 'muddle through'. . ." [and] readily concede that life is full of uncertainty, recognizing "the role of accident and approximation in human affairs . . . ."[233] This observation – if true – sits uneasily beside the study about partisanship and brain activity cited above. How can Americans be wired differently than Britons?

This perception that Americans are polarized concerning political opinions is further illustrated by a 23-question survey by Public Policy Polling in December of 2011. Mathematician Jordan Ellenberg made a scatterplot of the results and found a heart-shaped polarity. Those that were more opinionated formed dense concentrations of dots that resembled left and right lobes in the diagram:

> As the voters get more informed, they don't get more Democratic or more Republican, but they do get *more polarized*: lefties go farther left, right-wingers get farther right, and the sparsely populated space in the middle gets even sparser. In the lower half of the graph, the less-informed voters tend to adopt a more centrist stance. The graph reflects a sobering social fact, which is by now commonplace in the political science literature. Undecided voters, by and large, aren't undecided because they're carefully weighing the merits of each candidate, unprejudiced by political dogma. They're undecided because they're barely paying attention.[234]

Maybe Ellenberg is right about centrist voters – that they are uninformed and apathetic. I would like to change that (if he is right). Some of the questions, though, are those of political opinion, like "Do you approve or disapprove of the job [Senate Minority Leader, at the time] Mitch McConnell is doing?" Does a question like that measure "informedness" just because you have a firm opinion? Firmly answering "yes" does not make you informed if, in fact, he is doing a bad job or even vice versa. It could be that the centrist voters are actually weighing things carefully or honestly indicating that they do not know. Better it is to not know – and say so – than to proclaim you are informed simply because you have an opinion. What

---

[233] Terry Eagleton, *Across the Pond: An Englishman's View of America* (New York: W.W. Norton and Company, 2013), 127-129.

[234] Jordan Ellenberg, *How Not to Be Wrong: The Power of Mathematical Thinking* (New York: The Penguin Press, 2014), 345-46.

are the informed *informed about?* Are they simply better informed about what their favorite conservative or liberal sage, or pettifogger, says about an issue? In other words, do they have comprehensive knowledge about the topic or issue from many sides and perspectives, or are they merely conversant with *what their ideological camp says about it?*

If we are indeed encrusted in our ideological worldview and change our minds with difficulty, then we need to learn to agree to disagree about certain areas, and look for common ground in others. Even a *deeper awareness* of how partisan we are may serve to infuse our discourse with a little more charity and openness. If common ground is unattainable, members of each ideological group can at least consider the evidence that their opponents present, exude civility in debate, and even have the humility to concede a good point or two. In a debate about policy or political philosophy, there is certainly a pitfall: the reluctance to concede, sympathize, or understand a well-supported point or two by your political opponent for fear that members of your own group may perceive you as giving comfort and aid to the enemy.[235] Such an attitude, though, is a shame because it enervates reasonable debate and discussion. Politicians, believers, cynics, and other persons invested in an ideology or belief – and those without them – should have the courage to dismiss such a zero-sum view of ideological competition. A second pitfall that may be more serious in blocking productive agreement is that various propositions – whether religious, political, or economic – are "embedded in a context" of other propositions and beliefs that make up an entire worldview for that camp, so it is difficult to challenge one of them without having implications for the others. Carefully disentangling these beliefs or positions from the others might take considerable effort, but could be attainable. Since carping at a stance on a particular issue may have implications for other issues, remember that one may cause committed followers to dig in and defend their entire corpus.[236]

Another route to civility and some modest cooperation is distinguishing between ends and means. Liberals and conservatives are vigilant in their

---

[235] Simon Blackburn, *Truth: A Guide* (New York: Oxford University Press, 2005), xxi.
[236] Ibid., 144. Blackburn refers to this approach as holism. It makes it difficult to take one belief "at a time." His concerns, though, were more general in nature about philosophical notions of truth.

devotion to certain principles and goals – their ends – so maybe they can subject the means to those ends to "reasoned deliberation."[237] The means consist of the pragmatic, day-to-day maneuverings that leaders employ to navigate toward their goals. Each side, with a grudging wink, recognizes that everyone is not going to get all points of their program accomplished. The party or ideology in control makes compromises to get most, or a large portion, of what they want while the opposing side strategically obstructs a total version of their opponents' ends and bides their time until the political and electoral winds change. When the loyal opposition gets hold of the reins, the process begins anew with new ends sought through the same means of negotiation and a continued recognition of limits to what gets accomplished. Edmund Burke, often considered a father of conservatism, recognized this when combating the radicalism of the French Revolution and trying to prevent its spread to England. He aimed for "equipoise" when dealing with political actors that demanded strict adherence to abstract principles about political rights. One has to give way sometimes to maintain balance and stability.[238] The following statement was bandied about quite a lot during the political debates over raising the debt ceiling and hammering out a budget in 2013 and 2014 in the United States: nobody is going to get everything they want.

Another angle on how both camps can utilize "ends and means" thinking has been highlighted by Richard Striner in *Lincoln's Way* (2010). He has traced a style of leadership from Lincoln to John F. Kennedy. In order to ensure "prosperity and power" for the United States, both Republicans – Lincoln, Theodore Roosevelt, and Eisenhower – and Democrats – FDR, Truman, and Kennedy – have used "Hamiltonian means for Jeffersonian ends." Alexander Hamilton, the first secretary of the treasury, crafted a program for dealing with the initial debt accumulated after the American Revolution that created a strong, national government. Jefferson, on the other hand, was a champion of individual liberty and limited government. The above presidents used the strong arm of the government (Hamiltonian means) to ensure employment, security, prosperity and political equality (Jeffersonian ends) for American citizens within "a political and cultural synthesis [that reconciled] enough of the conservative and liberal traditions

---

[237] Clor, 34-35.

[238] Yuval Levin, *The Great Debate: Edmund Burke, Thomas Paine, and the Birth of Left and Right* (New York: Basic Books, 2014), xvii, 133.

to soften the harshness of left-versus-right dialectics." Striner, I must add, does not see this synthesis as one of moderation, though.[239]

I can only conclude with the observation about religion and unbelief in chapter two. Perhaps conservatives and liberals need each other. Sniping at, arguing with, and refuting one's ideological opponent helps refine, sharpen, and invigorate one's position. The other side keeps one from settling into an ideological complacency. In fact, having to explain your position in a detailed way actually leads to moderation. In one study, participants were asked to provide fuller explanations of a political or economic position held. They often "reveal[ed] their ignorance when asked to provide a detailed explanation without the aid of Google." As a result, they were only able to provide a broad sweep of a position or belief and became less committed to that stance afterward. Talking it out led to moderation even though that was not the intention.[240] Ideally, one could progress from this realization that you do not know as much as you thought about a topic and then intentionally devote time to questioning your own assumptions, beliefs, and policy preferences. You can be your own best opponent, as noted by Ellenberg: "I find it's a good habit to put pressure on all your beliefs, social, political, scientific, and philosophical . . . To the greatest extent possible you have to think as though you believe what you don't believe. And if you can't talk yourself out of your existing beliefs, you'll know a lot more about *why* you believe what you believe."[241] To sum up, the way to get along in the political world is to recognize common ground, concede that one will not get everything one wants, distinguish between ends and means, chasten ourselves with our awareness of how partisan we are, and acknowledge that each side needs the other to clarify, improve, a better communicate their positions.

---

[239] Richard Striner, *Lincoln's Way: How Six Great Presidents Created American Power* (Lanham, MD: Rowan and Littlefield Publishers, Inc., 2010), 5-14.

[240] David McRaney, *You Can Beat Your Brain: How to Turn Your Enemies into Friends, How to Make Better Decisions, and Other Ways to Be Less Dumb* (London: Oneworld Publications, 2013), 199 – 200.

[241] Ellenberg, 434.

Chapter Five

Knowledge: How Do You Know That?

It's much easier to reveal a lie than to reveal the truth.[242]

Russ Kick

The quality of our lives is determined by the quality of our decisions, and the quality of our decisions is determined by the quality of our thinking. By improving the quality of our thinking, then, we tend to improve the quality of our lives.[243]

Theodore Schick, Jr. & Lewis Vaughn

To cast off the idiot Questioner who is always questioning,
But never capable of answering; who sits with a sly grin
Silent plotting when to question, like a thief in a cave;
Who publishes doubt & calls it knowledge . . . . [244]

William Blake in *Milton*

As a college instructor, I often wonder what my students will remember from my courses five years from completion. Ten years after completion? Twenty? Did they actually learn anything?[245] One of my favorite

---

[242] Russ Kick, ed., *You Are Being Lied To: The Disinformation Guide to Media Distortion, Historical Whitewashes, and Cultural Myths* (New York: The Disinformation Company, 2001), 6.

[243] Theodore Schick, Jr. & Lewis Vaughn, *How To Think About Weird Things: Critical Thinking for a New Age*, 3rd ed. (Boston: McGraw Hill, 2002), 147.

[244] Quoted in Harold Bloom, *Genius: A Mosaic of One Hundred Exemplary Creative Minds* (New York: Warner Books, 2002), 700.

[245] I am aware that I may be asking the wrong question. One of the current questions in higher education is, what have students learned to *do* in your course? In other words,

psychology instructors when I was an undergraduate gave a lecture that has stayed with me over the years, and I often incorporate parts of it into my own lectures whenever I can. He delivered it in either a statistics or research methodology course. I can only hope that a few students of mine will remember and contemplate one of my lectures years later like I absorbed and retained this one. Most people would probably yawn or politely turn up their nose when they hear the philosophical field this lecture addressed: epistemology – the study of the nature of knowledge and its limits. To put it more simply, how do you know what you think or perceive is true? When considering such important topics like religion, economics, or politics, this question is foundational. The field of epistemology examines the different ways of knowing by delving into the strengths and weaknesses of these different avenues to knowledge. Given my preference for the abstract, this topic is good stuff.

He identified six different ways of knowing: revelation, authority, intuition, empiricism, rationalism, and science. First, revelation was knowledge gained from God. If there was a God and this God was omniscient, then this God may choose to *reveal* knowledge or messages to chosen people. These people presumably proclaimed this knowledge to other humans or recorded it as sacred scripture, and God ensured that its translation from divine into human communication, from perfect to imperfect, retained the gist of the message. Second, knowledge by authority was gained by heeding or repeating the advice, proclamations, or findings of some authoritative expert or official, like a pastor, scientist, researcher, professor, physician, or magistrate. Since these individuals know so much more about selected topics than the average person – and we often do not have the time, energy, ability, or desire to do our own research – we often defer to their expertise concerning an area of knowledge and accept their assertions as largely credible or valid. Third, intuition is a route to knowledge characterized by the "gut feeling." We do not have any evidence or reasons to believe something, but are still convicted of its truth since we can feel it in our bones. Fourth, empiricism is the idea that knowledge is generated from the sensations we experience through our five senses – it's true or reliable because I can see, hear, taste, feel, or smell it. Fifth, rationalism bestows credibility on truth claims if they make sense and are

---

skills should be the proper focus, not just knowledge.

logical. Here's a well-known example that any student in an introductory philosophy course should recognize:

All humans are mortal

Socrates is a human

Therefore, Socrates is mortal

Rationalism values coherence and non-contradiction, the determination of which is not dependent on your five senses. In the above syllogism, if the first two premises are true, the conclusion has to follow necessarily. And finally, science is often considered as a sixth way of knowing. We have already covered the scientific method in chapter two. For the purpose of this chapter, you can consider science as a strategic combination of empiricism and rationalism under controlled conditions, with appeals to authority thrown in. A scientist's hypothesis can indeed arise from intuition but must be tested in the end.

With television and online mediums, we are awash in a sea of information. There is so much at our fingertips that we certainly can lose our way wading through all of it. What information is really important? How can you tell? Is it accurate? There is certainly a gargantuan amount of disinformation on the internet and, even worse, information that is only half true. Factual claims that are a mixture of truth and falsehood are worse because it often takes more time to disentangle credible facts and arguments from those that are not. Given this state of seemingly anarchic knowledge, it is even more imperative to be skeptical about what we hear and read and to be familiar with the philosophical issues about the generation of knowledge.

Most of us have busy lives and do not have the time or energy to (continually) develop intellectual discipline or allow our curiosity to roam. Nothing would make me giddier than to know that a healthy slice of my former students, once graduated from college, have been inspired by their college courses, at least mine, to continue reading books about history, politics, philosophy, etc. and evaluating the information they encounter. It would also be encouraging that Americans read in-depth articles online rather than surfing for surface content. After reading the article, they check out a few of the sources used by the author to fact-check his claims. The powers-that-be know that many of us are too tired, preoccupied, or lazy to challenge what we read by checking the footnotes or hyperlinks, if any. Perhaps that is why so much disinformation can be slipped into political and other narratives that we just take for granted as true. If this is the case, I can only continue to offer some guidelines and suggestions.

Nurture skepticism

I am not advocating skepticism for the sake of skepticism, but for the purpose of ferreting out bad reasoning or inaccurate information, and even approaching the truth of the matter. Let's face it. The person who constantly questions everything, every sentence, every judgment, is downright annoying. There is such a thing as overkill. No one can live a purely skeptical life – even a famous skeptic like David Hume admitted as much.[246] There comes a point when you have to make decisions firmly: crossing the street, signing a contract, purchasing a house, getting married. When it comes to information that you come across every day on television or online, claims and knowledge that do not have an immediate, direct impact on your life, one should adopt an attitude of "this may be true or not" until more information sheds additional light. Is this claim firsthand or secondhand? What evidence supports such a claim or story? Is the author biased in any way? What assumptions need to be assessed? This skeptical analysis should not be reserved only for religious or political positions that you already disagree with, but should be extended to even your own set of beliefs about religion, politics, and society. For those that think that skepticism is a depressing, crotchety philosophy, Guy Harrison convincingly argues otherwise: "Skepticism is the brain's perfect diet. It trims away the fat and turns you into a lean thinking machine. It dumps unnecessary ballast and clears the way ahead so that you can get to all the good stuff out there waiting to be discovered. . . . Anyone who tries to tell you that skeptics are pessimistic party poopers or that the scientific process is dull and takes the thrill out of life has no idea what they are talking about."[247] There is no

[246] Bryan Magee, *Confessions of a Philosopher: A Journey Through Western Philosophy* (New York: Random House, 1997), 99.
[247] Guy Harrison, *Think: Why You Should Question Everything* (Amherst, NY: Prometheus Books, 2013), 30-31, 43.

shame in hesitancy when it comes to many claims about reality – "it's about withholding belief until you know."

My advocacy of skepticism, though, should not be seen as synonymous with a populist attack on expertise.[248] We need experts. Yes, they are often wrong – no one is omniscient – but it is usually other experts or meticulous researchers that find their mistakes, whether in facts, reasoning, or methodology. This vetting process is very akin to the self-correcting nature of science mentioned in a previous chapter.

Require evidence and evaluate it evenhandedly

Let's start with a famous maxim of William K. Clifford's: "It is wrong always, everywhere and for anyone to believe anything upon insufficient evidence."[249] This principle has been chewed over, I'm sure, by philosophers and intellectuals, but let us take it as good, general advice with the meaning of "wrong" and "insufficient" subject to variable definitions under variable circumstances.[250] When confronted with a truth claim or an argument, the most immediate question that should pop into one's mind is: what is the evidence? In addition, one should scrutinize the evidence for one's own beliefs just as rigorously as you would the evidence presented by an ideological opponent. For instance, Christian thinkers claim that Clifford's Principle is often used mostly against religious belief rather than being evenly applied to unbelief. This tendency to apply rigor unevenly is closely related to confirmation bias, a pesky tendency that we have encountered in this book several times. In fact, readers are probably weary at this point, if not well before, with each additional mention of it. We accept evidence that supports our positions with little question, but apply stricter tests to

---

[248] For an excellent overview on the danger of sustained attacks on expertise, see Tom Nichols, *The Death of Expertise: The Campaign Against Established Knowledge and Why It Matters* (New York: Oxford University Press, 2017).

[249] http://www.ling.rochester.edu/~feldman/philosophy152/11-knowledge.htm

[250] As always, Bryan Magee is always helpful and clarifying: "For example, what counts as "evidence" has an all-pervadingly different logic and structure in a court of law from what it has in a physics laboratory, and is quite different again for the historical researcher: to the historian hearsay counts as evidence, in fact it is very often the only evidence he has, whereas for the judge it is inadmissible as evidence, while for the physicist the question does not even arise. So the word 'evidence' means something materially different in each context." (117)

contrary evidence, if we consider contrary evidence at all.[251] With the evidence that we do accept, have we considered whether that same evidence can be marshalled to support other plausible explanations or "different conclusions?"[252]

Read books and other printed matter respectfully but carefully

Hey, I'm a book snob and proud of it. I believe that books, newspapers, and magazine articles held in one's hands are superior to those found online. Printed materials, as I never tire telling my students, undergo more scrutiny through peer review and the sharp eye of editors than the electronic versions found online. I must admit that online books and articles have become more sophisticated and reliable because of more website filters to separate the chaff from the wheat. But I'll continue to stand my ground. Nonetheless, you should not be naïve enough to swallow everything read in books. Reid Buckley, brother of conservative spokesman William F. Buckley, has admitted: "I used to believe anything I read in a library was true, or it wouldn't be there." He quickly learned that "even books from reputable publishing houses aren't totally safe." Yes, those books, hopefully, have undergone a strict evaluation process before the publishing company is willing to tag its name to them. But those books are also subject to error and authorial bias, especially books and other publications that come from ideological organizations or "any sort of power system."[253] Yes, even this book you hold in your hands or displayed on your device is probably laced with bias and inaccuracies – but I don't think I am a key player in any power system that I know of.

Read the original source, if available and accessible

---

[251] Brooks Jackson and Kathleen Hall Jamieson, *UnSpun: Finding Facts in a World of Disinformation* (New York: Random House, 2007), 69-70, 76-77, 127; Thomas H. Morris, ed., *God and the Philosophers: The Reconciliation of Faith and Reason* (New York: Oxford University Press , 1994), 44-45; Schick & Vaughn, 138.
[252] Bill Kovach and Tom Rosenstiel, *Blur: How to Know What's True in the Age of Information Overload* (New York: Bloomsbury, 2010), 99.
[253] Reid Buckley, *Speaking in Public: Buckley's Techniques for Winning Arguments and Getting Your Point Across* (New York: National Review Books, 1988), 36-37; Noam Chomsky, Peter R. Mitchell, & John Schoeffel, *Understanding Power: The Indispensable Chomsky* (New York: The New Press, 2002), 323-324.

Essayists, writers, researchers, and historians have to build their assertions and narratives out of something. In the world of historical scholarship, there is a distinction between primary and secondary sources. The latter consist of books, articles, and other publications that are removed from their topic by time and space, say, a book about the Civil War (1861-65) written in 2009. A primary source can be compared to a building block that historians use to reconstruct the past: a series of letters, journal entries, a recorded speech, a newspaper article, or most any written documentation from the time period under investigation. In a similar manner, journalists and columnists use sources to write their stories or columns. As Brooks Jackson and Kathleen Hall Jamieson have exhorted, "Track your information upstream. Be wary of secondhand accounts, and even more wary of thirdhand stories."[254] The message and details get garbled with each retelling. Jackson and Jamieson ought to know, for they both help write for and direct the award-winning website, FactCheck.org. Now, a skeptic may well ask, "I thought you distrusted information from the internet." I do, but I recommend this website for two reasons: they provide footnotes or hyperlinks for their reports and they periodically issue corrections. Admitting you are wrong on occasion only increases reliability and transparency. Finally, even original and primary sources are not 100% reliable and should be read with a grain of salt. *Mein Kampf* is a primary source, for hyperbolic example, and most reasonable people read it with a truckload of salt. The authors of original sources can be biased, suffer from faulty or selective memory, and often tailor their message to their audience.

Be wary of the <u>selective</u> use and clever deployment of statistics

Cynics often quote one of Benjamin Disraeli's dictums: "There are three kinds of lies: lies, damned lies, and statistics," a quip attributed to him in Mark Twain's *Autobiography* (1924).[255] The following is not meant to attack the use of statistics, a very sophisticated tool that we need in modern life, research, and science. A responsible statistician tries to practice his profession with honesty, and generally adheres to the standards of his

---

[254] Jackson and Jamieson, 160-62.
[255] Thomas Cathcart & Daniel Klein, *Aristotle and an Aardvark Go To Washington: Understanding Political Doublespeak Through Philosophy and Jokes* (New York: Abrams Image, 2008), 109-110; Elizabeth Knowles, ed., *The Oxford Dictionary of Quotations* (Oxford: Oxford University Press, 1999), 271.

discipline. However, ideological and cause-centered groups often use those statistics to advance their cases and positions, often cherry-picking only those statistics that they contend prove their argument – confirmation bias, again. For instance, did you know that there are different levels of unemployment? The "official unemployment rate" consists of unemployed people that are "actively seeking" work (U-3). A second level includes the above workers plus those that have thrown up their hands in despair and have stopped looking (U-4). A third level consists of the above groups plus those that haven't searched for work in the "last four weeks" but would take a job if offered (U-5). A fourth group, the largest, is made up of all of the above-mentioned groups in addition to part-time workers that actually want full-time work but cannot find it (U-6). This menu of statistics is a politician's buffet. If you are the political party in power and the economy has been struggling, then you can confidently cite U-3 when the rate keeps consistently dipping a little at a time, but if you are the party out-of-power, then you can choose a higher number from the other options, especially U-6. This actually happened in 2012 when the U-3 official rate had fallen to 8.3% in January, a rate that represented a three-year low since the onset of the 2008 economic meltdown, a rate that the Obama administration – in an election year – could confidently point to as evidence that economic conditions were getting better under his watch. But the Republican hopefuls Mitt Romney and Newt Gingrich, vying for the Republican nomination in primary season – and trying to outdo each other in landing punches at the Obama administration – cited the higher rates from the other unemployment levels. Although Romney technically cited the U-5 groups, he mentioned the U-6 rate of 15.1%, the worst rate among the options to remind voters that the economic climate under Obama's administration was still evidence of failure.[256]

Sometimes, statistics can be misleading. Here's a notional example: A local anti-free enterprise group notes that the Acme Company increased their profits by 200% in 2009! If you look at the absolute numbers, it may not be that impressive. To use a simple example, the company's profit in 2008 was $10,000, and it cleared $30,000 in 2009. That is undoubtedly a nice net gain for a small to medium-sized company, but does not sound as exponential as 200%. Or, Brand Acme is the best-selling brand on the

---

[256] http://factcheck.org/2012/02/whats-the-real-jobless-rate/

market! "Best-selling" may incline one to believe that they sell a good majority of all those particular products, but if you look at the distribution of all the competitors, Brand Acme may only have 23% of the market and its closest competitor comes in with 21%, followed by all the others. Technically, they can claim to be the best-selling, but they are not as dominant as that commercial adjective implies.[257]

Partisans are often wary of statistics put forward by an opponent. For example, Walter Williams has criticized a 1993 Environmental Protection Agency study about the deadly effects of secondhand smoke. The EPA concluded that secondhand smoke causes the death of 3000 Americans annually. Williams objects to the study because the results were determined using a 90% confidence level (i.e., that there was a 10% chance that the results could be due to chance, not secondhand smoke) rather than a conventional 95% level: "That has the effect of doubling the margin of error and doubling the probability that mere chance explains those 3000 deaths."[258] Williams may be right, but his focus serves as a further admonition, that *one should extend the same skepticism toward the statistics cited by one's own political party or ideological institution.* As Patrick Grim has noted, ". . . an informal statistic on statistics [is that] most people are far more critical of statistics offered for a view they don't support than they are of statistics offered for a view they agree with."

In addition to sharpening your awareness about the selective use of statistics, how they are cleverly presented, and our propensity for applying more scrutiny to adversarial statistics, one should also trace statistics back to the original source, as noted above, and perform simple math. A notorious example is provided by Joel Best, a sociologist at the University of Delaware. A widely-cited statistic in the quiver of gun-control advocates was that the number of American children killed in gun-related deaths had doubled each year from 1950 to 1994. If you started with one child killed by guns in 1950 and doubled the number each year, one would find that one billion kids had been killed by guns by 1980 – which was way more than the

[257] Nicolas Capaldi, *The Art of Deception: An Introduction to Critical Thinking: How to Win An Argument, Defend a Case, Recognize a Fallacy, See Through Deception, Persuade a Skeptic, Turn Defeat into Victory* (New York: Prometheus Books, 1987), 58.
[258] Williams, 58.

number of people that inhabited the United States. Best traced the source of the statistical claim back to a report in 1994 by the Children's Defense Fund: "Since 1950, the number of American children gunned down every year has doubled." The number of children that had died as a result of gunfire had doubled since 1950 – not that the fatalities had doubled each year – a much less extraordinary claim since the population of the United States increased by 72 percent between 1950 and 1994, accounting for much of the rise in deaths. Since statistics can be fired like bullets (pardon the pun), concise and precise, they are quickly cited, endlessly repeated, and "can mutate faster than it's possible to check," almost like a virus. They are indeed wonderful tools because you can roll a bulky package of information into a "tidy" number, but lots of information is left out, with the researchers deciding which information to include and exclude.[259] As the researchers and writers of FactCheck.org frequently caution, a single number cannot tell the whole story. That's the price we pay for efficiency of information for easy digestion.

Be wary of polls and survey results

Surveys try to determine the general opinion of a large group of people, whether Americans, Europeans, scientists, clergymen, Christians, teenagers, or farmers, about an issue or question by polling a select number of them through types of questionnaires, either written or oral.   To take an imaginary example, after polling 1,000 Americans, 34% believed that the country was headed in the wrong direction. Pollsters try to take the pulse of America by selecting a much smaller group from the actual population of Americans, and then take the results as a general sense of what Americans are thinking, usually with a margin of error in either direction. However, one should be aware that it takes skill to pick a sample of people that is representative of the group that you are trying to assess. Like statisticians, pollsters are trained professionals and strive for as much accuracy as possible by adopting a rigorous methodology.

Some polls, though, suffer from serious flaws. A famous (or infamous) example comes from the 1936 election between Democratic candidate

---

[259] Patrick Grimm, *The Philosopher's Toolkit: How to Be the Most Rational Person in Any Room,* The Great Courses *(Chantilly, VA: The Teaching Company, 2013), 330 - 35.*

Franklin Delano Roosevelt and Republican challenger Alfred Landon. It is an extreme example, yes, but should stand as an easily understood one for demonstrating how flawed methodology can badly skew results, although other questionable polls are nowhere near as glaring. The poll, conducted by *Literary Digest*, asked people culled from the phonebook who they were going to vote for in the upcoming election. The poll numbers projected that Alfred Landon would win decisively. Roosevelt, however, won in a massive landslide, 523 to 8 electoral votes. What was wrong with the poll? The poll conductors called people on the telephone and asked their preference. The problem is that better-off Republicans tended to own telephones and struggling Roosevelt supporters did not, thus leaving out a wide swath of voters that could have made the poll more representative. Now, if one wanted to be a contrarian, then you could object by asking what a random sample is and how to achieve it. Or with our poll of 1000 Americans, one could certainly object that the sample is too small for a nation with over 300 million people. Okay, then, what is an adequate sample? 10,000? 100,000? One million?[260] Another famous cautionary example comes from Alfred Kinsey's seminal work *Sexual Behavior in the Human Male* (1948). He found that 10% of men were homosexual or had those tendencies. However, it was later revealed that 25% of his sample respondents were in prison, and men in prison only comprise 1% of the entire male population in the United States. Inmates are more likely to have those types of interactions since the surrounding population is completely male, which will drive up the percentage. Undoubtedly, this is another "really egregious case of sample bias," but the lesson should be clear.[261] Keep in mind, though, that people often remember the blatant examples of error, but are unaware of, or do not count, all the polls that predicted something correctly, the latter far exceeding the former.[262]

Suppose the poll has been conducted in a methodologically accepted manner. The poll's aim may be straightforward – like measuring public attitudes toward Obamacare (the Affordable Care Act), an actual poll taken

---

[260] Capaldi, 106, 134.

[261] Whyte, 142.

[262] In an ironic inversion, people often remember what psychics predict correctly, but don't bother to keep count of how many incorrect predictions are on their ledger. The number of misses far outweighs the hits, and that's putting it kindly.

in October 2010. One overwhelming percentage can be cited for effect, or one can pick and choose percentages from the other questions, combine them, and spin something in the opposite direction:

Percentage of people opposed to Obamacare	52%
Percentage of people that favor repeal	37%
Percentage of people that wish to leave the ACA as is	15%
Percentage of people that wish to expand the ACA	36%

Ellenberg jokes that Fox News and MSNBC would simply pick the percentage that would confirm their conservative or liberal audiences' opinions respectively: *"Majority of Americans oppose Obamacare!"* Fox News could gleefully report while MSNBC could smugly assert that a *"Majority of Americans want to preserve or strengthen Obamacare!"*[263]

Numbers and terms are meaningless unless compared to other numbers or terms

Middle-school students, for an imaginary example, improved their math scores on some standardized test by an average of 23 points. Okay, we can at least say that they improved. How much did they improve, though? Was the total number of points on the exam 100, 500, or 1000? If 100, that is a significant increase that students, teachers, and school boards can showcase. If it is 23 out of a 1000, then the accomplishment is not that great, even though a slight improvement. Was this 23 point-advance over last year, or over the past five years, or ten? The baseline, or frame of reference, that you put a number to can make a world of difference in its interpretation. In an actual political dispute, Democrats charged that the Bush administration put or allowed "more arsenic" in the nation's drinking water in 2001. It did not. In fact, the dispute was over how much to reduce the amount, and when the proposed reduction by Republicans was lower than the Clinton administration's, this became twisted into the charge that Republicans were

---

[263] Ellenberg, 368.

adding "more arsenic" to the drinking water. Since 1942, the federal government allowed 50 parts per billion (ppb) of arsenic. Before leaving office, Bill Clinton advocated a regulation that would have reduced this cap to 10 ppb. The Bush administration suspended the rule for further study, concerned that the new regulation would cost communities money. Bush officials proposed amounts up to 20 ppb, and then later adopted 10 ppb years later. Arsenic levels were actually mandated downward. [264]

Use multiple sources and look for a "convergence of evidence"

Instead of reading one book about Abraham Lincoln and thinking that you know most of what you need to know, read several books about him. Authors have different viewpoints and assemble different facts in different ways and leave out others. Find out what a particular author is leaving out by reading another author. As for news, do not limit yourself to just one media station, outlet, or program. If you watch CBS News, watch CNN occasionally to see how the stations differ in their coverage. If you read articles from The *Washington Post* on a regular basis, diversify your exposure to opinion by reading columns from the *Wall Street Journal* to get a different perspective on an issue. Sole reliance on just one news source can have serious consequences for the development of critical thinking, for "if one receives most of one's news from a single cultural or national source, the likely impact on the mind will be that of distortion and deception. Most people, as a result, are trapped in one world view . . . ." Consulting multiple sources not only helps diminish tunnel vision and enables you to hear other sounds outside of an echo chamber, but the activity can help you better determine accurate or at least probable information. Whenever two sources that are ideologically different from one another actually agree on something, it obviously increases the credibility of the story or fact. In the same way that different methodologies can give broadly the same results, say, about the number of homeless people in America, the more certain you can be about the validity of a story or news that you glean from multiple sources with opposing ideologies or beliefs. Any good debater before a public audience knows this: "If you can find two authorities with otherwise conflicting opinions who nevertheless agree with your position on a specific issue, this tends to impress the audience with the fact that you are so right

---

[264] Capaldi, 59-60; Jackson and Jamieson, 32-33.

that almost everyone has to agree with you." Michael Shermer, for instance, has publicly debated Holocaust deniers and has repeatedly pointed to a "convergence of evidence" from a variety of sources: official documents, eyewitness testimony by survivors *and* Nazi officials and doctors, photographs, etc. When "different methods and different source materials" point to the same thing or have substantial overlap, the more certain one can be.[265]

Correlation does not imply causation

This pivotal assertion is probably the one main maxim that I remembered from my undergraduate days as a psychology major since it was hammered into our heads. Just because your study has found that men with higher IQs tend to have smaller feet does not mean that intelligence inhibits foot growth or that small feet increase intelligence. That two phenomena or variables occur in conjunction with each other does not mean that one causes the other, or is either necessary or sufficient for the occurrence of the other. Now, there actually may be a causal relationship between two variables, but it must be determined through a controlled experiment and then replicated. For example, patients with lung cancer also tend to be habitual smokers. Without testing this relationship through the scientific method, one cannot say definitively that smoking causes lung cancer simply based on "correlational data." As is commonly known, legitimate experiments have confirmed this causal connection, though.

Another example is the scare whipped up about the causal link between power lines and cancer. In 1992, the National Academy of Sciences released an extensive study of the effect of electromagnetic fields generated from power lines on health and concluded that "the current body of evidence does not show that exposure to these fields presents a human health hazard." Still, those who continue to be spooked by living close to power lines can point to communities with a litany of health problems near huge power lines with stations nearby. However, those that raise those fears often commit

---

[265] Capaldi, 55; Jackson and Jamieson, 113,140; Richard Paul and Linda Elder, *The Thinker's Guide For Conscientious Citizens on How to Detect Media Bias and Propaganda in National and World* News (The Foundation for Critical Thinking, 2004), 10; Michael Shermer, *Why People Believe Weird Things: Pseudoscience, Superstition, and Other Confusions of Our Time* (New York: W. H. Freeman and Company, 1997), 211-241.

the Texas sharpshooter fallacy: a gunslinger fires bullets at the side of a barn and then walks over and draws a bull's eye around the bullet holes no matter how spaced out they are on the barn's side. They focus on cases in a certain area that confirm their suspicions of a dangerous link and ignore other instances that fall well outside of their irregularly-shaped, after-the-fact bull's eye.[266]

What are you going to replace it with?

One of my all-time favorite movies is *Jaws*. In one of the last scenes, as the characters have run out of options as the boat is sinking and the huge great white shark is circling in for another opportunity to churn up the water with blood, Richard Dreyfuss's character, Matt Hooper, an oceanographic specialist, suggests that they should lower the shark cage into the water and try to shoot a lethal dart into the shark. The sheriff objected that the shark would rip the cage to pieces, and the captain implied that the small dart would barely scratch the skin. Hooper, frustrated, yells back, "Do you have any better suggestions?" It is often easy to be a critic. You can come in from the sidelines and find a whole host of errors or just ridicule an idea or theory from afar. Criticism is certainly a useful thing, but can the critics offer a better explanation, plan, or scenario? We have seen three examples in previous chapters: (1) defenders of the military – industrial complex can wonder if the opponents of the system can offer a better one, (2) defenders of evolution deflect creationist critiques by challenging them to provide a better alternative that is authentically scientific, accounts for the physical evidence, and makes useful predictions, and (3) defenders of thoroughgoing materialism could challenge critics – who complain that our own thinking would be suspect if our brain, as part of the natural world, is subject to molecular and biological determinism – to offer up a more reliable method of determining causation and ensuring accuracy. To be fair, David Henige, a historian that has examined the nature of historical evidence and argumentation, asks, "Should the skeptic feel bound to replace discredited ideas with better ones?" He asserts, "It is not necessary for skeptics to provide a satisfactory counter-hypothesis, which merely begs the question

---

[266] Robert Park, *Voodoo Science: The Road from Foolishness to Fraud* (New York: Oxford University Press, 2000), 140-161; Chris Spatz & James O. Johnston, *Basic Statistics: Tales of Distributions* (Pacific Grove, CA.: Brooks/Cole Publishing Company, 1989), 82-83.

of sufficient evidence."[267]   If the skeptic has done a workmanlike job in dismantling or landing punches at an idea, argument, or interpretation, his job is done.   Besides, that's what Socrates probably did: he steadily undermined a position with relentless questions but did not offer any solutions or systematic replacements himself.[268]

You cannot separate the media, money, and the market

TV and radio stations, as well as major networks, are owned by corporations, and corporations naturally try to turn a profit every year. To turn a profit, one must continue to provide a product that people will consume.

The Audience: The generation and presentation of the news is certainly different than that of automobiles or hamburgers, but the hard reality is that news purveyors have to please their audience (consumers): "As long as the mass of people want high-fat processed foods, the market will sell high-fat and processed foods to them.   And as long as the mass of people want simplistic news articles that reinforce" their worldview and opinions, "the news media will generate such articles for them." [269] So, networks like FOX News and MSNBC know who their audiences are and handcraft the on-air news, shows, and personalities accordingly.   To please the audience, tell them generally what they want to hear, with a devil's advocate segment or dissenting comment here and there to give the impression of fair-mindedness and independent thought.   As the population ages and your network starts to lose younger viewers, add younger, good-looking news analysts to the payroll and offer more segments on sports and celebrity scandals.   Finally, just wink at those charges of bias, for industry execs know that if a different program or network peddles opinions that Mr. Jones agrees with, then that venue is "objective" in his eyes, but if it offers viewpoints that he disagrees with, that station or network is obviously "biased."   Hey, the customer is always right!   This type of news, which offers

---

[267] Henige, 36-37.
[268] Thomas F.X. Noble, *The Foundations of Western Civilization*, The Great Courses (Chantilly, VA.: The Teaching Company, 2002), 200. Noble poses Socrates' method as a question: "[D]id [Socrates] formulate a positive body of doctrine, or did he really [just] poke holes in what was out there?" I will go with the latter.
[269] Paul and Elder, 9, 28

the audience content, examples, and anecdotes that reinforce their belief systems and worldview, has been labeled by Bill Kovach and Tom Rosenstiel as "the Journalism of Affirmation, for its appeal is in affirming the preconceptions of the audience, assuring them, gaining their loyalty, and then converting that loyalty into advertising revenue."[270]

The Advertisers: As pointed out in the last chapter, not only must corporate news keep the audience in mind, they have to keep an eye on what their advertisers think or how they may react to a news story or primetime guest.[271] If an advertiser is offended by what a host or one of her guests said on her show, then it might withdraw ads from the show, or even the network, and take their money with them. Since these corporations that own media are huge and multi-faceted, content-deciders and deliverers must keep in mind that the parent company owns a lot of other companies, and care must be taken not to run stories that criticize or otherwise cast mother's offspring or adoptees in a bad light.

The Content: Hard-nosed, analytical, investigative journalism is expensive.[272] Media corporations have to keep an eye on the bottom line like any other business and can cut costs with the best of them. In the highly competitive world of corporate media, sometimes the best thing is the ability to beat the others to the punch. Breaking stories pull in more of an audience than those that are built up by patient research, source-checking, and good writing. Both newspapers and the world of television news are skimping on serious journalism and long stories that may strain the increasingly-shrinking attention span and – some say – the information literacy of the average consumer of news. Instead, stations and networks start to rely on "official" sources and boilerplate press releases by other corporations and groups in the news. Seeing himself as one of the last of his breed, gadfly investigative journalist Greg Palast grouses about spineless reporters and establishment

---

[270] Kovach and Rosenstiel, 45. The authors contrast this model with the Journalism of Assertion – where news providers merely report the news and allow or encourage unsubstantiated rumors and allegations, or moderators allow partisans to present their dueling opinions without substantial challenges – and the Journalism of Verification. The latter involves a rigorous vetting process where sources and evidence are scrutinized in a transparent way. The authors champion the latter.
[271] Ibid., 22
[272] Ibid., 24

journalists: "One good, slick explanation from a politician or corporate chieftain and it's *case closed,* investigation over." This ready dependence on these types of sources greatly restrains the angles one can develop, and certainly restricts journalists to only the facts or canned version that the government, some business, or group strategically wishes to release.[273] Some segments are simply advertising – a story is generated that gives airtime exposure for a product or service, usually paid for by the company that peddles them. These "fake news" stories (which predate Donald Trump's favorite variety) are known in the business as video news releases (VNRs). Government agencies, corporate publicists, and other self-promoting groups put these presentations together and package them to sound like news stories. A majority of the news programs do not disclose the creator and funder of the segments.[274]

The Study: Journalists, producers, and on-air personalities are certainly not experts in many of the fields they cover and are subject to time restraints in a fast-paced business, so they often make appeals to authority by citing a study. Readers beware. One should find out who foots the bill for a study or report referenced by a news article or TV host. Many studies are conducted and offered to news media by ideological organizations – such as the Heritage Foundation or Greenpeace, conservative and liberal respectively. The writers and researchers for these organizations will naturally present findings that uphold the ideological leanings and positions of their employer. On top of that, the foundations and organizations themselves are funded by wealthy individuals and groups with political commitments. Granted, bankrolled research does not mean that it *necessarily* has slanted or inaccurate information or fallacious reasoning, but it should make one wary, or at least aware, of the sponsorship.[275] For example, a group of 32 scientists co-authored an article in *Science* magazine and claimed that there was no oil in the water or on the beaches after the BP oil spill in the Gulf in 2010. Palast and a team of researchers found that 31 of the 32 scientists had received at least a slither of half a billion dollars from BP for researching the oil spill. Palast quotes "biologist" Yogi Berra: "It's amazing what you can see

[273] Greg Palast, *The Best Money Democracy Can Buy*, 14-15; Paul and Elder, 22-23.
[274] Peter Phillips, ed., *Censored 2008: The Top 25 Censored Stories* (New York: Seven Stories Press, 2007), 274-76.
[275] Jackson and Jamieson, 148-49, 165.

when you're looking," which, for this cadre of scientists, can also mean that it is amazing what you can't see if you are not really looking because of "BP's dollars taped over your eyes."[276] Not only biologists are susceptible. Often, countries that allow archeologists to dig in their country often fund the research and expect results that contribute to national goals and "self-identity": "Since most funding comes from official or quasi-official sources, there is a built-in temptation to satisfy benefactors. Archeology requires the long-term goodwill of the host government, and with this comes a sense of obligation that might manifest itself in various regrettable ways."[277]

Let me emphasize again, though, that research funded by an ideologically-invested organization or think tank is not invariably unreliable because of the sponsorship. One has to be careful not to deploy the "Motive Fallacy" – dismissing someone's or a group's claim because they have a motive to espouse it.[278] It's a version of the ad hominem argument: attempting to refute a claim by questioning the author's credibility instead of honestly evaluating the evidence the author presented for that position.

The FCC: If you are worried about the increasing consolidation of the media under a few mega-corporate umbrellas, don't count on the FCC to police these behemoths very closely, especially after the Telecommunications Act of 1996, which allowed corporations to buy up more stations. The Center for Public Integrity issued a study (I know, be wary) that showed that FCC officials have been entertained at conferences and lavish hotels to the tune of almost $2.8 million in exotic locations like Paris, Rio de Janeiro, and Las Vegas. Who paid the bill? Corporate media.[279]

Immerse yourself in literature

Okay, now for some special pleading for the humanities. I firmly believe that one should read the great writers of history for the mere pleasure of reading, not to uncover the racist or sexist themes of those works; or to "deconstruct" them to reveal hidden attempts to maintain power and

---

[276] Palast, *Vulture's Picnic*, 127.
[277] Henige, 73-74.
[278] Whyte, 16-17.
[279] Peter Phillips, ed., *Censored 2004: The Top 25 Censored Stories* (New York: Seven Stories Press, 2003), 87, 130.

hegemony by white European males. Those scholarly exercises do have merit, though, if done in the spirit of traditional criticism. I do not want to get into the whole dispute about which authors and works belong to the corpus of "Great Books." These famous works of literature, far from being a monolithic structure of monotonous themes and values, actually express a wide variety of opinions about a range of human activities and aspirations. They have plenty of examples of characters that question authority and subvert the status quo that can give inspiration and intellectual ammo to the oppressed and excluded groups of history. Now, my concern is how a steady appetite for good literature sharpens your mind. Jonathan Franzen has noted that literature helps nurture linguistic precision and a suspicion of simple explanations, a creeping expectation that something more profound or even sinister lurks under the surface. Howard Bloom would add that good literature and poetry have healthy portions of irony. Repeated exposure to these classics, I would like to think, would hone readers' ability to recognize similar ironies in politics, economics, and religion. In addition, reading great literature helps forge an "autonomous self" – which might make one less of an ideologue on either the left or the right.[280]

Awareness of limitations results in more careful thinking

We have already seen repeatedly that confirmation bias can be a pitfall: we actively search for information, evidence, examples, and data that support our ideological or religious viewpoint, and downplay, ignore, or more rigorously question the evidence cited for an opposing position. Recent books for a general audience have identified more pitfalls by providing compelling syntheses of the remarkable research in the social sciences about human cognition and behavior.

Overconfidence: Daniel Kahneman, in *Thinking, Fast and Slow*, has shown that we underestimate the role of luck and emotion in our successful choices and overestimate how much we think we know. We may grudgingly admit to making mistakes, but we also find "it is easier to recognize other people's mistakes than our own."[281]

---

[280] See Harold Bloom, *Genius* and *How to Read and Why* (New York: Scribner, 2000), 195; Jonathan Franzen, *How to Be Alone: Essays* (New York: Farrar, Straus, and Giroux, 2002), 90-92.
[281] Daniel Kahneman, *Thinking, Fast and Slow* (New York: Farrar, Straus and Giroux,

<u>Patterns and Coherent Stories</u>: It seems that we are prone to discern causality and patterns where none exist. As David McRaney has put it, "you find it irresistible to connect the dots" when searching for a comforting explanation for events and things both ordinary and extraordinary. We reshape our memories to make our story more coherent, and the reshaping gets further refined the more the past recedes behind us. It reminds us of the caution that historians often spotlight, that there's the past as it was, the past as recorded, the past we actually remember, and the past as the way we would like to remember it. Telling these coherent stories – to ourselves and others – serves an adaptive purpose, though, for it helps us cope with life, make meaning out of it, and maintain a manageable equilibrium. [282]

<u>Asymmetrical insight</u>: We think we know our ideological opponents better than they know themselves. And your opponents think that they know your side better than you know your own side. Not only that, but each camp thinks that the other is less nuanced than themselves, whereas your own group of like-minded individuals shows evidence of complexity and "shades of gray" – for we are far more sophisticated in our thinking than they are. And they think the same way about your group.[283]

<u>Digging in our heels</u>: Unfortunately, think of this as confirmation bias on steroids. Once an opposing side or individual offers contradictory evidence, we hunker down and assert our position even more firmly and heatedly with new counterexamples and talking points. The online environment has put this tendency into overdrive: "Most online battles follow a similar pattern, with each side launching attacks and pulling evidence from deep inside the Web to back up its position until, out of frustration, one party resorts to an all-out ad hominem nuclear strike."[284]

2011), 9-14, 28, 45

[282] Ibid., 114-15; David McRaney, *You Can Beat Your Brain: How to Turn Your Enemies into Friends, How to Make Better Decisions, and Other Ways to be Less Dumb* (London: OneWorld Publications, 2013), 7,13,40; Harrison, 126; Noble, 166.

[283] McRaney, 196-197.

[284] Ibid., 148; Joseph T. Hallinan, *Kidding Ourselves: The Hidden Power of Self-Deception* (New York: Crown Publishers, 2014), 91.

I would like to address some possible objections to the idea of religious, economic, and political moderation and my summary of the principles, attitudes, criticisms, and assertions cited throughout this book. First, concerning the latter, I readily acknowledge that my areas of focus are incomplete. For instance, I have said very little or nothing about some undoubtedly important topics: the health care debate, immigration, LGBTQ+ rights, mass shootings and gun control, campus protests and free speech, just to name a few. Some readers may find that some of the general observations I have methodically listed to represent one ideological camp are trivial issues compared to the ones identified in the oppositional camp, or that the generalizations are shot full with many possible exceptions. The topics are exceedingly broad: religion, politics, economics, and even knowledge itself. Experts in these fields, and the various subfields, can easily poke holes by identifying what I have left out, demonstrating the complexity of a topic that I have only superficially covered, and finding instances where I should have taken my own advice and traced sources back to the original one. I know my limitations and can imagine those of this book. I can only respond that I – like everyone that I have exhorted so far – should be open to new evidence, topics, and arguments, and hope that this book will be a starting point for a bigger, more encompassing conversation about moderation and humble skepticism. I certainly don't claim that the summary of positions and purported insights are comprehensive, but are simply themes that I chose to examine.

Second, one may ask, are there some issues that you can't be moderate about? How is it possible to adopt a moderate position between rationality and irrationality? Can you be moderate about Donald Trump, whether a supporter or opponent? Take rationality, for instance: determining who has the rational position is complicated when groups or individuals claim the mantle of rationality for themselves. The most common example is when atheists and other unbelievers charge Christians or other types of religious believers with irrational beliefs. But Paul Copan and William Lane Craig have retorted that it is the "new atheists" that are not making the grade, in either rationality or civility: "Rather than sticking to rational, carefully reasoned arguments, they have taken off the gloves to launch angry, sarcastic, and sloppily argued attacks."[285]   Moderation (and rationality, it seems) is in the eye of the beholder, for conservatives and liberals may see each other as the unrealistic extremists and their own respective positions as moderate and reasonable.   For instance, liberals may read my summary of advice about achieving an informed moderation and exclaim, "Hey, you're talking about us and what we believe and practice!" For instance, Eric Alterman has surveyed liberal intellectuals' attempts to crystallize the essence of liberalism: the promotion and practice of toleration; the ability to deliberate in a reasonable fashion when adopting policies and genuinely respecting opponents when doing so; a generous capacity for self-criticism; and openness to experimentation and new ideas. All of the above practices and attitudes are sprinkled with restraint and humility.[286]   Does that mean that conservatives are intolerant, unreasonable, unreflective, and close-minded?   Sophisticated voices of conservatism in the mold of a William F. Buckley, George Will, or David Brooks would object to such a characterization.   Older, more traditional conservatives would argue that it is conservatives who uphold the value of Western civilization and the values that have historically accompanied it: the rule of law, the advance of applied science and technology, open debate and free speech, human liberty, religiously-motivated morality, the eager acceptance of innovation, and a constrained government – surely a list of things that are reasonable and productive of both order and happiness.

Recently, a British historian, David Cannadine, has surveyed world history and determined that our common humanity has been overshadowed by our differences. Conflict gets most of the attention while cooperation and coexistence are overshadowed. Perhaps the reason for this is that conflict makes for a more gripping historical narrative. He examined the clashing dichotomies that historians have constructed over gender, race, class, religion, nation, and civilization. Undoubtedly, these clashes are real and regrettable. He complicates these divisions, though, by providing many counterexamples of cooperation and coexistence in more localized contexts

---

[285] Paul Copan and William Lane Craig, eds., *Contending With Christianity's Critics: Answering New Atheists and Other Objectors* (Nashville, TN: B and H Academic), vii.
[286] Eric Alterman and Kevin Mattson, *The Cause: The Fight for American Liberalism From Franklin Roosevelt to Barack Obama* (New York: Viking), 355-56.

and on a personal level, and he reveals that each side is not as united as often portrayed, for there are often internal divisions.[287] If I situate my brief survey within Cannadine's broader context, perhaps I have perpetuated this conflict-ridden view of the world. But I hope that a plain unfolding of the arguments, evidence, and mentalities of the religious, economic, and political groups in recent American history – along with the enumerated signs of moderation, as laid out in the first chapter – will result in a more democracy-affirming, evidence-based, bias-aware, context-dependent, fallacy-averse, consensus-seeking conversation among ordinary Americans and leaders.

Finally, another way of viewing the concept of moderation is as a manifestation of American pragmatism. I am not speaking only of the conventional – and largely true – assertion that Americans favor a can-do practicality to arid theory and sterile academic concerns, but the American philosophical tradition of pragmatism as typified by William James and Charles Pierce and, more recently, that of Richard Rorty. "Truth" – whether asserted by liberals or conservatives, interventionists and free marketeers, plumbers or lawyers – is not the proper aim. Instead, we should break down those age-old divisions between objective and subjective, fact and value, truth and falsity, reality and appearance, realism and idealism, and build up a consensus on whether a position taken or policy adopted will really make a difference and have positive results. As Rorty has argued, we need to adopt "another vocabulary." This fresh vocabulary is amicably, or at least civilly, nurtured in a conversational – not confrontational – atmosphere where tolerance is urged, attentiveness is nurtured, and agreement is achieved by persuasion. We should deliberate, not debate. The goal is not to arrive at the "truth" about theology, economics, or politics, but to devise methods and adopt policies that will produce better people: "We should think of human progress as making it possible for human beings to do more interesting things and be more interesting people, not as heading toward a place which has somehow been prepared for us in advance."[288] This

---

[287] David Cannadine, *The Undivided Past: Humanity Beyond Our Differences* (New York: Alfred A. Knopf, 2013).

[288] Richard Rorty, "Science as Solidarity" in *The American Intellectual Tradition*, edited by David A. Hollinger and Charles Capper, Vol. II, 6th edition (New York: Oxford University Press, 2011), 533-43. Rorty's positions are controversial in the halls of academic philosophy and also among liberal and conservative pundits. He is often criticized for defending "fuzziness" (his breaking down of standard philosophical dichotomies) and

questioning of a monolithic version of truth or a predetermined end goal in life was also embraced by Raymond Aron and Isaiah Berlin, two thinkers that Aurelian Craiutu identified as advocates of moderation. Aron decried any notion that the historical process was headed to some scientifically determined end point of bliss and perfect order, while Berlin questioned the notion that there is one truth or path to get there (as well as the concept of a teleological end point).[289]

Admittedly, this hopeful scenario is more applicable to legislative decisions and the adoption of policy than to religious belief, scientific studies, and historical scholarship. Christians would argue that people are sinful and cannot be made better without divine assistance. And insisting that we should not be heading toward a place which has somehow been prepared for us in advance would flatly nullify a central Christian belief. Believers would not be open to negotiation when it comes to those two beliefs. Christians, scientists, and historians (not mutually exclusive groups) would question whether you should put the word "truth" in quotation marks, for such a signifier would imply that truth is not absolute, that it can be subject to diplomatic haggling and finessing. Historians, for instance, strive to achieve factual accuracy and truthful narratives, even if in service to a debatable interpretation of a past event. Perhaps we can suggest that such tentative hesitancy in asserting truth claims – or putting such efforts aside – does not mean that truth on various levels does not exist. Truth exists, but we imperfect humans can only approximate it. This assertion of limitations should please both Christians and hardcore nonbelievers and scientists. For the former, an admission of human incapacity seems compatible with Christian theology's emphasis on human depravity and its debilitating impact on human rationality. For the latter, an admission of human incapacity to ever approach the truth is consistent with the self-correcting nature of science, that a theory should always be open to falsification.

---

trying to complicate any efforts to consign him to the relativist camp. These intellectual battles are well summarized and evaluated – with engaging, entertaining prose – in Carlin Romano, *America the Philosophical* (New York: Alfred A Knopf, 2012), 126 – 157.

[289] See Aurelian Craiutu, chapters two and three.

Using the pragmatist approach as a blueprint, then, these tolerant conversations and trial-and-error adoptions of solutions to problems should value creativity, imagination, and originality over assertions of unalterable truth. We should strive to find creative ways to solve our political and economic problems rather than each side issuing platforms and manifestos with sentences like this: "We believe that . . . ." The trial-and-error mentality of the great tinkerers of the past like Thomas Edison should be applied to our religious, economic, and political conflict. The approach partakes of the "If we were able to put a man on the moon, then why can't we do X" aspiration, where X could be balancing the budget, investing in education, or ensuring affordable healthcare, all in a manner that is cost-efficient, fair to all taxpayers, and effective. One should be aware, though, that a critic could rightfully point out that a trial-and-error approach can be, at best, inefficient and, at worst, dangerous – if the proposed trial somehow causes considerable errors that result in inconvenience, injury, or even death.

I can't prove that a steady diet of the following will produce moderation: reading books, informed articles, and literature; a contextual awareness of viewpoints from a variety of sources and perspectives; an awareness of our vulnerability to confirmation bias; our overconfidence in our reasoning abilities as we construct stories and patterns to make sense of life, whether those patterns are actually there or not; and an acknowledgement that both camps on a religious, economic, or political issue are not monolithic. It is more of a hope than a thesis.

As stated in the first chapter, moderation is not seeking out a bluff near the center of the spectrum and looking down self-righteously on the partisans on either side. In fact, moderation means recognizing that there are multiple spectrums – one for each issue, problem, or topic. Your position on each one depends upon reaching conclusions via the methods, cautions, and attitudes listed throughout this book. For instance, you may fall on the conservative side of the spectrum regarding health care but on the liberal end when it comes to the legalization of marijuana. Or, after deliberation, an individual may oppose stifling regulation in general but agree that regulation in a certain area of the pharmaceutical industry is gravely needed. In other words, with a multitude of spectrums, your position is not determined by an ideological or theological checklist of items that must be checked off with the correct answer of agreement or disagreement. A moderate is not afraid to unbundle a package that the ideologically or religiously committed insist be accepted in a unitary, all-or-nothing, systematic worldview. The moderate recognizes that, for those committed to an array of beliefs within a political or religious worldview, the issues that you carefully study on a case-by-case basis are often linked, and unlinking them without substantially diluting other vested positions within that political or religious universe can be complicated – but not impossible.

Bibliography

"A Growing Environmental Disaster." *The Week*, June 4, 2010.

Alterman, Eric. *What Liberal Media? The Truth About Bias and the News.* New York: Basic Books, 2003.

Alterman, Eric and Kevin Mattson. *The Cause: The Fight for American Liberalism from Franklin Roosevelt to Barack Obama.* New York: Viking, 2012.

Alston, William P. "A Philosopher's Way Back to Faith." In *God and the Philosophers: The Reconciliation of Faith and Reason*, edited by Thomas V. Morris, 19-30. New York: Oxford University Press, 1994.

Anderson, Martin. *Imposters in the Temple: American Intellectuals Are Destroying Our Universities and Cheating Our Students of Their Future.* New York: Simon and Schuster, 1992.

Armstrong, Karen. *A History of God: The 4000-Year Quest of Judaism, Christianity and Islam.* New York: Alfred A. Knopf, 1994.

_____. *The Battle for God.* New York: Alfred A. Knopf, 2000.

_____. *The Bible: A Biography.* New York: Atlantic Monthly Press, 2007.

Asimov, Eric. "The Fate of Interstate Wine Shipments." Diners Journal. http://dinersjournal.blogs.nytimes.com/2010/10/19/the-fate-of-interstate-wine-shipments/.

Bamford, James. *The Shadow Factory: The Ultra-Secret NSA from 9/11 to the Eavesdropping on America.* New York: Doubleday, 2008.

Barofsky, Neil. *Bailout: An Inside Account of How Washington Abandoned Main Street While Rescuing Wall Street.* New York: Free Press, 2012.

Beard, Henry and Christopher Cerf. *Spinglish: The Definitive Dictionary of Deliberately Deceptive Language.* New York: Blue Rider Press, 2015.

Berman, Morris. *Dark Ages America: The Final Phase of Empire.* New York: W.W. Norton and Company, 2006.

_____. *The Twilight of American Culture.* New York: W. W. Norton Company, 2000.

Berman, William C. *America's Right Turn: From Nixon to Bush.* Baltimore, MD: The Johns Hopkins University Press, 1994.

Biskupic, Joan. *American Original: The Life and Constitution of Supreme Court Justice Antonin Scalia.* New York: Sara Crichton Books, 2009.

Blackburn, Simon. *Think: A Compelling Introduction to Philosophy.* Oxford: Oxford University Press, 1999.

Bloom, Harold. *Genius: A Mosaic of One Hundred Exemplary Creative Minds.* New York: Warner Books, 2002.

_____. *How to Read and Why.* New York: Scribner, 2000.

Bodenhamer, David J. *The Revolutionary Constitution.* New York: Oxford University Press, 2012.

Boghossian, Peter. *A Manual for Creating Atheists.* Durham, NC: Pitchstone Publishing, 2013.

Bork, Robert H. *Slouching Towards Gomorrah: Modern Liberalism and American Decline.* New York: Regan Books, 1996.

_____. *The Tempting of America: The Political Seduction of the Law.* New York: Touchstone, 1990.

Boyd, Gregory A. *Cynic Sage or Son of God? Recovering the Real Jesus in an Age of Revisionist Replies.* Wheaton, Ill.: BridgePoint/Victor Books, 1995.

Brinkley, Douglas. *The Great Deluge: Hurricane Katrina, New Orleans, and the Mississippi Gulf Coast.* New York: William Morrow, 2006.

Brock, David. *Blinded by The Right: The Conscience of an Ex-Conservative.* New York: Crown Publishers, 2002.

Brookfield, Stephen D. and Stephen Preskill. *Discussion as a Way of Teaching: Tools and Techniques for Democratic Classrooms*, 2nd ed. San Francisco: Jossey-Bass, 2005.

Brooks, Arthur C. *Gross National Happiness: Why Happiness Matters for America- and How We Can Get More of It.* New York: Basic Books, 2008.

Brooks, David. "What Moderates Believe." *New York Times,* August 22, 2017. https://www.nytimes.com/2017/08/22/.../trump-moderates-bipartisanship-truth.html
_____. "What Moderation Means." *New York Times.* October 26, 2012. www.nytimes.com/2012/10/26/opinion/brooks-what-moderation-means.html

Brown, David S. *Moderates: The Vital Center of American Politics, From The Founding To Today.* Chapel Hill, N.C.: University of North Carolina Press, 2016.

Buckley, Reid. *Speaking in Public: Buckley's Techniques for Winning Arguments and Getting Your Point Across.* New York: National Review Books, 1988.

Cannadine, David. *The Undivided Past: Humanity Beyond Our Differences.* New York: Alfred A. Knopf, 2013.

Capaldi, Nicolas. *The Art of Deception: An Introduction to Critical Thinking: How to Win An Argument, Defend a Case, Recognize a Fallacy, See Through Deception, Persuade a Skeptic, Turn Defeat into Victory.* New York: Prometheus Books, 1987.

Cathcart, Thomas and Daniel Klein. *Aristotle and an Aardvark Go To Washington: Understanding Political Doublespeak Through Philosophy and Jokes.* New York: Abrams Image, 2007.

Chaffee, John. *The Thinker's Way: Eight Steps to a Richer Life.* Boston: Little, Brown and Company, 1998.

Clor, Harry. *On Moderation: Defending an Ancient Virtue in a Modern World.* Waco, TX: Baylor University Press, 2008.

Coates, David. *Answering Back: Liberal Responses to Conservative Arguments.* New York: Continuum, 2010.

Conason, Joe. *Big Lies: The Right-Wing Propaganda Machine and How It Distorts the Truth.* New York: Thomas Dunne Books, 2003.

"Conservatives on Obama's stay-in-school speech: "Indoctrination," "Brainwashing," Communist China, Hitler Youth." Media Matters, Sept2, 2009. http://mediamatters.org/research/200909020012.

Coyne, Jerry A. *Faith vs. Fact: Why Science and Religion Are Incompatible.* New York: Viking Penguin, 2015.

____. *Why Evolution Is True.* New York: Penguin Books, 2009.

Craig, William Lane. *Dawkins's Delusion.* In *Contending With Christianity's Critics: Answering New Atheists and Other Objectors*, edited by Paul Copan and William Lane Craig, 2-5. Nashville: B & H Publishing Group, 2009.

Craiutu, Aurelian. *Faces of Moderation: The Art of Balance in an Age of Extremes*. Philadelphia: University of Pennsylvania Press, 2017.

Crossan, John Dominc and Jonathan L. Reed. *Excavating Jesus: Beneath the Stones, Behind the Texts.* New York:HarperSanFrancisco, 2001.

Davidson, James West and Mark Hamilton Lytle. *After the Fact: The Art of Historical Detection*. 5th ed. New York: McGraw Hill, 2005.

Dawkins, Richard. *The God Delusion.* Boston: Houghton Mifflin Company, 2006.

____. *The Greatest Show on Earth: The Evidence for Evolution.* New York: Free Press, 2009.

De Botton, Alain. *The Consolation of Philosophy*. New York: Pantheon Books, 2000.

Delbanco, Andrew. *College: What It Was, Is, And Should Be.* Princeton: Princeton University Press, 2012.

Denby, David. *Great Books: My Adventures with Homer, Rousseau, Woolf, and Other Indestructible Writers of the Western World.* New York: Simon and Schuster, 1996.

Early, John F. "Reassessing the Facts About Inequality, Poverty, and Redistribution." Cato Institute, April 24, 2018. https://www.cato.org/publications/policy-analysis/reassessing-facts-about-inequality-poverty-redistribution#full

Ehrman, Bart D. *Did Jesus Exist? The Historical Argument for Jesus of Nazareth*. New York: HarperOne, 2012.

___. *Jesus Interrupted: Revealing the Hidden Contradictions in the Bible (and Why We Don't Know About Them)*. New York: HarperOne, 2009.

___. *Lost Christianities: The Battles for Scripture and the Faiths We Never Knew* (New York: Oxford University Press, 2003

___. *Misquoting Jesus: The Story Behind Who Changed the Bible and Why*. New York: HarperSanFrancisco, 2005.

Elder, Linda and Richard Paul. *The Art of Socratic Questioning*. Dillion Beach, CA: Foundation for Critical Thinking, 2007.

Ellenberg, Jordan. *How Not to Be Wrong: The Power of Mathematical Thinking*. New York: The Penguin Press, 2014.

Epstein, Joseph. *Snobbery: The American Version*. Boston: Houghton Mifflin Company, 2002.

Evans, Craig A. "How Scholars Fabricate Jesus." In *Contending With Christianity's Critics: Answering New Atheists and Other Objectors*, edited by Paul Copan and William Lane Craig, 126-147. Nashville: B & H Publishing Group, 2009.

Feinman, Jay M. *Law 101: Everything You Need to Know About American Law*. 4th ed. Oxford University Press, 2014.

Fernandez-Armesto, Filpe. *Truth: A History and a Guide for the Perplexed*. New York: St Martin's Press, 1997.

Flew, Anthony. *How to Think Straight: An Introduction to Critical Reasoning*. Amherst, NY: Prometheus Books, 1998.

___. *Thinking About Social Thinking*. 2nd ed. New York: Prometheus Books, 1995.

Folsom, Burt. *The Myth of the Robber Barons: A New Look at the Rise of Big Business in America*. 5th ed. Herndon, VA: Young America's Foundation, 2010.

Foner, Eric. *Who Owns History? Rethinking the Past in a Changing World*. New York: Hill and Wang, 2002.

Frank, Robert. *Richistan: A Journey Through The American Wealth Boom and the Lives of the New Rich.* New York: Three Rivers Press, 2007.

Franzen, Jonathan. *How to Be Alone: Essays.* New York: Farrar, Straus, and Giroux, 2002.

"GAO Authority Undermined." OMBWatch, March 10, 2003. http://www.ombwatch.org/node/1244.

Gardner, Martin. *Did Adam and Eve Have Navels? Discourses on Reflexology, Numerology, Urine Therapy, and Other Dubious Subjects.* New York: W. W. Norton and Company, 2000.

Genovese, Eugene D. *The Southern Tradition: The Achievement and Limitations of an American Conservatism.* Cambridge, MA.: Harvard University Press, 1994.

Golob, Eugene O. *The ISMs: A History and Evaluation.* Freeport, NY: Books for Libraries Press, Inc., 1954, 1968.

Gould, Stephen Jay. *Rocks of Ages: Science and Religion in the Fullness of Life.* New York: The Ballantine Publishing Group, 1999.

Gregory, Chad. "Judges, Lawyers, and Historians: Parallel Developments in Historical Interpretation and Legal Thought." Unpublished manuscript, 2009.

Grim, Patrick. *The Philosopher's Toolkit: How to Be the Most Rational Person in Any Room.* The Great Courses, transcript book. Chantilly, VA.: The Teaching Company, 2013.

Habermas, Gary R. "The Resurrection of Jesus Time Line: The Convergence of Eyewitnesses and Early Proclamation." In *Contending With Christianity's Critics: Answering New Atheists and Other Objectors*, edited by Paul Copan and William Lane Craig, 113 – 125. Nashville: B & H Publishing Group, 2009.

Hacker, Jacob and Paul Pierson. *Winner-Take-All Politics: How Washington Made the Rich Richer – And Turned Its Back on the Middle Class.* New York: Simon and Schuster, 2010.

Hallinan, Joseph T. *Kidding Ourselves: The Hidden Power of Self-Deception.* New York: Crown Publishers, 2014.

Harrison, Guy. *Think: Why You Should Question Everything.* Amherst, NY: Prometheus Books, 2013.

Hazlitt, Henry. *Economics in One Lesson.* New York: Arlington House Publishers, 1979.

Hecht, Jennifer Michael. *Doubt: A History, The Great Doubters and Their Legacy of Innovation from Socrates and Jesus to Thomas Jefferson and Emily Dickenson.* New York: HarperSanFrancisco, 2003.

Henderson, David. *The Joy of Freedom: An Economist's Odyssey.* New York: Prentice Hall.

Henige, David. *Historical Evidence and Argumentation.* Madison, Wisc.: The University of Wisconsin Press, 2005.

Herman, Arthur. *The Cave and the Light: Plato Versus Aristotle, and the Struggle for the Soul of Western Civilization.* New York: Random House, 2013.

Higgs, Robert. *Against Leviathan: Government Power and a Free Society.* Oakland, CA: The Independent Institute, 2004.

Hofstadter, Richard. *Anti-Intellectualism in American Life.* New York: Vintage Books, 1963.

Ivins, Molly and Lou Dubose. *Bushwacked: Life in George W. Bush's America.* New York: Random House, 2003.

Jackson, Brooks and Kathleen Hall Jamieson. *Unspun: Finding Facts in a World of Disinformation.* New York: Random House, 2007.

Jacoby, Susan. *The Age of Unreason.* New York: Pantheon, 2008.

Johnson, Paul. *A History of Christianity.* New York: Atheneum, 1976.

Kahneman, Daniel. *Thinking, Fast and Slow.* New York: Farrar, Straus and Giroux, 2011.

Kaye, Harvey. *"Why Do Ruling Classes Fear History?" and Other Questions.* New York: St. Martin's Griffen, 1997.

Keener, James P. "Confessions of a 'Weird Mathematician'." In *Professors Who Believe: The Spiritual Journeys of Christian Faculty,* edited by Paul M. Anderson, 86 – 93. Downers Grove, Ill.: InterVarsity Press, 1998.

Kick, Russ, ed. *You Are Being Lied To: The Disinformation Guide to Media Distortion, Historical Whitewashes, and Cultural Myths.* New York: The Disinformation Company, 2001.

Klein, Naomi. *The Shock Doctrine: The Rise of Disaster Capitalism.* New York: Picador, 2007.

Knowles, Elizabeth, ed. *The Oxford Dictionary of Quotations.* Oxford: Oxford University Press, 1999.

Koplow, Douglas and Aaron Martin. "Fueling Global Warming: Federal Subsidies to Oil in the United States." http://archive.greenpeace.org/climate/oil/fdsuboil.pdf; http://www.mineralweb.com/owners-guide/leased-and-producing/royalty-taxes/depletion-allowance/.

Kovach, Bill and Tom Rosenstiel. *Blur: How to Know What's True in the Age of Information Overload.* New York: Bloomsbury, 2010.

Kreeft, Peter and Ronald K. Tacelli. *Handbook of Christian Apologetics.* Downers Grove, Ill.: InterVarsity Press.

Krugman, Paul. *The Conscience of a Liberal.* New York: W. W. Norton and Company, 2009.

Lewis, C. S. *Christian Reflections.* Grand Rapids, MI.: William B. Eerdmans Publishing Company, 1967.

____. *Mere Christianity.* New York: McMillan Publishing Company, 1960.

Limbaugh, Rush. *See I Told You So.* New York: Pocket Books, 1993.

____. *The Way Things Ought to Be.* New York: Pocket Books, 1992.

Linville, Mark D. "The Moral Poverty of Evolutionary Naturalism." In *Contending With Christianity's Critics: Answering New Atheists and Other Objectors*, edited by Paul Copan and William Lane Craig, 58-73. Nashville: B &H Publishing Group, 2009.

Lodge, David. *Small World* in *A David Lodge Trilogy.* New York: Penguin Books, 1993.

MacLean, Nancy. *Democracy in Chains: The Deep History of The Radical Right's Stealth Plan for America.* New York: Penguin Books, 2017.

Magee, Bryan. *Confessions of a Philosopher: A Journey Through Western Philosophy.* New York: Random House, 1997.

Mattson, Kevin. *Rebels All! A Short History of The Conservative Mind*. New Brunswick, NJ: Rutgers University Press, 2008.

Meyer, Steven. *Signature in the Cell: DNA and the Evidence For Intelligent Design*. New York: HarperOne, 2009.

Mitchell, Peter R. and John Schoeffel, eds. *Understanding Power: The Indispensable Chomsky*. New York: The New Press, 2002.

Morris, Thomas V. "Suspicions of Something More." In *God and the Philosophers: The Reconciliation of Faith and Reason*, edited by Thomas V. Morris, 8-18. New York: Oxford University Press, 1994.

Muller, Jerry Z. *Adam Smith in His Time and Ours: Designing the Decent Society*. New York: The Free Press, 1993.

Murray, Michael J. *"Seek and You Will Find."* In *God and the Philosophers: The Reconciliation of Faith and Reason,* edited by Thomas V. Morris, 61-76. New York: Oxford University Press, 1994.

Nash, George. *The Conservative Intellectual Movement in America Since 1945*. Wilmington, DE.: InterCollegiate Studies Institute, 2006.

Nichols, Tom. *The Death of Expertise: The Campaign Against Established Knowledge and Why it Matters*. New York: Oxford University Press, 2017.

Noble, Thomas F. X. *The Foundations of Western Civilization*. The Great Courses, transcript book. Chantilly, VA.: The Teaching Company, 2002.

Palast, Greg. *Armed Madhouse: Who's Afraid of Osama Wolf?, China Floats, Bush Sinks, The Scheme to Steal '08, No Child's Left Behind, and Other Dispatches from the Front Lines of the Class War*. New York: Dutton, 2006.

____. *The Best Democracy Money Can Buy: The Truth About Corporate Cons, Globalization, and High-Finance Fraudsters*. New York: Plume, 2003.

____. *Vultures' Picnic: In Pursuit of Petroleum Pigs, Power Pirates, and High-Finance Carnivores.* New York: Dutton, 2011.

Park, Robert. *Voodoo Science: The Road from Foolishness to Fraud*. New York: Oxford University Press, 2000.

Paul, Richard and Linda Elder. *The Thinker's Guide For Conscientious Citizens on How to Detect Media Bias and Propaganda in National and World* News. The Foundation for Critical Thinking, 2004.

Phillips, Kevin. *American Theocracy: The Peril and Politics of Radical Religion, Oil, and Borrowed Money in the 21st Century*. New York: Viking, 2006.

____. *Wealth and Democracy: A Political History of the American Rich*. New York: Broadway Books, 2002.

Phillips, Peter, ed. *Censored 2003: The Top 25 Censored Stories*. New York: Seven Stories Press, 2002.

____. *Censored 2004: The Top 25 Censored Stories*. New York: Seven Stories Press, 2003.

Phillips, Peter and Andrew Roth, eds. *Censored 2008: The Top 25 Censored Stories of 2006-07*. New York: Seven Stories Press, 2007.

Pierce, Charles P. *Idiot America: How Stupidity Became A Virtue in the Land of the Free*. New York: Doubleday, 2009.

Piereson, James. *Shattered Consensus: The Rise and Decline of America's Postwar Political Order*. New York: Encounter Books, 2015.

Rampton, Sheldon and John Stauber. *Banana Republicans: How the Right Wing Is Turning America into a One-Party State*. New York: Jeremy P. Tarcher/Penguin, 2004.

Reiff, Patricia H. "Three Heavens – Our Home." In *Professors Who Believe: The Spiritual Journeys of Christian Faculty*, edited by Paul M. Anderson, 55-64. Downers Grove, Ill.: Intervarsity Press, 1998.

Rizzo, John. *Company Man: Thirty Years of Controversy and Crisis in the CIA*. New York: Scribner, 2014.

Roberts, Michael. *Evangelicals and Science*. Greenwood Guides to Science and Religion. Westport, CT: 2008.

Roberts, Paul Craig. *How the Economy Was Lost: The War of the Worlds*. Oakland, CA.: CounterPunch and AK Press, 2010.

Romano, Carlin. *America the Philosophical*. New York: Alfred A Knopf, 2012.

Rorty, Richard. "Science as Solidarity." In *The American Intellectual Tradition*, edited by David A. Hollinger and Charles Capper, 533-543. Vol. II. 6th ed. New York: Oxford University Press, 2011.

Rubenstein, Richard E. *Aristotle's Children: How Christians, Muslims, and Jews Rediscovered Ancient Wisdom and Illuminated the Dark Ages.* New York: Harcourt, 2003.

Schick, Theodore Jr. and Lewis Vaughn. *How to Think About Weird Things: Critical Thinking for a New Age.* 3rd ed. Boston: McGraw Hill, 2002

Sherman, Arloe & Stone, Chad & Taylor, Roderick, and Trisi, Danilo. "A Guide to Statistics on Historical Trends in Income Inequality." Center on Budget and Policy Priorities, May 15, 2018. https://www.cbpp.org/...inequality/a-guide-to-statistics-on-historical-trends-in-income

Shermer, Michael. *How We Believe: The Search for God in an Age of Science.* New York: W. H. Freeman and Company, 2000.

____. *The Borderlands of Science: Where Sense Meets Nonsense.* New York: Oxford University Press, 2001.

_____. *Why Darwin Matters: The Case Against Intelligent Design.* New York: Times Books, 2006.

____. *Why People Believe Weird Things: Pseudoscience, Superstition, and Other Confusions of Our Time.* New York, 1997.

Sinclair, James Daniel. "At Home in the Multiverse? Critiquing the Atheist Many-Worlds Scenario." In *Contending With Christianity's Critics: Answering New Atheists and other Objectors*, edited by Paul Copan and William Lane Craig, 6-25. Nashville: B & H Publishing Group, 2009.

Smith, Huston. *Why Religion Matters: The Fate of the Human Spirit in An Age of Disbelief.* New York: HarperSanFrancisco, 2001.

Sowell, Thomas. *Basic Economics: A Citizen's Guide to the Economy.* New York: Basic Books, 2000.

Spatz, Chris & James O. Johnston. *Basic Statistics: Tales of Distributions.* Pacific Grove, CA.: Brooks/Cole Publishing Company, 1989.

Stiglitz, Joseph E. *Freefall: America, Free Markets, and the Sinking of the World Economy.* New York: W.W. Norton and Company, 2010.

____. *Globalization and its Discontents.* New York: W.W. Norton and Company, 2002.

Strobel, Lee. *The Case for Christ: A Journalist's Personal Investigation of the Evidence for Jesus.* Grand Rapids, MI: Zondervan Publishing House, 1998.

___. *The Case for Faith: A Journalist Investigates the Toughest Objections to Christianity.* Grand Rapids, MI.: Zondervan Publishing House, 2000.

Suppe, John. "Ordinary Memoir." In *Professors Who Believe: The Spiritual Journeys of Christian Faculty*, edited by Paul M. Anderson, 65-73. Downers Grove, IL: Intervarsity Press, 1998.

Swinburne, Richard. "The Vocation of a Natural Theologian." In *Philosophers Who Believe: The Spirtual Journeys of Eleven Leading Thinkers,* edited by Kelly James Clark, 179-202. Downer's Grove, Ill.: InterVarsity Press, 1993.

Trachtman, Joel P. *The Tools of Argument: How The Best Lawyers Think, Argue, and Win.* North Charleston, S.C.: CreateSpace Independent Publishing Platform, *2013.*

Wainwright, William J. "Skepticism, Romanticism, and Faith." In *God and the Philosophers: The Reconciliation of Faith and Reason*, edited by Thomas V. Morris, 77-87. New York: Oxford University Press, 1994.

Wallace, Daniel B. "How Badly Did the Early Scribes Corrupt the New Testament? An Examination of Bart Ehrman's Claims." In *Contending With Christianity's Critics: Answering New Atheists and Other Objectors*, edited by Paul Copan and William Lane Craig, 148-166. Nashville: B & H Publishing Group, 2009.

Weisman, Jonathan. "US Declares Bank and Auto Bailouts Over, and Profitable." *New York Times.* Dec. 19, 2014. https://www.nytimes.com/2014/12/20/business/us-signals-end-of-bailouts-of-automakers-and-wall-street.html

Wells, Jonathan. *Icons of Evolution: Science or Myth? Why Much of What We Teach About Evolution is Wrong.* Washington, DC: Regnery Publishing, Inc., 2000.

Wells, Steve. *The Skeptic's Annotated Bible: The King James Version from a Skeptic's Point of View.* SAB Books, 2012.

"Where America's Jobs Went." *The Week.* March 25, 2011.

Whyte, Jamie. *Crimes Against Logic: Exposing the Bogus Arguments of Politicians, Priests, Journalists, and Other Serial Offenders*. New York: McGraw Hill, 2005.

Wiker, Benjamin. *Ten Books Every Conservative Must Read: Plus Four Not to Miss and One Imposter.* Washington, D.C.: Regnery Publishing, Inc., 2010.

Williams, Walter. *Liberty Versus the Tyranny of Socialism: Controversial Essays.* Stanford, CA: Hoover Institution Press, 2008.

Wilson, Edward. *Consilience: The Unity of Knowledge.* New York: Alfred A. Knopf, 1998.

Wolpe, David J. *Why Faith Matters.* New York: HarperOne, 2008.

Wright, Jonathan. *Heretics: The Creation of Christianity from the Gnostics to the Modern Church.* Boston: Houghton Mifflin Harcourt, 2011.

Young, Matt and Taner Edis, eds. *Why Intelligent Design Fails: A Scientific Critique of the New Creationism.* New Brunswick, NJ: Rutgers University Press, 2005.

York, Anthony. "*National Review* Fires Anne Coulter." *Salon,* October 2, 2001.
http://www.salon.com/news/politics/red/2001/10/02/blue